THE COMPLEAT
CRAFTSMAN

THE COMPLEAT CRAFTSMAN

Compiled by
Martin Lawrence

Yesterday's Handicraft Projects for Today's Family

The Main Street Press

A Main Street Press Book

Universe Books   New York

Library of Congress Catalog Card Number 77-70473

ISBN 0-87663-968-6, pb
ISBN 0-87663-300-9, cloth

Published by Universe Books, 381 Park Avenue South,
New York, New York 10016

Produced by The Main Street Press, 42 Main Street,
Clinton, New Jersey 08809

Printed in the United States of America

Cover photograph by Eric Schweikardt

Contents

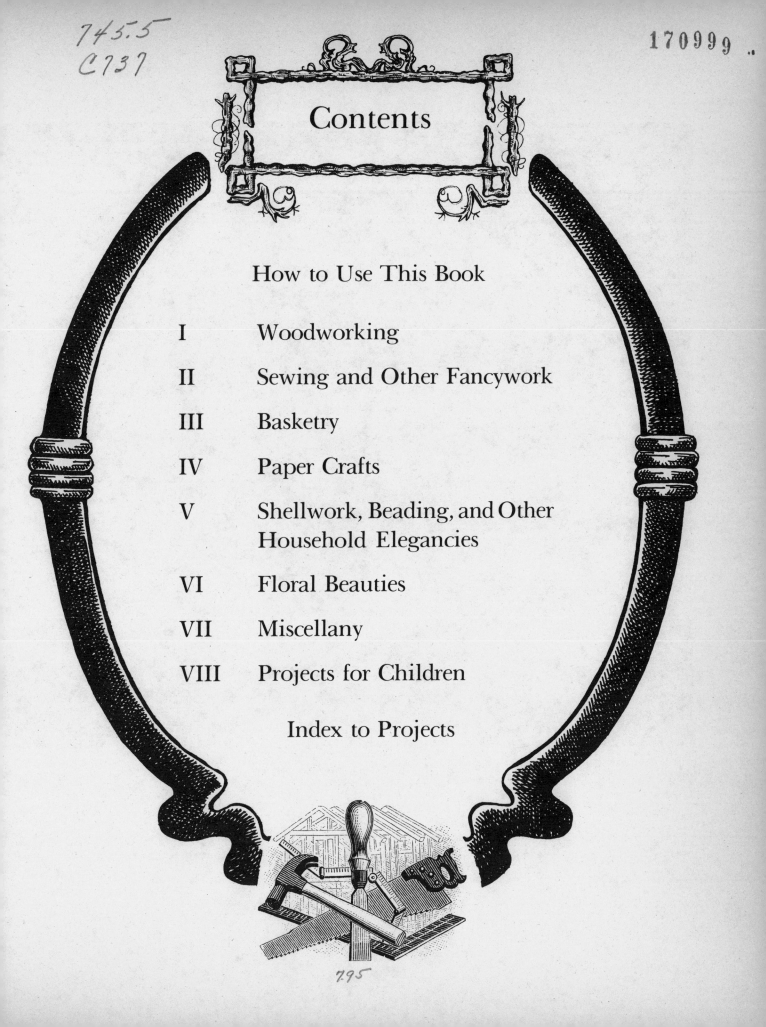

THE WHISTLE-MAKERS.—*Drawn and Engraved for the American Agriculturist.*

How to Use This Book

Handicrafts are just that—objects made by hand. Some may be the most amateurish of sorts, suitable only for the back of a closet or for a garage sale; others can be exquisitely worked objects selling for hundreds, if not thousands of dollars. The degree of craftsmanship is a measure of the skill of the hands, rather than the precision of a machine. While some types of machinery may be used in producing the component parts of a particular object, it is the most simple and intelligent of instruments—the human hand—which determines the final shape and aesthetic value.

The skills necessary for fine handicraft work have been practiced for many, many generations. In the nineteenth century, home craftsmen—men, women, and children—worked as imaginatively with wood, textiles, paper, metal, the needle, and other materials as any people before or since. Although the industrial revolution was well under way, this was still an age of natural materials; synthetics of various sorts were virtually unknown. A hundred years later we look back on this period with nostalgic longing. Even the patently ridiculous excesses of the time—overworked embroideries, maudlin or cloying designs in paper and wood—seem at least intriguing. Upon closer examination, however, we can see that there is much more than sentimental value in the busy-work of the past. These handicraft projects tell us something about the economic and social values of leisure time and of work, and of the proper use of natural resources. *The Compleat Craftsman* is a testament to the Victorian craftsman who wasted not and wanted not. The illustrative pictures are both instructive and amusing. As a compilation of hundreds of nineteenth-century craft projects, it is a book that can be used for personal profit and pleasure.

The crafts movement has assumed epidemic proportions in the 1970s in North America and Europe. Everyone, it would seem, wants to "make something" original. So tired have we become with ill-fitting clothes, shoddy toys, various defective household articles—and their grossly inflated prices—that we are now willing to try our own hand at their production. Commercial manufacturers, of course, have rushed to fill the new desire for "handmade" articles. Kits of every sort make even the most traditional of crafts seem as simple as "painting

ORNAMENTAL DESIGNS
—FOR—
Fret-Work, Scroll Sawing, Fancy Carving,
—AND—
HOME DECORATIONS.

Fret-Sawing has become an art of such wonderful popularity that the interest in it has been shared by both amateurs and professionals to an astonishing extent. Hundreds are earning large sums of pocket-money by cutting these beautiful household ornaments, and selling among friends or acquaintances, or at the art stores.

by the numbers," and various synthetic preparations allow the amateur to fashion something resembling a "craft." Some of these are truly useful improvements. Try to find such nineteenth-century necessities as gum tragacanth or dextrine or pink saucers at your local drugstore! But the majority of the twentieth-century nostrums are pure hokum, inferior and costly substitutes for imagination and skill. They are as real as the pressed-paper beams which are offered in place of hand-hewn timbers by the local lumber yard. *The Compleat Craftsman* will return you to the basics—flour paste, natural dyes, wool, cotton, silk, pine cones, shells, fret-work saws, willow reeds—which will save you money and your aesthetic sense.

Over 400 projects of almost every sort are offered in these pages. Each one has been selected with the interests of today's craftsman in mind and from a wide variety of English and North American sources—books, magazines, pamphlets—of the period from roughly 1840 to the turn of the century. Each has been edited and reset for readibility; how-to drawings and other illustrative examples are included when available. Editorial notations concerning various materials and processes are found where appropriate. *The Compleat Craftsman,* borrowing its title from Henry Peacham's *The Compleat Gentleman* and from Izaak Walton's *The Compleat Angler,* can complement your efforts to become an accomplished or "compleat" craftsman— or, if you prefer fashionable jargon, "craftsperson."

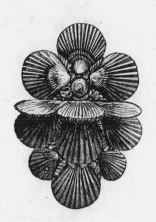

As recently as 1949 a distinguished writer on crafts, Allen H. Eaton, wrote of the misconception "that to produce by hand is a step backward because the machine is now paramount and is leading us, through mass production, into an era of abundance in which everyone may have the essentials of life." This conception of progress, fortunately, is now greeted as skeptically as the politician's promise to lower taxes. The danger present today, as Dorothy Canfield Fisher recognized with much prescience in her Foreword to Mr. Eaton's major book, *Handicrafts of New England,* is that we will oversentimentalize the past: "The prevalence of unsound, sentimental, and insincere talk about the value of making things by hand has created . . . a prejudice against the whole idea in the minds of many of the people who might casually pick up this book . . . . They are often the very men and women who, although they don't realize it, are starved and pining for a vitamin essential to their personalities.

HOUSEHOLD ELEGANCIES.

The most beautiful Ladies' Book ever published. Get it for your Work Basket
or Parlor. A Beautiful Gift to Friends.

BY HENRY T. WILLIAMS AND MRS. C. S. JONES.

VOL. 2—WILLIAMS' HOUSEHOLD SERIES.

A splendid new book on
Household Art, devoted
to a multitude of topics,
interesting to ladies ev-
erywhere.

CONTENTS.

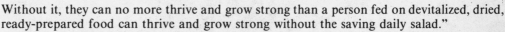

Without it, they can no more thrive and grow strong than a person fed on devitalized, dried, ready-prepared food can thrive and grow strong without the saving daily salad."

The reader of *The Compleat Craftsman* may just find something that suits his daily needs for meaningful and practical activity—toys built to last, which are in every sense "educational" tools; simple wood shelves or boxes useful for storing objects; everlasting or paper flower arrangements suitable for use the year 'round; embroidered or crocheted pillows, mittens, and other small objects. In addition, the reader will find it impossible not to learn something of daily life in the Victorian era—how men and women fashioned utilitarian articles with imagination and economy, how they brought color and amusement into their homes. Toilet articles such as a nose picker and an ear probe are unlikely to be made again; the washstand splasher is probably doomed to oblivion. But the Kate Greenaway figures appliqued on wall decorations during the 1880s and fish-scale embroideries and shellwork popular in the '70s might just have a comeback! Fashion is, indeed, a fickle mistress, coming and going at will.

The craft projects found in this volume are divided into eight categories from woodwork to those which can be made for or by children. Victorian woodworkers were able to use the newest kinds of saws and lathes to produce their ornate objects. Beginning in the 1850s fret-work saws could be found in hardware stores. Cigar boxes were often recommended for reuse as the bases of match safes. Friction matches came into widespread use at the time, and, as one writer noted in 1870, "The increased facility in obtaining fire has brought with it increased danger. The scratch that will bring the friendly fire will also bring the fire fiend to burn and destroy." Children and matches are still a problem, and the solutions recommended in the pages of this book are still functional and valuable. Larger boxes and crates were recommended for reuse as chairs, seats, storage containers, etc. Typical of the more ambitious projects tackled by craftsmen of the period was the building of a rowboat (pp. 27–29). Even an undertaking this complex, however, could be accomplished with the use of simple tools and materials.

Projects of greater interest to the Victorian woman were those involving needle fancywork, basketry, paper crafts, shellwork, and beading. Patterns for such useful items as ties, handkerchiefs, rag rugs, and tidies are included in these pages. Also covered are recipes for natural dyes capable of supplying long-lasting, pleasing colors almost foreign today. Paper products, of course, were used again and again for a variety of objects including lampshades and covers for books and other articles. Cardboard was especially prized and utilized for frames, holiday decorations, etc. Crepe and tissue paper came into great use at the end of the century for artificial flowers, household decorations, and costumes. "Flowers made of fine tissue paper are most elegant," one enthusiast wrote at the time, "and the art of forming them is capable of being carried to a high state of perfection. Unlike the art of forming wax flowers, this may be made to give satisfaction in the hands of a mere amateur." So right! The present writer, it is admitted, failed utterly to make sense out of the many waxwork projects found in books and pamphlets of the time; they have not been included here. The reader will find, however, that the taste for the unusual in crafts is more than plentifully supplied by those projects employing shells, fish scales, feathers, straw, hair, and even popcorn.

Basket weaving was once thought only appropriate for residents of homes for the insane and non-Ivy League colleges. The making of such containers is now a national pastime, and directions are included for those made from willows and straw. That crafts of this sort were once the special domain of the mentally ill does say something, however, about their true therapeutic value then and now. Two miniature chairs suitable for a doll's house are included in these pages (216–17) and were, according to the discoverer of them in 1882, the product of a feeble mind. "It was my sad pleasure not many weeks since to visit at a home for the insane, a friend I had not seen in thirteen years, and who, in the interval had from a series of misfortunes become deranged. Deplorable as her state is, I was glad to find that her hallucinations were pleasant and comfortable ones. In the midst of all these wanderings, she keeps her room, clothing, and person in perfect order, and except when talking to visitors, is very busily engaged.

"As the matron said, 'She made a thousand and one pretty notions.' Her walls were covered with picture frames and brackets, and her tables with really beautiful articles. I examined

everything carefully and wondered how a mind so restless and imaginative could fashion so many things, perfect in shape and harmonious in color."

If basketry was once considered suitable to calm one's nerves, woodworking was *de rigueur* for boys; and the making of dolls and their clothing, for girls. Today these lines are not as clearly drawn, but, in practice, they probably were frequently crossed during the Victorian period. The frontispiece illustration for the 1870s (p. 2) shows children of both sexes and all ages busily at work on their needlework, just as the Victorian engraving on p. 207 shows a girl *and* a boy happily playing with dolls. Both young boys and girls enjoyed paper cutouts. Indeed, one craftsman of the time commented: "Children find wonderful pleasure in the use of scissors. Give them something that is lawful to cut, or they will probably cut off their eyelashes or front locks of hair, or scallop their own little frocks. At first they lust for the pure pleasure of cutting, but soon they want to 'make something.'" There are plenty of projects here for them to make: kites, doll's clothes, simple dolls from vegetables or clothespins, easy magic tricks. There are also more complicated objects such as locomotives, a croquet set, doll's house furniture, and various other toys which require the special skill of an adult. All can be made without kits, without costly materials.

Victorian children introduced to various crafts at an early age developed the skills which we celebrate today—an ability to use tools and instruments of various sorts, to fix things, to create objects of solid beauty and character. Accomplished craftsmen working in this past tradition are small in number at present, but their number could increase if current interest in handicrafts is sustained in homes and schools. These skills could well prove more useful in the future than they have in the dim past. As we are forced to reexamine the necessities of life in a fragile environment and on a reduced budget, resourcefulness in the use of natural materials may again establish itself as the norm rather than the exception. *The Compleat Craftsman* is a book to be used by any and all, of whatever age, who are willing to rediscover the pleasures and benefits of working with one's hands. It is not meant to be an instructional book, although there are plenty of explicit steps which can be followed if you wish. It is not history tidied up and cosmeticized to fit today's needs; the Victorians were as gifted and as creatively looney as we are. Use this book not to escape from the present, but to prepare for the future and to enjoy it.

I. Woodworking

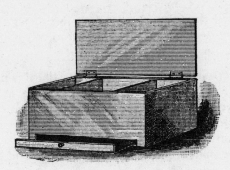
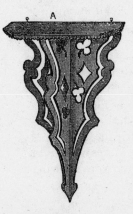

Designing for Scroll Sawing

A simple method of making designs for scroll work is as follows: Procure several sheets of thin plain white paper of any suitable size, a common pen, ink, pencil, eraser, a ruler and a compass. Determine what article to design and its size. Every part must be supported so as to prevent splitting off. Make as few openings as possible, consistent with beauty and fitness for the purpose intended.

An example: To design the back of a comb case 12 inches wide and 17 inches long, with but three openings in the pattern, place a sufficiently large sheet of paper on a board or table, its narrow side towards you, and draw a line across its middle the longest way. Mark on this line two points 17 inches apart. Through these points draw two very light parallel pencil lines across the paper. Three inches above the lowest point draw a line across the paper at right angles to the long first line. Four inches above this draw another line parallel to it. Then 6 inches on each side of the long line, draw lines parallel to it. You will have a space 12 inches wide and 4 inches high, the place of the comb box. Your drawing will appear like *figure 1*.

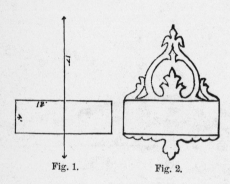

Fig. 1.   Fig. 2.

Now study the whole space, 12 by 17 inches, thinking of the design you desire. All above and below the box space (of 12 by 4 inches) is to be made ornamental. With a pencil lightly sketch the pattern as you design it in mind. It may be composed wholly of curves, or of curves and straight lines combined. After making a sketch of a suitable design, re-mark half of it (on one side of the long middle line), retouching here and there to perfect the pattern, erasing all unnecessary lines. The drawing will now appear as in *figure 2*. In the half pattern finish the lines carefully with pen and ink. Fold the paper against a pane of glass through which strong light is shining. Press the two folds close together. The ink lines of the drawing will show plainly through. Carefully trace with a pencil all the ink lines, and both sides of the design will be alike in every detail and part. *Figure 3* shows how the pattern will now appear. This will be a design for the back part of the comb case.

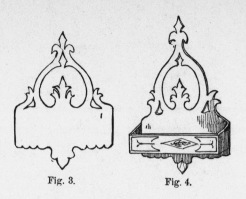

Fig. 3.   Fig. 4.

The front of the case will of course be like the back, after sawing through. In this instance the ends of the box will be 3¾ inches long by 3 inches wide. The front is made plain, 2¾ by 12 inches, the bottom 3¼ by 12 inches. The front may be line-carved in any appropriate design, and then the completed comb case will appear as in *figure 4*. The right and left sides of all scroll designs may be duplicated in like manner.

Designs with large openings like this may be pasted on medium thick cardboard. Tack the cardboard to the wood to be made up. Following the pattern lines, saw through cardboard and wood, preserving the card carefully. This card pattern may be used as long as required, by marking around it and sawing to the lead pencil lines. (1883)

Wall Decorations: A Bracket

A book called *Hints on Household Taste*, by Sir Charles Eastlake, an eminent English painter, has been reproduced in this country in elegant style by Osgood & Co. The work is a vigorous fight against shams in architecture, furniture, and all household adornments. Most of his suggestions are so excellent that one would like to follow them, if it could be afforded, but for the present we must accept machine-made furniture instead of handmade, and must use veneered articles because we can not afford the solid. He is very radical in his proposed reforms in household furnishings of all kinds, and while we cannot follow him in all things, we can accept and make use of many of his hints.

When there are many pictures in a room, he suggests that the monotony be broken by introducing brackets here and there for the reception of a statuette, vase, or other object. Brackets are now in very common use, and are sold in various styles in the fancy stores. Mr. Eastlake finds the ordinary brackets too unsubstantial,

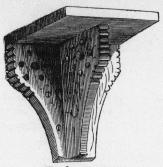

Fig. 3.—BRACKET.

and gives an engraving of one made according to his views, which we here reproduce. This is certainly a good, honest, solid bracket, and able to bear any reasonable weight. Moreover, it is more easily made than the more fragile ones. Ordinarily a portion of the bracket is cut in openwork ornamental figures, this being especially the case with the centerpiece that supports the shelf. Our author objects to this, and insists that all ornament shall be subordinate to the thing itself, and whatever ornament there is, should be cut *out* of the work, as shown in the engraving. It will be seen that when the work is done he does not hang it by any concealed hooks, but puts it up with good, honest

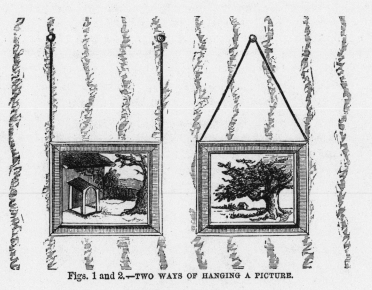

Figs. 1 and 2.—TWO WAYS OF HANGING A PICTURE.

screws. This idea of honesty in construction runs all through the book, and we hope the work will lead to something of reform in our household decorations. (1872)

Cigar-Box Ornaments, Brackets, Etc.

A leisure hour and a jackknife are often well employed in executing some tasteful device which may serve to ornament a room or be valued as a gift by some friend. There are so many little gems of photographs nowadays, so many pretty statuettes, and various ornamental objects suitable for placing upon brackets, that we give the accompanying engraving of a bracket made of the wood of a cigar box.

Its construction is evident from the picture, and so simple that it needs no description. Similar brackets are made with but one support, placed under the center of the shelf. This writer happened to have the little owl's head (which is a natural one), the design was made with a view to its accommodation. One's friends value such little things much on account of the neatness of execution, but more on account of the beauty and originality of design. There is really no limit to the variety of styles and forms which may be made of this common and very cheap material. (1864)

A Lamp Bracket

Mr. Editor.—You said you admired the lamp brackets you saw at our house the other day, and as that pleases me well, I send you a description of how they are made, and, if you will excuse the egotism of my saying so—I must add that I admire them myself, not so much for their beauty,—you may pass judgment upon that—but for their utility. Well, then, you must know I have been trying a long time to get Father to saw me out some semi-circular pieces of board, with brace pieces, to make them of, but it has been busy time with him and all the

15

rest of *man*kind, so I could do no better than help myself.

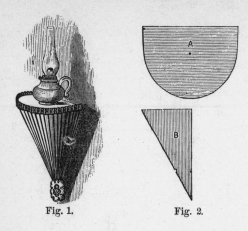

Fig. 1.   Fig. 2.

The piece *A, figure 2*, was made of a portion of the head of a nail keg, part being split off and the corners sawed square, and the sides thus formed rounded into the curve of the head as best I could with a hand saw. *B*, represents the brace, a triangular piece of half-inch clapboarding. *Figure 3* shows how the two, with one

Fig. 3.

nail to hold them together, were nailed to the wall; one nail going through a gimlet hole at the notch in the brace piece, and another driven slanting through the top. I was lucky in striking studs in the wall.

Before this, however, the cloth covering was tacked on to the top. This covering I made of plain muslin (if striped, the stripes to run up and down), cutting a piece a little wider than the brace piece is long, and long enough to allow for a frill at the top. This piece was hemmed on the top and a thread run ⅜ of an inch from the edge to draw the frill by, and it was drawn so as just to go round the top piece which was covered with the same material. A thread was also "caught in" at regular intervals along the bottom edge of the cloth so as to draw it into regular plaits, and then this cover was tacked to the top, the gathering thread being covered by a fancy braid ¼-inch wide. Then the bracket was nailed up, the bottom gathered and tied to the front of the brace, and a rosette was made and pinned on. Thin stuff requires a lining to prevent the light showing through, for which brown paper will do.

I made a pair and placed one on each side of the mirror at the toilet stand, so high that lamps set upon

them will shed a good light upon the head of a person before the glass." (1866)

Cone and Plain Brackets

The cone bracket, *figure 1*, may be made at a trifling expense by anyone of moderate skill and taste. Cut the bracket of any desired shape from pine; stain with powdered umber mixed with a little water. After the two pieces of the bracket are nailed together, a piece of wood 2 inches square and 1 inch thick should be glued to the center of the lower piece close to the top. This gives strength to the bracket, and raises the work in the center.

Fig. 1.—CONE BRACKET.

Have a good assortment of cones, acorns, etc., at hand and dispose them on the frame to suit the fancy. This may be done in a great variety of ways. The engraving shows one, the central figure of which is a large open pine cone; at the top and bottom, smaller cones not open; at the sides, butternuts, spruce and hemlock cones, with large and small acorns. The border is made of inverted acorn-cups—a row on the edge of the frame and one on the surface. These must be of uniform size and shape.

Now have good glue and fasten each piece, beginning at the center. When this is done, let the work dry thoroughly, after which varnish with thin furniture varnish, and it is complete.

Fig. 2.—BRACKET.

16

Figure 2 shows a bracket to be cut with a narrow saw and penknife. It can all be done with the knife, but the saw makes much more rapid work. It is finer work than that shown in the former illustration, but it requires little skill after the pattern is marked upon the board. This should be of thin stuff, about three-eighths of an inch in thickness, after it is planed down.

The shelf is fastened by glue and by small brads or screws driven in at the back. The support underneath may be put on with glue or with a small brass hinge. A board 7 or 8 inches wide is sufficiently large for work of this pattern. Pine, white wood, black walnut and butternut are suitable woods for this kind of work. The latter, unfortunately, is quite overlooked as an ornamental wood. It is nearly as dark and handsome in the grain as black walnut, and in many parts of the country much more accessible. (1867)

REVOLVING BIRD HOUSE.

A Revolving Birdhouse

Herewith is an engraving of a bird house. Blue birds take a special liking to it, and will raise several broods there each year. The advantage is that the door is always turned from the storm. The arrow is made of inch hardwood board, with a plate of iron for the "feather-end." A quarter-inch iron pin in the top of the pole runs through the arrow, the whole answering for a vane.

(1883)

Pigeon Houses

Pigeons are valued both as ornamental birds and as furnishing an exceedingly delicate article of food. If kept for use, or if reared purely for fancy, pigeons must be kept in rooms secure from cats, rats, weasels, etc.,

over the stable or some outbuilding. This gives the owner access at all times to the birds and their nests. The houses are subdivided by latticework partitions into as many apartments as are desirable.

We give herewith some engravings of simple "pole houses" and one which may be appropriately set *(figure 3)* upon a roof. For convenience of examination, pigeon houses should have the roofs attached so that they may be lifted off. The roofs should have wide, projecting eaves and gable ends to keep out the rain; and the houses should be fastened very securely by iron straps shaped like an inverted "L" and screwed to the bottom of the houses, and to the side of the post. The post should be very smooth for several feet below the top and painted to prevent vermin getting to the pigeons.

Fig. 1.—RUSTIC PIGEON HOUSE.

Figure 1 and *plan 1* represent a simple house, 20 × 20 inches, for a single pair of pigeons. This has two brooding rooms, and a vestibule or outside room connecting them. The pigeons will make a nest in one room which is spacious, hatch a pair of young ones, and before they are old enough to take care of themselves, the hen will make another nest in the other room, leaving her mate to take care of the squabs which, by the time the hen is broody again, will be set adrift.

Plan 1.—20 × 20 in.   Plan 2.—24 × 30 in.

During the warm weather pigeons multiply rapidly, and the squabs must be provided for in some way, or brought to the table, if the accommodations are not more spacious than these we are considering. This house, as is also the Log Cabin, *figure 2,* is constructed of round and half-round sticks of as nearly a uniform size as possible, which, after drying with the bark on, are tacked upon a box made or adapted to the purpose.

Fig. 2.—LOG CABIN PIGEON HOUSE.

The Log Cabin is a good deal larger than *figure 1*, and will accommodate as many pairs of birds as there are distinct apartments. In *plan 2* the four rooms measure 12 × 15 inches each. No vestibules are provided, but each tenement is big enough for two nests if needed.

Fig. 3.—SWISS COTTAGE.

The Swiss cottage house, *figure 3*, is more elaborate, and will require a skilled hand and patience to make it. Each story of the house should be made separate. The lower one should be at least eight inches high, and the lower piazza eight inches wide. The stones upon the roof should be wired to the cross-strips. *Plans 3* and *4*

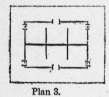

Plan 3.   Plan 4.

represent the lower and upper stories respectively; 4, 6, or 8 pairs may be accommodated, according to the internal arrangement. (1869)

Picture Frame

A very good thing for the amateur to try his hands at is a simple frame for a small photograph or other picture. The outline for the frame shown in the engraving, if

neatly cut out from a piece of cigar box or other thin wood, will make a pleasing design.

PICTURE FRAME.

It may be made more elaborate by the addition shown by the dark portion of the engraving. This may be cut from black walnut or some very white wood, either of which would afford a marked contrast of color and add much to the effect, and glued on.

The frame may be made of any convenient size. The pattern should be first made of paper, taking care to get both sides exactly alike; and then, by laying this upon the wood, the form may be drawn with a pencil, or the paper can be pasted upon the wood, from which it can be readily removed by slightly moistening it. (1869)

Fig. 2.—FRAME.

Oval Frame

Figure 2 represents an oval frame for a photograph. It is made from a piece of a cigar box, but any other thin, dark colored wood will answer as well. It is about 3½ by 4 inches.

It is first marked out with a paper pattern and pencil, and then cut away with a sharp knife. The frame is finished off with file and sandpaper and rubbed with linseed oil. A small ring is attached to the back with a loop of tape and glue for the purpose of hanging the picture. (1868)

Window Gardening

A mode of having plants and flowers, and for spring and summer the best of all, is to have boxes neatly made of wood to fit on the outside of the window, and then filled with flowering plants. These make a kind of miniature garden and at the same time form an excellent screen. Shades may be dispensed with, as the plants are sufficiently close to prevent persons seeing into the room, but, at the same time, not preventing those inside from observing through the foliage and flowers everything taking place outside.

WINDOW GARDEN.

These boxes can be made quite plain or ornamented, and afterwards painted a light green. Stocks, scarlet geraniums, and mignonette succeed well, grown in boxes of this description. The outer edges, next to the street, should be planted with the pretty blue lobelia, verbenas, and other trailing plants, which, falling over the sides of the boxes, add much to their effect. The ends of the boxes may be planted with morning glories (*Convolvulus major*), and canary bird flower (*Tropaeolum peregrinum*), to be trained on wires up and around the windows.

The edging of the box, shown in the engraving, can be readily made of willow or rattan. Besides the plants mentioned above, almost any of our annual and bedding plants may be grown. Water them as often as may be needed, taking care to avoid overwatering. (1867)

Rustic Window Boxes

Many people would have flowers in their rooms if it were not for the trouble entailed by a number of pots. The earth in pots soon dries out and separates, and frequent watering, with its attendant drip and "muss," makes the care of them a task. When a cold snap comes on it is often necessary, especially in country houses, to remove the plants to some warmer quarter, and the carrying about of a dozen or two pots is no light task. Then pots of themselves are undeniably unsightly, unless one buys very expensive ones; and if they are not filled with plants that are particularly attractive, the collection as a whole, pots and plants, is not altogether satisfactory as an ornament to the dwelling.

All of these objections may be overcome by the use of window boxes. The earth does not dry out rapidly; if the plants must be moved they can all be lifted at once; the box can be made of a pleasing appearance and is an ornament in itself should the plants not be especially attractive, or even if it contained no plants at all.

Here are some delightful window boxes that can be made by almost any one. They are so thoroughly rustic that engravings have been made of them as a guide to those who wish to try they hands—or to direct *somebody else* to try his hands—at making them. The foundation in all cases is a box of sound pine, which need not of necessity be planed. The size of the box should have reference to that of the window. Some windows have sills broad enough to hold the box, but where this is not the case it may rest upon a couple of brackets screwed to the wall. Wooden brackets may be used, or cast-iron ones. The box should be thoroughly nailed and strong in its make. Then it is to be covered, and the engravings show three styles of doing it.

Fig. 1.—BOX COVERED WITH CEDAR STICKS.

In *figure 1* cedar sticks, straight and of the same size, are split in halves, the bark left on, and firmly nailed to the box. In *figure 2* is shown what to many tastes is an exceedingly beautiful box. It is covered with some well-marked bark; in the case of the one figured, that of the

Fig. 2.—BOX COVERED WITH BARK.

Fig. 3.—BOX WITH MOSAIC WORK.

whitewood or tulip tree, common throughout all the Western states, is used. The engraving shows the manner of laying it on. *Figure 3* shows a more elaborate style, which in reality is more effective than can be shown in the engraving. The ornamentation here is done with halved sticks, those shown light being of white birch, the silvery bark of which showed in strong contrast with the darker pieces, which are apparently laurel or some dark-barked wood. In this last case the wood was varnished, which is not necessarily an improvement. Either of these boxes is of a most pleasing exterior, and while it would not seem out of place in the most elegant parlor, would grace and add an air of refinement to the humblest kitchen. So much for the outside of the box, which any one who really sets herself about it can accomplish without difficulty.

As to the inside: If you wish to do the best thing, get a pan of sheet zinc or galvanized iron made to exactly fit it. If this expense should not be warranted use the box without it, but in case of over-watering it may drip, and if not thoroughly and carefully nailed the sides may warp; but a little foresight will avoid these difficulties. A good mechanic can make a box quite watertight by putting thick white lead or a strip of paper dipped in tar between the joints before nailing.

Now, to fill it, put in the bottom—whether it has a pan or not—an inch or two in depth, according to size, of broken flowerpots if you have them, if not, bricks broken to the size of walnuts; or if neither of these is available, use small stones or hard coal. This is what gardeners call drainage. Then over this place a layer of moss, of any kind, sufficient to keep the earth from working down among the drainage. The reason for this preparation is: if the earth should happen to receive too much water, the excess will pass down into this bottom layer and the roots of the plants receive no injury.

For the earth the object must be to have it moderately rich and so porous that it will not bake hard. Good garden soil may do without addition; if heavy, mix some sand. Earth from the woods, garden soil, and sand mixed in proportions to make a light porous soil will be capital.

Of the plants themselves, suffice it to say that any usually grown in the house in pots will do well in such a box, and each one will have her own preference. If one has no house plants, and can not readily procure them, a box of this kind may be made an object of beauty and interest without expense. Go to the woods and take up sods of moss that have partridgeberry, princess pine, and such plants, or get cranberry plants from the bogs, or even strawberry plants from the garden. With green moss, such ferns as appear to be evergreen, and low-growing plants from the woods, a fine cheery bit of green may be kept up all winter. But a box filled in this way should not be kept in a very warm room. (1873)

Boxes in the Window

Few who have not tried it are aware of the brightness a bit of living green brings into a room. Flowers are well, but all cannot have them, and some must be content with the green. Whether it be the one livingroom of the "pioneer," or a richly-furnished room in the "mansion," green brings cheer, and is welcome.

A box at the window is better than pots. It may be a handsome box, inlaid with costly tiles, with a zinc lining, but the plants will give no more pleasure than if in a cheap box put together with the materials at hand. All houses do not have broad window sills upon which

Fig. 1.—A WINDOW-BOX.

the box can be set, but if there is a mere ledge, the box can be at the window. If there are a few inches of projection upon which one edge of the box can sit, the rest is easy.

Put a strong screw in the end of the box near the top and front; fasten a stout bit of copper wire to this, and carry the other end of the wire to another screw in the window casing, and the box will stand firm. *Figure 1* shows one end of a box thus secured; of course, the place for the upper screw will depend upon the kind of casing.

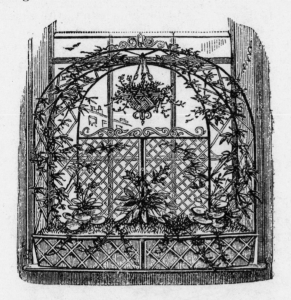

In order to have a really satisfactory window box, it must be thought of, and made ready in season. Those who provide such pleasing window decorations do not always make the most of them. Few seem to be aware of the great improvement that may result by the addition of a light trellis, or lattice work, over which vines are allowed to run. A low, light arch, like that shown in *figure 2*, or a much taller one, nearly doubles the ornamental capabilities of a window box. Such a frame may be made of rattan, or equally well of straight willow shoots, and may bear an ivy, or some more rapid-growing climber. If boxes were not prepared beforehand, one may find means even later in the growing season to bring in a bit of green; seedling evergreens from the woods may be taken up, or, in the absence of these, a few carrots planted in the soil will give a mass of filiage, which for beauty is equal to that of many costly exotics. Morning glory seeds, if sown at the ends of the box, will soon give vines for a trellis.

Window boxes also have a practical end in view. Such a box, three or four inches deep, will supply a garden of moderate size, with plants of early cabbages, tomatoes, lettuce, etc., and allow such vegetables to be enjoyed at least a month earlier than those from seeds sown in the open ground. It will be well to have at least two such boxes, one in which to sow the seeds, and the other to hold the plants, or a part of them, when large enough to transplant. If soil was not laid in before cold weather, it may be difficult to find a supply for the boxes. If properly treated, the soil beneath the manure pile should not be frozen, and will answer the purpose. (1883)

Chair Made from a Wood Packing Box

A very comfortable and handsome chair can be made from an ordinary packing box. The box should be about 1½ feet wide by 2 feet long, and not more than 14 inches deep. If deeper it will make the chair too high, and so take away much from its ease. A caster should be fastened firmly to each corner; after which the box is ready to cover.

Cut from large-flowered chintz as many breadths, 16 inches deep, as are necessary to go around the sides of the box three times, and run them together. Make a hem an inch deep around the bottom, and pleat it into 1½ inch side pleats. Let the lower edge of the flounce come slightly below the bottom of the box, and lay the extra length over on top of the box, where it is fastened with small tacks, so that when the cushion is on the tacks will be covered.

To make the cushion, cut two pieces of strong muslin, or partly-worn ticking, the first piece the size of the top of the box. The second is a piece 3 inches deep which is to be sewed between the top and the bottom of the cushion as for a mattress. One side should be left unsewed until the stuffing has been put in. For this hay or straw can be used, or worn-out comforters or quilts. Enough of whatever is used must be put in to fill the cushion tight.

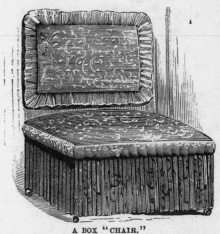

A BOX "CHAIR."

Cut from the chintz a piece the size of the top of the cushion and make a strip 5 inches deep, and long enough to go once and a half around the cushion. Gather this strip and sew one side to the piece of chintz. Draw over the cushions and sew the other edge of the puff to the underside. The cushion can be tacked firmly to the box along the front by holding it up from the back and catching the tacks through the edge of the puff where it is sewed to the cushion.

For the back, make a pillow 4 inches less in length than the box, and not quite as broad as long. Feathers make a good stuffing for this, or it may be filled with whatever is used for the cushion on the box. Cover the pillow with chintz, and put a ruffle of the chintz 2 inches wide around it. The ruffle looks better if made double instead of hemmed.

Three loops of cord are sewed to the top of the pillow, one at each corner and one in the center, far enough below the edge to keep them from showing above the ruffle, and by these the pillow is hung on nails against the wall back of the covered box. This is one of the most satisfactory of homemade chairs. (1882)

A Combined Table and Book Rack

The wish expressed by many, that books in daily use should be conveniently kept, has led to a plan for a portable and handy book rack which does not take up much room. At first the plan was for a book rack and nothing more, but a top has been added to it, and the result is a combination rack and table which is quite an ornamental and useful piece of furniture.

The legs are made on a scroll saw from butternut boards. The entire table is made of butternut, oiled well, and not varnished. Varnished surfaces show every little scratch plainly, and lack the rich appearance of unvarnished surfaces. Between the legs are fastened shelves for books; two on each side. Casters are fixed to the legs, thus making it easy to move the stand about the room or to any place where the family gathers. The top has a covering of pretty cretonne, edged with fringe.

Children can use it for their school books. Little drawers might be added, like those fastened to the lower side of sewing machine tables, to hold attachments. These could be used for pencils, pens, ink, stationery, etc., thus adding to the usefulness of the table, and making it a sort of portable library and writing desk. About four inches above the center of each shelf a straight piece of wood runs across from leg to leg, forming a support for books put in from each side. (1883)

An Ironing Board

This simple contrivance, though much used, may not be known to all, and an account of it is given with the suggestion that those who have never made use of a similar help in ironing should try it at once.

AN IRONING-BOARD.

The method of construction is to take a board 5 or 6 feet long, 1 foot wide and 1½ inches thick. The board is covered with two or three folds of woolen material, and over this is put a piece of linen or flannel, which is lightly tacked on, in order that it may be taken off and washed when necessary.

In use, the ends of the board rest upon the backs of two chairs, or they may be supported at the proper height in any other convenient manner. A board of this kind is almost indispensable in ironing dresses or skirts, as no part gets rumpled while the rest is being ironed—a thing which always happens when the ironing is done upon a table. The board is to be put into the skirt in the manner shown in the engraving. Shirts can be ironed by the aid of this board, and it will be found to greatly reduce the trouble of ironing the bosoms. Every man that has any taste for dress (and the most of them have), especially prides himself upon a perfectly smooth shirt front. If a board of this kind were in general use, there would be less frowning over badly ironed shirt front than there is at present. (1871)

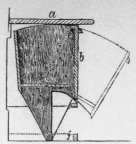

Fig. 2.—SECTION OF FLOUR-BOX.

deep, and lettered. They set in a case made of ⅜-inch whitewood. The molding board (g) is slid behind them when not in use. The drawers (m and n) are always useful for sugar, graham flour or buckwheat, towels, baking tins, and a score of things; the closet (k) for syrups, lard, butter, eggs, etc., etc. Three shelves are in the corner, though only one (j) is shown."

Now, if any husband is coaxed by his better half to get one made for her, he may lay the blame to J. F. R. (1872)

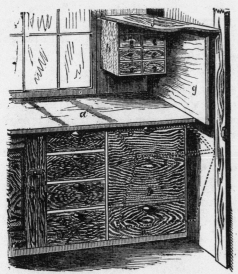

Fig. 1.—FLOUR-BOX AND ACCESSORIES.

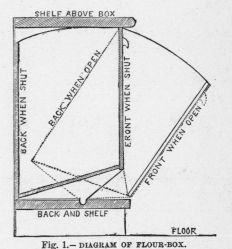

Fig. 1.— DIAGRAM OF FLOUR-BOX.

A Flour Box

Mrs. J. F. R. writes: "Having recently made a few improvements in our pantry, the best of which is a flour box, differing from any I have ever seen, and which is admired by all the ladies who have seen it, here is a sketch of it. It is easily made, and there is no patent on it. It can be made without the four drawers, closet, and spice drawers, though these are all very handy.

"The top, a, I made of 1¼-inch pine, 22 inches wide. The flour box, b, is 16 inches wide inside at the top, and 14 inches at the bottom. Depth: 15 inches inside. Length of end boards: 30 inches. Width of front: 19 inches. Length: 24 inches outside. These dimensions may be varied, but the form of the ends, c, figure 2, should be preserved. They rest on pieces of thick leather, fastened to them and to the floor when finished.

A strip (e) is screwed under the top for the box to shut and open against. The back should be screwed on firmly. The spice drawers are made of tin, 6 inches by 6 inches, with black-walnut fronts, 2 to 3 inches

Another Flour Box

Construct the base, 5 inches high and 17½ inches wide. Place one standard between the boxes and one outside of the two boxes. They are 17 inches wide, 26 inches high, upon which place a shelf, 18 inches wide, which forms the base of a cupboard. Cut the end pieces (figure 2) of the boxes 26½ inches long and 16 inches wide. Make a line, ½-inch above the bottom end, and on that line, 5½ inches from the front edge of the board, make a point and draw a 1-inch circle, to form a foot (a) to hold the box in place.

23

Fig. 2.—END-PIECE.

Measure up the front edge from the line just mentioned 3½ inches, and make a point (*b*). Draw a line from that point to the center of the inch-circle. Saw it to the circle, and saw also from the back edge on the line first mentioned to the circle, leaving a foot 1 inch wide by ⅝-inch long.

Cut a furrow across from the two lower corners on the inside of the end pieces, to receive the bottom. From the top on the back edge of the end piece, measure down 1⅞ inches, and round the end to that point.

Use ¾-inch lumber for front and back, rabbeting it to ½-inch. Measure in from the front of the dividing stands 6 inches, and with an inch-gouge cut a socket or place for the foot to rest in the base-shelf, being particular about bringing the face of the box and the dividing stand even when the box is shut.

Cast handles are put on with screws, the feet are placed in the sockets, and the boxes are thus completed. The boxes will stay open or shut, as desired. (1872)

A Convenient Cooking Table

Mrs. M. S. W. sends the following account of a contrivance which she has found very convenient in the kitchen of an old-fashioned house where pantries and closets were omitted by the builder: "Having for several years walked miles each day while doing my cooking and dairy work, and now having the comfort of a cooking table established within eight steps of my cooking stove, I will describe it, hoping some woman of many steps may be induced to supply the need for herself.

"My cooking table is eight feet long, and is placed in a recess between the chimney and a window, the size of which decided its length. It is two feet seven inches high, and should be two feet three inches wide on top. Below, it is enclosed at the back and ends, and has doors in front. It has no floor, but stands directly upon the floor of the room, and is movable. The enclosed space below is divided into three compartments. The right hand closet contains the flour barrel; a door coming down to the floor opens to admit it, and closes tightly again until the next barrel is needed. Inside, there is space to hang baking pans by their rings on the partitions; over the flour barrel is a lid that is raised whenever flour is to be taken out; the sieve and scoop remain in the barrel. The lid is a part of the surface of the table, and opens over the whole width of the flour compartment.

"Above the door of the middle closet there is a drawer without back or sides, which is the bread board. When drawn out and turned around, the front becomes a back, and is very useful in preventing the scattering of flour in rolling pastry, etc.; when returned to its place the roller can remain upon the board. Below this drawer is a closet with a door, and a shelf large enough for a pan of milk, or bowls and pudding dishes; below the shelf is space for a bucket of sugar, jar of lard or cream, and molasses jug.

"The left hand closet has at top a drawer divided into two compartments, one for eggs, the other for spices, yeast powders, nutmeg grater, cake cutter, etc.; a shelf below holds boxes of saleratus, a bag of salt, boxes of rice or tapioca, jug of syrup, jars of preserves while in use, etc., or is an excellent place to keep pies. I can assure any woman who has not better conveniences that it is a great saving of time in cooking to have all these within reach of her hand, without stepping from her place. The table, including its surface, being about an inch and a half higher than a flour barrel, a short woman cannot roll pastry or mould bread easily without something to stand upon. I have a narrow piece of board about two feet long, with two pieces of inch board nailed across its underside. This is one of the best conveniences of all, for on a cold morning when I have biscuit to bake, I warm my wooden cricket by the fire, and it saves me from any uncomfortable chilliness, and as the closet door swings over it, is not in the way.

"The table may be of pine, and stained or not in front, or of black walnut. There should be a narrow strip of wood nailed upon the back of the surface of the table, and one across between the principal part of the table and the flour division, to keep water from flowing over the back or into the division containing flour, when washing the table after cooking." (1868)

A Cellar Closet

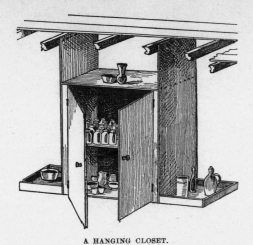

A HANGING CLOSET.

The engraving shows how a cellar closet may be cheaply and easily made. Two wide boards, forming the sides of the closet, are nailed to joists by their ends. A board is nailed to the bottom of the side pieces and extends a foot or more upon each side. These ends, when bordered with a lath, make very convenient shelves. The top board of the closet also furnishes a place for holding many articles.

The number of shelves within the closet is determined by the length of the side boards and the size of the articles to be kept in the closet. A lock may be easily fitted upon one of the doors, the other being fastened by hooks inside at the top and bottom. A hanging closet of this sort may be convenient in the wood shed, farm shop, or other outbuilding and is easily constructed. (1883)

A Homemade Extension Lounge

Anybody can knock up such a lounge with a few carpenter's tools. It is a very convenient thing to have in the house since it is so easily turned into a bedstead when an extension is required.

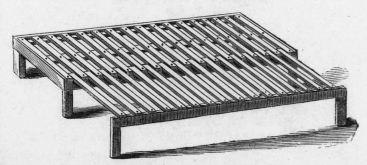

A HOME-MADE EXTENSION LOUNGE.

There is, first, the light frame of an ordinary lounge, made with four posts, held in place by four light narrow boards on the sides and ends, with narrow slats nailed across the top from side to side. There should also be a support running through the middle of the top of the lounge from head to foot. A few of the slats are nailed to this support if it is not sufficiently firm without. The slats should be narrow, not more than 1½ inches in width, and placed evenly a little more than 2 inches apart. This completes the lounge frame without the extension.

To make the extension, make two more posts like the other lounge posts, and unite them by a narrow board like the sides of the lounge. Nail to the top of this side board as many slats as there are spaces in the top of the lounge, taking care that they are narrow enough to slip into these spaces easily, and all evenly placed and nailed. This is all there is of the extension, and it looks frail enough by itself. But place it upon the lounge so that it has the support of the side pieces and middle "stringer,"—well, then you have quite a respectable lounge. You may convert it into a serviceable bedstead when need requires—a wide bed or a narrow one, as you please.

A good way to fit up the lounge: Make a thick box mattress to fit the shape of the lounge. Make two other mattresses of equal thickness, each half as large as the lounge mattress. Fill them (very full) with straw or husks, or whatever suits you. Cover them with strong pretty calico, and stand the two half mattresses up on their sides at the back of your broad lounge when they are not needed for the bed, thus making a comfortable back to the lounge. You can pull out the extension just enough to let these half-mattresses slip down back of it, so as to make the lounge wider and the back not quite so high—just as you like. One or two large pillows, covered like the lounge ticks, would add to the comfort of the concern.

Unless the lounge posts are ornamental, a curtain tacked across the front, and separate ones tacked across each end, would add to the good looks.

Dimensions of the frame: 1 foot high, 6 feet long, 2 feet wide. (1873)

A Footrest

In the "sanctum" of a friend is an odd looking piece of furniture, the use of which is not easy to conjecture. It consists of two hardwood boards, each 16 inches long and 12 inches wide, put together as shown in the engraving, the horizontal piece being fastened 3 inches

FOOT REST.

below the top of the upright one, and braced by semicircular pieces let in at the edges. It is not an easy matter to warm or dry the feet by a stove, where the fire is at a distance from the floor, and the ordinary way is to rest them upon a chair. You will find this rest to be much more comfortable and convenient, as it accommodates itself readily to any slight movement or change of the position of the body. (1868)

Stools

There are nice large highchairs, a little lower than regular baby highchairs, to be found at some furniture stores, but many parents neglect to procure them when baby No. 1 is dethroned by baby No. 2. But no child of six or seven is large enough to sit comfortably and gracefully at table in a chair made to suit a grown person, especially if not allowed to put its feet upon the chair-rung. Its feet do not reach the floor, and are apt to swing about in a way to fret nervous people, and in a way that certainly is not graceful. And its elbows are not high enough to give it easy command of its plate and knife and fork.

Fig. 1.—OFFICE STOOL.

So, in teaching table manners, look first for the comfortable seating of your children. A cheap piano stool does very well for an intermediate seat between highchair and common dining chair. Any man with tools can make one on a rainy day, if it seems too much to purchase a second highchair.

Fig. 2.—STOOL FOR TABLE.

A friend of ours purchased a high, yellow office stool for a dollar. This was sawed off, to suit the needs of a child of six, above the lower rungs. A second very comfortable and useful seat was made of the part sawed off, by putting a square board atop, and cusioning it with gay woolen patchwork. (1872)

Fig. 3.—LOW STOOL.

A Seat in the Grove

A BASKET YARD SEAT.

A tree that has been felled, leaving a stump of convenient height, can provide a pleasant woodland resting place. The top of this is made level, and surmounted with a cover of a peach basket which is made of elastic splints. When this cover is attached by a strong nail in the center, it forms an inviting and convenient seat. (1883)

A Rustic Seat

A seat of some kind is needed in the grounds, whether they be extensive or of only moderate dimensions. What is called rustic work, that is, limbs as nearly as possible in their natural form and condition, seems to harmonize with the surroundings better than anything of a more artificial character. The engraving is taken from a rustic settee presented by D. J. Young, Esq., to the Cove (Oyster Bay) Ladies Soldiers' Aid Society.

A Rustic Seat.

It appears to be made of the wood of the laurel (*Kalmia latifolia*), and a great deal of ingenuity is displayed in the selection of the crooked limbs and fitting them together. The bottom, which is not shown very distinctly, is curiously inlaid with half round pieces, forming a sort of mosaic work. One who has a fair share of mechanical skill, can readily make work of this kind, and find pleasant occupation for stormy days. The woods of the laurel and red cedar are the kinds most suitable for such work. (1864)

How to Build a Boat

Rivers and lakes being so plentifully interspersed, boats become articles of great convenience, or absolute necessity, and the ability to construct one, however rude it may be, is a useful accomplishment.

Fig. 1.—THE BOAT IN USE.

Here are directions for constructing a boat capacious enough to carry two good-sized men and a fat buck, if they should ever be so lucky as to be compelled to carry one home. The boat is at the same time sufficiently light to enable it to be carried about easily when required to be removed from one piece of water to another.

The boat is flat-bottomed, and the keel or bottom is of board ¾-inch in thickness, of white pine, or other light wood that will not readily split. The length of the boat represented is 9 feet, width 2 to 3 feet, depth 18 inches. These proportions may be varied to suit circumstances.

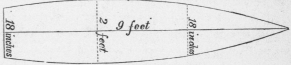

Fig. 2.—THE BOTTOM OF THE BOAT.

To shape the bottom or keel, take two boards of the character before mentioned and 12 inches wide. Join them together by a tongue-and-groove joint. Make the joint watertight by means of pitch, and fasten a cleat across with clinch-nails or screws, to prevent its spreading. Mark out with a pencil the shape represented in *figure 2*. Cut this out very accurately, and plane very smoothly to line, with a slight bevel upwards. The more carefully this is done, the closer the joint and the dryer the boat will be.

Fig. 3.—THE STEM.

The stem is made, preferably, of a tamarack "knee;" if this cannot be readily procured, cut out of soft maple a "knee" 1 inch thick, as a substitute. This should represent an angle of something over 90 degrees, so as to give a forward rake, as in *figure 3*. The front of the upright portion should be beveled to a fine edge, the bottom dressed square, and fitted to the keel in its place with screws, or wrought nails riveted over burrs.

27

Fig. 4.—BOAT TURNED TO SHOW BOTTOM AND STERN.

The stern (*figure 4*) is of similar stuff to the keel, cut 6 inches wider at the top than at the bottom. The side boards should be of ¼-inch spruce stuff, well seasoned, and dressed, at least on the outside, to present the least resistance to the water.

To give the boat the proper shape, cut out patterns representing the cross section of it at those parts crossed by the dotted lines. The sides should spread a little, that is, should be wider at the gunwale than at the keel, say 6 to 12 inches. The patterns should be cut accordingly and be tacked lightly to the keel-board to hold them in their place until done with. The dotted lines which cross the boat are drawn at equal distances, and show the width at those places which is greatest a little back of the center (*figure 2*).

It is a great point in hunting to have a boat that will make no ripple, and this gradual decrease of width towards the stern avoids all noise as the boat passes along. A boat of this pattern will do this perfectly, and will be found easier to row or paddle.

When the molds are properly placed, take the boards—which should have been previously soaked at the ends in water—and fit them to their places, holding them with a clamp, until securely nailed to the stem and stern. All nails which pass through the boards where they overlap, should be clinched on the inside; boat nails should be used. When the first board, which is the bottom one, is put on, fit the next, allowing ¾-inch to lap.

Between the boards, at the lap, place a piece of thick cotton cloth, dipped in tar, which will make the joint watertight, or nearly so, and calking will be unnecessary. Then fit on the top board, taking care the upper edge has a proper sweep. When the boards are fastened, put in two ribs, which should be of white oak, ½-inch thick, and 1½ wide. Soak them thoroughly, until they are pliable enough to bend into their places, and secure them by nails clinched on the inside. These should be placed midway between the molds, and not only strengthen the frame, but give a bearing for the feet of the rower. A piece of tin should be bent over the stem, and nailed from bottom to top, for a cutwater. Before putting this piece of tin on, fill in well with pitch and tallow.

The molds may now be removed. A strip 2 inches wide and ½ thick should then be nailed all around on the inside. Cleats are to be nailed on for the thwarts (or seats), which should be placed 6 inches below the gunwale or edge. The hinder seat may be made of the lid of a locker or box, in which tools, nails, lines, a supply of putty, tallow, pieces of tarred canvas and tin, should be stowed away, as resources in case of damage or leaking. The bow of the boat should have a similar place made to hold a supply of eatables when necessary. A baling dipper should be stowed away in one of these lockers. The bottoms of the lockers must be elevated 2 or 3 inches above the keel, to keep the contents dry. *Figure 5* shows the arrangement of the lockers and seat.

Fig. 5.—BOAT, SHOWING RIBS, LOCKERS, AND SEAT.

A ringbolt and cord, sufficiently long, should be attached to the bow, for the purpose of tying up. To finish up the job, the seams must be gone over carefully, and putty and white lead be applied to every crack. Then two coats of paint ought to be laid on. With the name painted on the stern, she is ready for the launch.

A pair of oars may be made of ash, or, what is preferable, a pair of paddles, like the one shown in *figure 6*. When properly made and used, paddles are much more convenient and efficient than oars. In using a paddle, one has his face to the front and can see all ahead of him. In rowing, it is necessarily the opposite to this. If oars are used, rowlocks must be fitted on to the sides.

Fig. 6.

To make a paddle, take a piece of inch board (cedar is the lightest and best, but an oak paddle is very durable), 6 inches wide. Dress out the blade ¼-inch thick at the edges, ½-inch at the center, gradually increasing the thickness towards the handle. The handle may be whittled down until it fits the hand comfortably. Then dress it with sandpaper perfectly smooth, and rub with oil; a smooth handle will not blister the hands.

A boat thus made will look very nicely, but if means and time are wanting to finish it as here described, a rough one may be put together very quickly and cheaply by using the same or lighter materials in a rougher fashion. In place of three side boards, one wide board (12 inches) may be used, and the seats laid across flush with the top. (1871)

How to Build a Rowboat

Those who live near the water are quite sure to have a boat of some kind, if it be only a roughly made skiff, or a "dug-out." Rowing is capital amusement and good exercise, and a boat is not only a source of pleasure but is, in certain localities, of great use.

Fig. 1.—THE BOAT COMPLETE.

Oak is the most durable material, but white cedar or even pine will make a much lighter boat. *Figure 1* gives a general view of the boat which is intended to be 16 feet long, and 3 feet wide. Two boards 16 feet long and 16 inches wide will be required for the sides; three boards of the same length and a foot wide will be needed for the bottom, besides material for the stern and other parts.

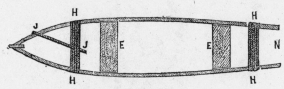

Fig. 2.—SHAPING THE BOAT.

The boards for the sides have two blocks, *E,E,* each 2¾ feet long, placed between them, and they are bound tightly by means of a rope, as shown at *H, H,* in *figure 2.* Insert a strong rod between the ropes at *J,* and twist it gradually until the ends of the boards nearly meet. Now insert the cut-water, seen in *figure 2* at left or prow end, which should be a strip 18 inches long, 3 inches wide, and an inch thick. Twist the ropes until the cut-water is held fast.

Secure the stick, *J,* so that the ropes cannot untwist, and then bore several holes through both side boards and the cut-water, and secure all three firmly with screws.

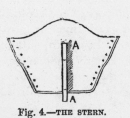

Fig. 4.—THE STERN.   Fig. 5.

The stern is shown in *figure 4.* It is 36 inches wide at top and 18 inches deep. It is fixed firmly to the end of the boat by means of long screws.

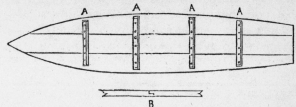

Fig. 3.—THE BOTTOM OF THE BOAT.

The bottom of the boat is made of three pieces, as in *figure 3,* the edges being rabbeted, as shown at *B.* The boards are held together by four pieces, *A, A,* screwed on firmly. The bottom is secured to the sides by means of long, slender screws, carefully put in, the cross-pieces being uppermost. The keel should be a strip an inch square, and firmly fixed along the bottom, exactly in the center.

The rudder is shaped as in *figure 5,* with a cross-piece at the top to which small ropes may be attached for the purpose of working it. It has two iron hooks, *D, D,* to enable it to be hung to a strip, *A, figure 3,* which is placed exactly in the middle of the stern, and is furnished with two iron eyes or screw rings to receive the hooks.

Row locks and seats are to be provided as in *figure 1.*

The boat is now to be caulked in every seam or crevice, and melted pitch should then be poured over these spaces. If all has been thoroughly done, the boat will be water-tight, and may then be painted inside and out of such color as may suit the taste. (1869)

An Open Wood Box

The engraving illustrates a convenient wood box. The "shelf" is a 1½-inch plank, 1 by 2½ feet. The end pieces are 28 inches high, with the shelf nailed on 10 inches from the floor. A cleat is fastened along the front. The ends may be cut away to form legs, as shown above. Such an open box or rack cannot become a receptacle for the refuse commonly thrown into the ordinary wood box. (1883)

A WOOD RACK.

A Convenient Woodbox

The old-fashioned woodbox is a clumsy, inelegant, and generally inconvenient affair. It takes up a great deal more room than can be readily afforded in most kitchens and is always in the way of the broom and the mop. The labor of bringing in wood to fill the box, night and morning, is considerable, especially if done by the cook. If the children perform this labor, there is a good deal of tracking in of snow or dust that might be avoided by having a different receptacle for wood.

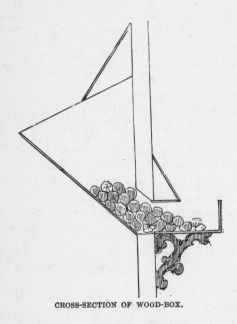

CROSS-SECTION OF WOOD-BOX.

Such an article is now in practical operation, and the women of the household count it a daily blessing. All there is to be seen from the kitchen is a box about 2 feet from the floor, supported by brackets. This box is about 2½ feet long, 1 foot wide, and 8 inches deep. On top is a cover which turns back against the wall. The box is placed close to the stove and the wood is handy. As fast as wood is removed from the kitchen part, that which has been piled into the reservoir of the outside part, in the attached woodshed, settles down, and thus there is always a supply, provided the filling of the box in the woodshed has not been neglected.

This outside woodbox is made large enough to hold fuel for a day's supply, and has also a cover. When both inside and outside covers are closed, there is no draft of cold air coming through the box. As the front of the reservoir is slanting, the weight of the wood crowds the sticks at the bottom forward into the opening in the kitchen. Such a woodbox is a vast improvement on the old kind, in handiness and in looks; the part belonging to the kitchen can be made as ornamental as desired. (1883)

Coal and Wood Boxes

A coal scuttle, or hod, as it is differently called, while it is a most useful household convenience, is not a very sightly thing to have in the sitting room or parlor. Of late years, the furnishing stores have kept coal boxes made of heavy sheet iron, and variously ornamented. True taste demands that a coal box should be honest, and that its appearance should be such as to lead anyone to suppose that it is anything but a receptacle for coal. Some of the coal boxes offered for sale are especially absurd. We noticed one in the form of a classic vase. It is bad enough to see these specimens of ancient art converted into flowerpots, but to have them used for coal boxes, made in iron, highly enameled, and ornamented with flowers, and furnished with a cover, is an outrage upon propriety. A vase with a cover! Another style nearly as bad is a short fluted column with a cover. Unless a column is solid it is worthless. Yet here we have one made hollow, and to hold coal!

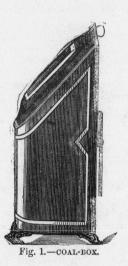

Fig. 1.—COAL-BOX.

The most sensible form of coal box offered for sale is shown in *figure 1*. It is made of heavy sheet iron, and has a handle at the front and rear to allow of its being readily carried. Some manufacturers ornament them profusely with flowers and other colored designs, which, as a matter of taste, had better be left off. There are many who would like to have a coal box who are beyond the reach of furnishing stores and of workers in iron who could make one for them. These must content themselves with a box of wood. One, made in the shape of *figure 1*, of wood, and lined if possible with galvanized or sheet iron or heavy tin, will answer. It is better to have the box lined, as a wooden one in a warm room will shrink so that the joints will allow dust to sift out. The wood may be varnished with shellac or other varnish.

Fig. 2.—RUSTIC WOOD-BOX.

Wood boxes are a necessity where there are wood fires, as, however carefully it may be managed, wood will make that dread of all good housekeepers—"a mess." In *figure 2* we give a design for a woodbox which may be of a size for one or two persons to carry, and which is susceptible of any desired amount of ornament. The essentials of a woodbox are that it shall keep the wood from contact with the carpet, and prevent the sticks from rolling off. The one we have figured may be made in a rustic style, with saplings and any thin boarding, and may be ornamented with whatever rustic work may be at hand. Its appearance may be improved by a coating of shellac or varnish. (1873)

Portable Clothes-Drying Posts

Many people are annoyed at seeing posts, for tying the clothesline to, standing permanently on the lawn. The difficulty, however, can be easily overcome by having movable posts, that can be placed in position for a few hours, when needed, and then taken down and laid away till next washing day. Here is a description of such a plan that has been used for some years and found to answer the purpose.

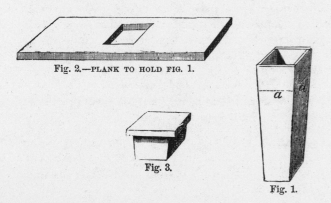

Fig. 2.—PLANK TO HOLD FIG. 1.

Fig. 3.

Fig. 1.

First make a box *(figure 1)* of 1½ or 2-inch plank, 18 inches long, 7 inches square at the top, and 6 at the bottom. Next get a plank about 3 feet long, 2 or 3 inches thick, and 12 or 14 inches wide *(figure 2)*, in which but a square hole which shall tightly fit the box at the dotted line, *a a*. Next make a wooden stopper *(figure 3)* to fit the top of the box *(figure 1)*. Nail the box firmly onto the plank *(figure 2)*, and plant them firmly in the ground, so that the top of the box is just level with the surface, ramming the whole well down. Make the end of your clothespost to fit the socket *(figure 1)*, and, when you remove it, be careful to cover the hole with the stopper. *Figure 4* shows a section of the whole when fixed for use. (1871)

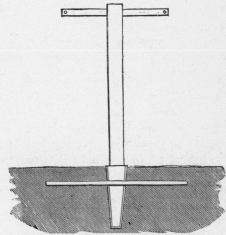

Fig. 4.—CLOTHES DRYING POST IN PLACE.

Homemade Trellises for Vines

Small trellises for supporting vines growing in pots can be bought in a great variety of shapes and styles, but those that will answer the purpose quite as well can be made at home with little trouble and at a very trifling expense.

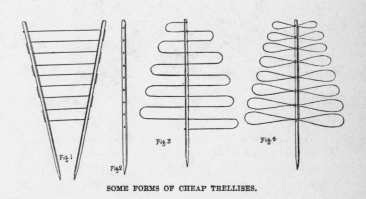

SOME FORMS OF CHEAP TRELLISES.

The form illustrated by *figure 1* is very easily made. Take two pieces of thin wood, *figure 2*, an inch wide, and 16 inches long, round off the top and sharpen the lower edges. With a gimlet make small holes 1¼ inches apart, and rub them smooth with a piece of sandpaper or a knife. Next take a piece of twine and thread it back and forth through the holes; fasten each end of the twine by tying in it a neat knot just large enough not to slip through the holes. After the trellis is drawn into the right shape, thrust it into a pot filled with earth to hold it at the right angle, and give it a coat of stiff varnish. When that is dry, add a coat of green paint. The trellis will be almost as firm and last quite as well as if made altogether of wood.

The trellis shown in *figure 3* is made by cutting square notches 1½ inches apart in a piece of wood 20 inches long, ½-inch thick, and ¾-inch wide. The supports are of medium sized wire put on as illustrated, and held firmly in place by binding once around the stick where the notches are cut out. After the wire is on, it is all painted green.

Figure 4 is made in the same way, but the wire is put on in a different shape. Instead of green the trellis may be painted a dark brown, or a light yellowish gray or brown, to look like cane or rattan. The sizes given are for trellises to be used in ordinary sized pots, and they can be made smaller or larger to suit the plant for which they are used. (1883)

Letter Box

Fig. 1.—LETTER BOX.

Figure 1 shows a letter box with three divisions that is very convenient for holding unanswered letters, envelopes, small notepaper, postage stamps, memorandum cards, and pencils. It is about 6 inches long, 3 deep, and

6 high at the middle of the back. It may be made of black walnut or butternut or of white wood or white pine, stained and rubbed with oil. The front shows open carved work with leaves and flowers, and is too elaborate for a beginner; but a part of the carving can be left off and still make a very convenient box.

It is put together with small iron pins and with wooden pegs and glue. It can either stand on the table, or be suspended from the wall in any convenient place. (1868)

Butter Molds

Here are directions for making useful butter molds at home. The difficulty lies in getting the stamp made. Anyone who can work a foot-lathe, can turn the mold and the plain stamp with the handle, but the device which ornaments the stamp troubles them.

Fig. 1.—BUTTER-MOLD.   Fig. 2.—BUTTER-MOLD.

To make this, take a piece of wood free from grain—a piece of soft maple or birch root is very good—and have it turned or dressed the proper size, and a smooth face made on it. Then either draw on the face, *the wrong way* (as shown in *figures 1* and *2*), or cut out letters from a newspaper and paste them on to the face of the mold, *the wrong way*, and make a border to suit the fancy, in the same manner. Then take a small, sharp gouge, like the one shown in *figure 2*, not larger than a ¼-inch in diameter, and smoothly cut away the wood beneath the letters, making them deep enough to show well when printed on the butter. About a ¼-inch would be right. The depression should be neatly smoothed out so as to make a neat, smooth print.

A pretty border for a mold is a quantity of clover leaves. They may be pasted on, and the wood then cut out as before described, or any other leaves would answer. (1872)

A Convenient Cutting-Board

LAP-CUTTING BOARD.

The board here figured is nothing new, but it is not in near as general use as it would be were it better known. A lady of our acquaintance who recently had one made, now wonders how she ever did without one. It is made to hold in the lap, and with a semicircular place cut out to accommodate it to the body. This board will be found very convenient in cutting and fitting work for the sewing machine, as it can be used without the fatigue that attends standing over an ordinary table. (1872)

A Support for Quilting Frames

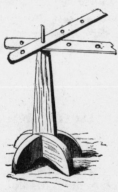

SUPPORT FOR FRAME.

Here is a little contrivance which will do away with the usual and awkward way of supporting a quilting frame upon the backs of chairs. The engraving explains how it works. The crosspieces, forming the foot, are 18 inches long, and the upright 31 inches high. A piece of stout wire is driven firmly into the top of the upright, and as it passes through the holes in both pieces of the frame, no pins are required. (1872)

Another Support for a Quilting Frame

Here is a simple device for supporting a quilting frame. The engraving shows one of the two supports required. It is made of any light wood, 3 feet wide and 4 feet high. The poles to which the quilt is attached are round, 7 feet long, or the desired length. In the crossbars of the support, holes (*a*, *b*) are bored to receive the ends of these poles, which are inserted in them. Gimlet-holes are made at *c*, down through the support and into the poles.

SUPPORT FOR QUILTING-FRAME.

W. M. Nixon, Clement, Ill., has supplied a sketch and description of his quilting frame. The construction of this frame is made clear by the engraving. the side pieces are of 2 by 4 inch dressed pine, 8 feet long. The frame may be taken apart and be closely packed away when not in use. (1883)

A Quilting Frame

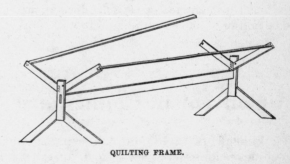

QUILTING FRAME.

The quilt is fastened to the poles in the usual manner, and rolled up upon one of them, except so much as is required to allow the ends of the poles to go into their places in the supports. The quilt, as the work progresses, can be readily rolled from one pole upon the other, and by boring a few holes in the ends of the poles at *a*, *b*, it may be stretched and held in place by the insertion of wooden pegs or nails. (1872)

A Spoon Case

A CONVENIENT SPOON-CASE.

Silverware is an article of table use that is not only expensive, but is easily injured by scratching, tarnishing, etc., and the spoons in particular should receive better care at the hands of the housekeeper than is generally given them. This is easily done by the use of a spoon case, or holder, similar to the one shown in the engraving.

It is simply a box, k, 2½ inches high, and of a length and width sufficient to place six teaspoons crosswise at one end, and three tablespoons lengthwise at the opposite end. The bottom may be filled half an inch in depth with wheat bran or sawdust, over which is fitted a piece of flannel, and upon this the spoons may be firmly pressed, to make a permanent indentation in the bran and the cloth.

Pieces of flannel, a, b, and h, are secured with glue or tacks to each end of the case. One of these pieces is spread over the spoons as soon as a course is laid; another is then added, and a second piece of flannel placed over it.

A hinged cover, e, may be attached to either end. A handle, p, is secured at the center. This is a very simple arrangement, and by the use of different colored flannels, and by the painting or papering of the box, a very neat and attractive receptacle is obtained for an expensive portion of table furniture. (1882)

A Convenient Clotheshorse

The clotheshorse here figured has several advantages over the old form. When opened to its full extent it has the capacity of a horse of the old style, and it can be used with one-fourth, one-half, three-fourths, or all of its slats spread. And when not in use it takes up but little room in its stable, which for this kind of horse is usually behind the kitchen door. After a trial of some weeks it was found an exceedingly convenient affair. It was invented by Mr. John A. Morfit, of Harlem, New York, who for a wonder has not patented it, but freely gives the design for the benefit of all readers.

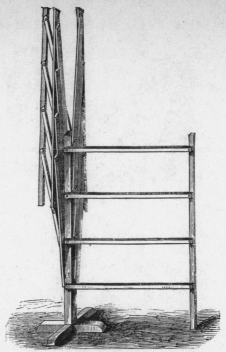

CONVENIENT CLOTHES-HORSE.

The engraving needs but little explanation. The central post, which has a foot to allow it to stand firmly, is of 1½-inch stuff, and is 4 feet 6 inches high. Each of the four sections consists of four horizontals of 1 × ⅜ inch stuff, 2 feet 8 inches long, and an upright of similar stuff 4 feet 6 inches high. The sections are all alike, and are put together by means of rivets and washers. If screws are used they will soon work loose. The central post is of pine, and the slats and uprights may be of ash or similar strong wood. This horse can be readily made by any one of ordinary mechanical skill, the chief item of expense being the rivets. (1873)

An Unpatented Clotheshorse

Many of the contrivances to hold clothes while they are drying or airing, are patented. Here is one invented by Mr. Chas. F. Diebert, Schuylkill County, Pennsylvania, that is not patented, and which is so simple that it can be readily made.

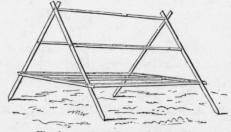

Fig. 1.—CLOTHES-HORSE EXTENDED.

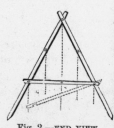

Fig. 2.—END VIEW.

The engraving shows a perspective view of the horse, which is 5 feet long and 4½ feet high. It requires in its construction neither nails nor screws, the whole being fastened together by wooden pins through the ends of the bars, which project through holes in the uprights, which are ¾-inch by 2 inches. The end view is given in *figure 2*. Perpendicular dotted lines show the manner in which the clothes hang, and it will be seen that those upon one bar will not come in contact with those upon another. The crosspieces at the ends are attached by one of their ends to one of the horizontal bars, and hook upon another bar by means of a notch near the opposite end. By unhooking the crosspieces, as shown by the dotted lines, and removing the lower center bar, the horse can be folded up and occupy but a small space. (1870)

A Convenient Stepladder

STEP-LADDER.

W.P. Hope, Kalamazoo County, Michigan, has supplied a drawing of a stepladder. The side pieces are 6 inches wide, any desired length. The top step is 1 foot wide and 2 feet long. The pieces nailed to the sides are 6 inches wide. The braces are 2½ inches wide; the length is proportionate to height of ladder. The posts are 2½ inches wide and 1½ inches thick, fastened to the upright with a pin. A brace, showing the notch to go on a pin in the posts, is seen in the engraving. This stepladder, when not in use, can be quickly folded and hung up on a good strong nail out of the way. (1883)

A Convenient Workbox

A very handy thing about the house is a suitable receptacle for needles, thimble, thread, scissors, bits of cloth, and odds and ends of sewing, which too often are

thrown carelessly about, or become lost or badly soiled and tangled up, etc., etc.

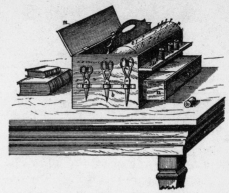

A CONVENIENT WORK BOX.

The engraving shows a new, neat, and desirable workbox that will prove very handy on the sewing table. The box proper is 8 inches long, 5 inches high, and 6 inches wide. At one side is a small drawer, *a*, extending across the bottom. The scissors may be secured to one end as at *b*, or placed inside as desired.

At the right of the handle is a pincushion, *e*, while at the left is a little box with lid, *m*. Above and parallel with the drawer, a strip, *p*, is tacked or glued, into which at proper intervals small pieces of wire are inserted; on these spools may be placed.

The box may be made from hard or soft wood, and embellished to suit the maker's fancy. (1882)

Fashions in Bootjacks

One would suppose that a bootjack was not susceptible of much improvement, and that a simple notched board, with a cleat to give it proper elevation, would be all that was required. Yet bootjacks have been improved, and have even been the subject of numerous patents.

Fig. 1.—COMMON BOOT-JACK.

Fig. 2.—IMPROVED BOOT-JACK.

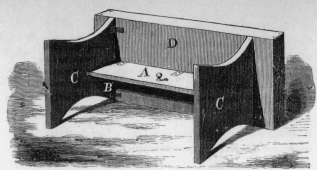

Fig. 5.—BOX AND BENCH FOR BLACKING SHOES.

If one has to use an implement daily, he desires it to be made in as comely a form as possible; hence it is pleasant to have the crude appearance of *figure 1*, with its sharp angles, modified into the neatly-rounded implement of *figure 2*. Those who travel much prefer carrying their own bootjack to trusting to the uncertain resources of ordinary hotels. For the convenience of packing in the trunk, the folded implement, shown in *figure 3*, has been contrived. Another folding style is shown in *figure 4*; the shorter portion has two stout pins, which, when in use, sufficiently elevates the end from the floor. When the parts are folded together, the pins fit into holes in the longer portion. All of the forms are easily made of wood, although numerous fancy patterns in iron must be purchased at the furnishing stores.

A Handy Boot Rack

One of the greatest troubles of the neat housewife in the country results from the muddy boots of those members of the family who have to work in the fields, the stables, and the barnyard. The wet boots must be dried, and are generally left under the kitchen stove, where their presence is very disagreeable. Now, to have a neat kitchen, there should be a book rack placed behind the stove, in which the damp boots may be placed to dry.

Fig. 3.—TRAVELERS' BOOT-JACK

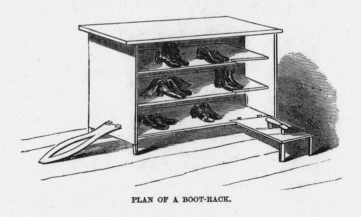

PLAN OF A BOOT-RACK.

Fig. 4.—FOLDING BOOT-JACK.

A bench for resting the foot while blacking, and which also serves as a box to hold the brushes, etc., is given in *figure 5*. It is made in such a manner as to shut up and occupy but a small space. The box, *D*, forms the top of the bench, and holds the blacking and brushes. The lid, *A*, serves, when open, to hold the two folding legs, *C*, in place. When packed away, the lid, *A*, shuts down upon *B*, and the legs are then folded together, and secured by a hook. (1871)

Such a contrivance as the one shown in the engraving has been found a great convenience. It has three shelves about 4 feet long, 10 inches wide, and placed a foot apart. At one end a bootjack is fixed by hinges, so that when not in use it is folded against one end of the rack and secured by a button. There is also a stand for cleaning boots at the front, which also folds up when not in use, and the blacking brushes are placed on the shelves behind the stand and are out of sight. The two feet of the stand are also hinged, and when it is folded they hang down out of the way. The rack should be made of dressed pine boards, and painted or stained of some dark, durable color. (1873)

Household Ornaments
A Match Safe

Household ornaments are not perhaps so essential in the country as in the city, where people are necessarily cut off from the fields and woods with their thousand beautiful things. But everywhere pretty articles of furniture are prized, and perform an important office in the education of children. The only objection to them in many houses is their cost. This book frequently presents illustrations of such ornaments and shows how they may be constructed. Anyone ingenious with the knife or handy with the needle can learn to make them and thus add to their own usefulness while they adorn their houses.

Fig. 1.—MATCH SAFE.

Figure 1 shows a match safe made from a common cigar box or any other thin bit of board. It is easy to have black walnut, butternut, oak, or other ornamental wood sawed thin for this purpose. The shield should first be marked out with a pencil according to the design. The cutting can all be done with a sharp penknife and will afford very good amusement for a winter evening. The large star in the centre forms the hole to hang up the box when finished. The box, made as shown in *figure 1*, can be put together and fastened to the shield with a little glue.

Such a match safe, hung up over the mantelpiece or near the stove where the fire is to be kindled or lamps lighted, will help essentially in the formation of orderly habits. There will always be a place for the matches, and the matches can be kept in their place. By enlarging the pattern, boxes can be made that will answer other purposes. (1867)

Match Safes

Friction matches allow us to kindle a fire with the least possible trouble. Housekeepers of the present day know but little of the difficulty those of older times had in getting a fire, and of the care exercised in keeping it. Perhaps some can recollect how cautiously the coals were covered with ashes at night, that the embers might be ready to start the morning fire; and when with all the care the coals were found dead, how irksome it was to go of a cold morning to a distant neighbor's to "borrow some fire," and convey it home in a pan or shovel, in order that the household machinery might be once more set in motion. But the cheapness of matches has done away with all this, and now a scratch with a match brings the needed servant to do our bidding.

The increased facility in obtaining fire has brought with it increased danger. The scratch that will bring the friendly fire will also bring the fire fiend to burn and destroy. Investigations by the proper officers in our large cities have shown that a considerable share of fires is to be attributed to carelessness with matches. There cannot be too much caution exercised in keeping matches, whether the stock for future use or those kept at hand to supply the daily needs. A match carelessly dropped may be ignited by the tread of the next passer, and give rise to a conflagration, or it may fall into the hands of a young child, and thus be the cause of disaster. Rats have been known to carry matches to their holes and thus add to their general mischievous ways by turning incendiaries.

Fig. 1.—SIMPLE MATCH-SAFE.

When a stock of matches is kept on hand they should be stored where none but the proper persons can have access to them, and in such a manner that there can be no possible danger of ignition by accident. A tin box is an excellent place. Equal care should be taken with those kept at hand for frequent use. Leaving them about upon the mantel shelf and in similar places should not be tolerated. There are match safes of various designs sold at the stores which may be had at little expense, but any box or receptacle that can be affixed in a convenient place will do as well. The important thing is to have the match safe in a fixed place, and have it understood that matches are to be found there and no where else. It is advisable that the receptacle have a rough surface for scratching the matches upon, as this will prevent much disfiguring of the woodwork. In rooms where there is no fire it is better to have a place to receive the ends of burnt matches. A half-consumed match is a small thing, but neat persons are often puzzled to know what to do with it, and all doubt upon the matter is done away with if a receptacle is provided.

Here are illustrations of match safes in which some ornamental work is introduced. They will serve as suggestions to those who would like to make such articles. Their woods of various kinds, including cigar-box material, are easily worked by the use of a sharp knife and a fine saw. (1870)

Fig. 2.—DOUBLE MATCH-SAFE.

Fig. 3.—CARVED MATCH-SAFE.

39

II. Sewing & Other Fancywork

An Embroidered Sachet

This pretty sachet, *figure 29*, is suitable for evening or dinner dress. It may be made of silk of two shades or colors. The form will be easily copied from the design shown in the illustration. The top has a double slide at

Fig. 29. Sachet-Embroidery.

the ends, in which strong elastic is run. Bows of ribbon ornament the ends, and the sachet is suspended by ribbon, with pearl buckles for ornaments. The outer part of the medallion is in buttonhole stitch. The whole of the embroidery is in purse-silk. (1876)

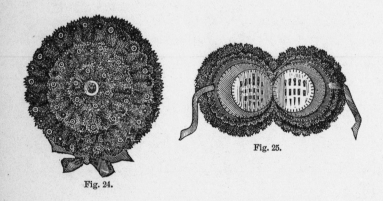

Fig. 24.

Fig. 25.

Ladies' Needlebook

Figure 24 shows a needlebook closed; *figure 25* shows it open. The leaves for holding the pins and needles are of fine cashmere edged with a buttonhole stitch. The outer part has a foundation of cardboard which is covered and lined with silk. Over this are little frills of silk, finely pinked, plaited, and ornamented with a bead in each plait. A bow of ribbon finishes the needlebook. (1876)

A Housewife (Caddy)

The housewife illustrated in *figure 18* is so good that with this description any lady can make one quickly. It is 6 inches wide and 10 long. The outside is made of green morocco, and the linings and pockets of green silk; it is bound all around with green galloon. The spools are held by a piece of strong wire which is fastened at one end into a round pincushion, and at the other fits into a piece of pasteboard covered with silk. The pincushion is fastened in by only half a dozen stitches so that the wire on which the spools are strung may be movable. This housewife may be rolled up and tied with a bit of ribbon. (1876)

Fig. 18. Housewife.

Children's Bibs

Common napkins do not serve the needs of children under six or eight years at the table so well as bibs that may be tied or buttoned around the neck. They should be long enough to tuck under the table, or to cover the child's lap. A small gore in front, with a band of right length, secures a good fit around the neck. A pattern (*figure 2*) is given for those who need it.

Bibs much like this are used for teething children. They are usually made of marseilles, or diaper-linen,

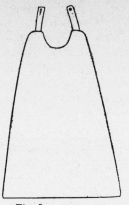

Fig. 2.—TABLE BIB.　　　　Fig. 3.—BIB.

and are lined. They may be scalloped and embroidered, or simply bound with braid. Some babies have them pinned down in front and behind with pretty little gold or fancy bib-pins. Here also is a pattern *(figure 3)* for a baby's bib, but it admits of variation. The table bib may be kept with the table napkins. A child should be encouraged to keep his bib clean and neat. (1872)

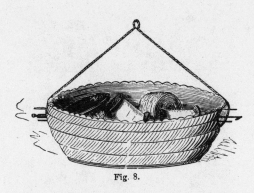

Fig. 8.

A Tatting-Boat

Those who are partial to tatting generally like to carry it with them to occupy a leisure moment, and to such persons is recommended the little boat shown in *figure 8*. It is made by crocheting an oblong piece in double crochet, using the coarsest cotton or fine cord, then stiffening with glue and forming while damp into the boat shape. Take also two small brass curtain rings, and crochet a cover for each; then insert them in the ends of the boat to hold knitting needles, crochet hook, etc. Plait or twist a cable cord, and fasten it in the upper part of the rings with little ball-buttons hanging from them. Varnish with copal, and when dry, line, if desired, with cherry-colored, amber, pink, or blue silk. When working, suspend from the belt by a ribbon passed through the rope handle. (1876)

An Ornamental Pincushion

A very pretty pincushion can be made in the following manner:

Cut a square piece of satin, wool, or silk, and embroider a grape vine with fruit, arranged in the form of a wreath, in the center. The leaves, stems, and tendrils should be embroidered with white silk in the overstitch, and upon each dot that represents a grape, fasten a bead of the size in *a*.

For the under side, cut a square like the one embroidered, and cover both over a cushion made of some common, thick material stuffed with cotton. Finish by fastening a quilling of white satin ribbon around the edge. The shape is improved by cutting each side of the material a little hollow. The color may be left to choice.

VINE FOR PINCUSHION.

A cushion of this kind makes a very pretty bridal present. The engraving shows a portion of the grape-vine wreath of about half the size needed for a large cushion. (1869)

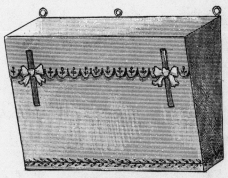

A DUST CLOTH CASE.

A Case for Dust Cloths

A tidy housekeeper cannot get along without dusters and wipers. A convenient place to keep such articles is a case made as shown in the illustration, and hung on the

43

kitchen wall. It has a division in the middle so that the dust cloth and the window cleaners can be kept separate.

The case should be made large enough to accommodate all the dusters and cloths in use, and a few others in reserve. Pieces for the back, front, bottom, and two sides, of the shape shown in the illustration, are cut from pasteboard. A third piece, the same size and shape as the sides, is fastened down the middle of the case, to make the two compartments. Each piece is covered with light oilcloth and bound around with woolen braid, a simple pattern having first been worked along the lower edge of the oilcloth with zephyr, same color as the braid. After the case is sewed together, the extra piece is fastened in the center by a few stitches top and bottom. A piece of oilcloth the width of the case, as shown, is scalloped at its base and sewn to the top front edge of the box. Three rings or loops of braid to hang the case up by are sewn to the back. Two pieces of braid on the flap and two on the front serve for fastening ties. (1883)

Catch-All

A CATCH-ALL.

To make this catch-all, cover a piece of tin or pasteboard, 20 inches long, and 4 wide, joined into a ring, with bright-flowered chintz. To the lower part of the ring run a strip of material 12 inches deep, and a yard long, seamed together. After it is sewed on, gather it at the bottom to make a full, fluffy bag, and add two small tassels of zephyr. Around the upper edge sew another piece of material, like the bag, 6 inches deep, and long enough to go around the ring easily. Sew a ribbon or braid an inch and a half from the upper edge to make a casing, in which run a narrow silk braid, or a cord, for a drawstring. Fasten a heavy worsted cord at each side, by which to hang it up. (1883)

Bags for Shoes and Slippers

The basic arrangement is one that can be used on the inside of the closet door in a bedroom. It contains 18 pockets (as shown in the figure), each of which will hold a pair of thin shoes; for thick shoes, a pocket each is required.

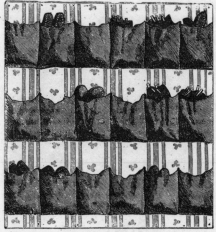

BAG FOR SHOES, ETC.

The backing foundation is 27 inches deep by 24 inches wide with a facing around the edge, underneath, to give it strength. For the pockets, take three strips, 7 inches wide by 42 inches long, and hem at top; a cord is sewn in the lower part of each to gather it to the size of the back foundation. Sew each strip tightly across the back, equidistant, commencing at the lower edge.

Each strip being divided into 6 equal parts, stitch them upwards in place, 4 inches apart. The pockets thus formed will receive the shoes, the size in all cases being proportioned to the requirements.

These articles are made with two rows for closets in spare rooms, and with shallow rows for small shoes in nursery and children's bedrooms. Simple square panels with 6 or 8 pockets are placed behind doors in servants' rooms to prevent their shoes being thrown in all directions about the room.

All of these are made of chintz, figured or plain, generally selected to correspond with the colors of the room. (1869)

A Sofa Cushion with a Lace Tidy

The model, *figure 40*, is 18 inches square, and may be made of two contrasting colors of silk or satin or of two shades of the same color. Instead of being covered with a

Fig. 40. Sofa-Cushion.

lace tidy, as in the engraving, the center of the cushion may be decorated with embroidery or cretonne appliqué. The space between the inner puffing and the two frills—the outer one and the ½-inch-wide frill which is fastened down by a box-plaiting—may be also filled up with a border of embroidery corresponding to the centerpiece. (1876)

An Embroidered Canvas Pillow

Figure 107 represents a finished pillow decorated with full ruchings of silk. The materials required are fine canvas, zephyr worsted in four shades of green, one of

Fig. 107. Pillow.

brown, and one of white; white and yellow embroidery silk; yellow and black twist silk; and two shades of blue floss silk.

Draw the outlines of the border, and then work the leaves in satin-stitch in two shades of green. The veins, stems, and tendrils are worked in long stitches with brown worsted taken double. The flowers and buds are likewise worked in satin-stitch of white zephyr-worsted, each petal further ornamented by a long stitch of white embroidery silk. Long stitches of green worsted taken double constitute the calyxes of the buds. Those of the flowers are represented by knots of yellow embroidery silk, and of this silk also, the loop at the stem of the corner bouquet is worked. The filling in is worked of two shades of blue, or any other lively color, in a pretty design of squares, each of which consists of five oblique stitches over three crosses, of canvas as is plainly shown in the illustration. The sprigs forming the design in the center are then worked in long loose stitches of black and yellow twist silk. A pretty monogram, or coat of arms, also forms a handsome centerpiece. (1876)

Designs for Chain-Stitched Handkerchiefs

Now that chain-stitched pocket handkerchiefs are all the fashion, we dare say the girls, and women too, will be glad of some pretty patterns to mark them. Let them

45

draw with a pencil the accompanying patterns, by placing the article to be worked over the designs, and then chain-stitch in red marking cotton. The designs are suitable for braiding also, and, to obviate the trouble of drawing the pattern on cloth, tissue paper may be used. Copy the designs through, on to strips of thin paper, baste these on the cloth to be braided, and sew through braid, paper, and cloth. The paper may be torn out when the work is finished. (1863)

Here is an engraving of a pattern for a tidy. It is made of simple Swiss muslin, which is cut square and hemmed with a narrow hem, and then "braided" with narrow white linen braid in any pretty pattern. That of the one presented is simple, yet pleasing.

In forming the points of straight parallel lines, braid of two different widths is used, with pretty effect. Finally, the tidy is bordered with a narrow white linen fringe, which may or may not have an open heading. These little affairs wash and "do up" very easily, so the ladies say, and are just as pretty as if they cost five or ten dollars. They may be made of different sizes to suit the backs of chairs or the arms of lounges; and if there are two or more used, it gives a pleasing variety, even if they are made alike, to arrange some with the points down and others horizontally. It is a useful practice, and quite a test of taste and ingenuity to devise pretty original patterns for the braiding. (1866)

Pattern for Crocheting or Netting a Tidy

The above pattern is intended for crocheting or for darning an openwork tidy. Those skilled in the mysteries of fancywork will have little difficulty in making an enlarged copy to work by; or by noticing the arrangement of the small squares, the design can be followed directly from the engraving. As will be gener-

A Very Pretty and Cheap Tidy

An especial interest in those articles of feminine contrivance called "tidies," was awakened in a man a few days since, by his setting down (in bachelor's quarters, of course), in a very comfortable rocking chair with a high back and inviting arms. The day was warm and damp, and the chair was a drowsy one, so he was very quiet for some minutes, and when finally aroused, found that he was held fast, Absolom like, by the hair of the head. That was a "stickler," and the increased regard for "tidies" will doubtless stick by him as long as the recollection.

worked in fancy colored silks, crimson, blue or buff, to suit the taste and complexion. The edges of the ends may be worked with either points and dots, or finished with a hem, and stitched or chain-stitched in one or two rows, with silk to match the principal design.

The cravat itself is best made of plain black, either ribbon or dress silk. To our individual taste the plain neckerchief or tie, without any such addition, is more becoming to any gentleman, old or young, but fashion decides otherwise, and most young men will be in the fashion if possible. A necktie neatly ornamented in this manner would be a very suitable present from a young lady to a gentleman for the holidays. Articles made by the hands of a friend are more highly valued than those purchased. (1863)

ally understood, the smaller figures at the top are samples of the border and corners. The space left between the chief ornament in the centre and the border will be regulated by the size of the tidy and the fancy of the maker. (1863)

Designs for Ornamenting Cravats or Ties

The accompanying designs are for ornamenting the ends of gentlemen's silk cravats or ties. They should be

Pattern for Marking a Handkerchief

Pattern for Marking a Handkerchief.

The above very neat design for marking the corner of a pocket-handkerchief may be readily copied upon tracing paper, and then used in embroidering. The pattern also may be marked directly upon the linen with a fine-pointed pencil, by holding the two together against a windowpane. (1864)

A Neat and Durable Tidy

An engraving is here given of a tidy which is easily made, is very pretty when done, and which can be washed and done up to look as good as new. The materials required are spool cotton thread, No. 12, and a frame 14 inches square, which can be readily made of half-inch strips.

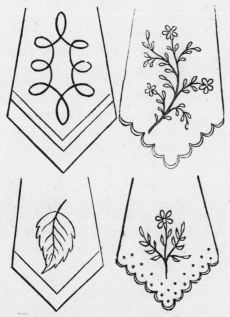

Designs for Ornamenting Cravats.

47

Fig. 1.—THREAD TIDY.

Upon the outer edge of each side of the frame are cut twenty notches, half an inch apart, beginning two inches from the corner. At each of these notches the frame is wound with thread, using from ten to fifteen turns, as the tidy is wanted heavier or lighter. When the frame has been wound in one direction, then wind the cotton in the same manner the other way. If the notches have been properly placed, the threads will cross at right angles, dividing the body of the tidy into squares.

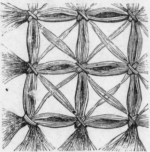

Fig. 2.—PORTION OF TIDY.

Then take a needle with double cotton and tie the thread fast, pass it diagonally across the square, pass the needle around the threads where they cross and tie a single knot. The whole is to be tied over in one direction, and then in the opposite. *Figure 2*, which shows some squares of the natural size, will enable the construction to be readily understood. When all the tying is done, cut the threads where they pass around the frame, and the fringe is formed. After washing and starching, it should be stretched in shape and pinned out to dry. It should not be ironed. (1868)

Tidies

A fresh, pretty tidy, either white or in colors, agreeing with or harmonizing the prevailing colors of the room, adorns both the room, and also the mistress of the household herself.

The first requisite is that the tidy should be appropriate to its place. A plain, substantial, white tidy, that evidently not only may be, but is, frequently changed and washed, is far prettier in a common sitting room than the most elaborate article in colors which can not be subjected to the same renovating process. Would it not be pleasant if all the rooms in a farmer's house were common sitting rooms?—at least, that there were fewer best rooms which scarcely ever see the beautiful sunlight—fewer parlors wrapped in covers, because too nice for use, and stowed away in the darkness and gloom of perpetual night?

But this useless appendage, the dark parlor, is fast becoming obsolete. Cheerful, open, light parlors, are superseding it, and soon, even in the most conservative regions, this prison room, in which every comfort of the house is confined; where the sofas and easy chairs are too nice for the tired father to rest upon at noon; where the senseless birds and flowers upon the carpets are too exquisite for little boots to crush; where the elegant bindings of the books are their only merit, will be the exception, and not the rule.

Fig. 1.—DIAMOND-PATTERN TIDY.

There is a great variety of patterns for tidies, so simple that any child can make them, and still pretty and serviceable. Any little girl who can knit a garter can make, with a very little assistance from mamma, or sister, a charming little tidy of this description, *figure 1*. All that is required is a skein of red woolen yarn, one of white cotton yarn, and two knitting needles. The red yarn should be of a bright scarlet color, and the white should be of the same size as the red.

Set up the number of stitches desired in the width of the strip—eighteen stitches is a very good width—and knit until the square is perfect, which will be about twenty-nine times across the needle. Then exchange the red for the white ball, twist the threads together for a few stitches, and knit twenty-nine times across with the white. Knit the red and white blocks alternately until the strip will extend from corner to corner of the tidy in view, beginning and ending with the red. The strips

Fig. 2.—BLOCK-PATTERN TIDY.

upon each side of the central strip will contain two blocks less than that, and the next ones two less than those. If the little child does not knit very evenly, it is better to let the strips run directly across the tidy, *figure 2*. A crocheted shell edge of either the white or red yarn, or both, forms a pretty finish, and will serve to give employment to many a dull afternoon. The strips should be neatly sewed together over and over, and pressed under a damp cloth.

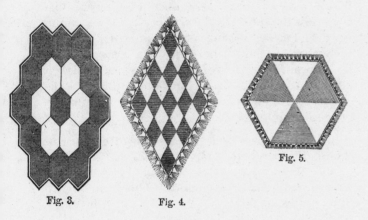

Fig. 3.   Fig. 4.   Fig. 5.

A more showy tidy is made by knitting thirteen red and six white blocks of the shape shown in *figure 3*. In knitting the first point, set up one stitch and widen the second stitch in each row; make the last point by narrowing the same. The blocks are sewed together in the form of a honeycomb, *figure 4*. A white initial letter embroidered in the central block produces a happy effect, and a white crocheted plain border makes a nice finish, provided all the angles are accurately preserved. If the border can not be neatly crocheted, the tidy looks better without it.

These tidies, *figures 4* and *5*, may be made in triangular blocks, or diamonds, to accommodate different tastes, or different chairs. The beauty or merit of these tidies consists in their being bright and cheerful in effect, where bright colors are appropriate, and yet, unlike the usual worsted Afghan **tidies**, they will wash and look as well as new ones, when soiled.

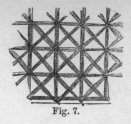

Fig. 6.   Fig. 7.

Sometimes a heavy tidy looks out of place. A very pretty and delicate one is made on a square frame, as in *figure 6*. This is constructed of pine sticks nailed together at the corners, with large-headed pins, or even common tacks driven in almost to their heads at intervals of half an inch, all around. Fasten one end of a spool of white cotton thread, number eight, to a corner tack, and wind the thread upon the tacks, three times in a place, both diagonally and horizontally over the frame, each way, which will make such a network at this, *figure 7*, held in its place by the tacks or pins.

Then begin again with a corner tack, fasten the thread to it, and with a needle weave the thread three or four times at the first intersection, fasten the thread in the center, and slip the needle through to the next crossing of the threads. When every crossing has been fastened in this manner, cut the tidy from the tacks, leaving the ends of the thread to form a fringed edge. When this tidy becomes soiled, it should be basted between two pieces of old and thin cloth, and, protected in this way, it can be washed, boiled, and starched, as easily as a more substantial one.

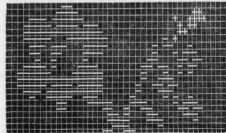

Fig. 8.—DESIGN FOR CROCHET.

Any pattern may be formed in crochet by drawing the designs upon paper and copying them as nearly as possible upon checkered paper, *figure 8*. Paper properly ruled is sold for this purpose, but this is probably only to be had in large cities, and we country people must rule it ourselves, which is not a very difficult job. A little practice will render one expert in making designs for working. (1867)

Recipes for Dyeing

Rain or other soft water should be used in these recipes, and the yarn should be thoroughly rinsed after dyeing.

Madder Red.—(Tried only on woolen yarn). To dye 2½ lbs of yarn take ¾ lb. alum, 1 quart of bran, and 1 lb. of pulverized madder. Dissolve the alum in sufficient water to cover the yarn, and boil the yarn in the solution for two hours, and then rinse, wring, and dry it. Boil the bran with two gallons of water and strain, add the liquor to the madder, which has been soaked the preceding night in strong vinegar, enough to wet it, add sufficient water to allow the mixture to cover the yarn and bring the whole to a scalding heat. Put the yarn into the dye and let it scald for half an hour without getting hot enough to simmer. When the yarn is removed from the dye it may be made a bright red by washing in soapsuds, or it may be made crimson by dipping it in weak lye slightly warmed.

Pink.—For dyeing 2 lbs. yarn, take ¾ oz. of cochineal, 1½ oz. cream of tartar and 3 oz. of chloride of tin. This last may be had at the drugstores under the name of muriate of tin, or tin mordant. Soak the cochineal in a quart of warm water, and add it to warm water enough to cover the yarn, add the cream of tartar and chloride of tin, and throw in the yarn and boil until the desired color is obtained. Double the amount of cochineal will produce a scarlet shade.

Yellow.—Make a strong decoction of black-oak bark, enough to cover the yarn, and for each lb. of yarn add ¼ lb. of alum, and 1 oz. of chloride of tin. Boil until the proper color is produced.

Orange.—Proceed as for yellow, but add madder in sufficient quantity to produce an orange color. Or instead, for dyeing 1 lb. of yarn take 1 oz. annatto, and 1¼ oz. of pearl ash (potassium carbonate). Slice the annatto into 3 quarts of water and dissolve the pearl ash in an equal quantity, and mix the two liquids and boil. Put in the yarn and simmer 15 or 20 minutes, and wash it in strong soapsuds as soon as it comes from the dye.

Dark Brown.—Into a vessel large enough to contain the yarn, put white-walnut bark enough to half fill it. Fill up the vessel with water and boil for an hour. Take out the bark and put in the yarn and boil. Remove the yarn and air it, and if not dark enough dip it in lye, increasing the strength of the lye if a very dark shade is wanted.

Light Brown.—Proceed as for dark brown, using white-ash bark instead of walnut, and dip the yarn in strong lye. The yarn, as it comes out of the dye, may be nearly white, but the lye will darken it, and if one immersion is not enough, dip it again. The lye will not injure the yarn if it be thoroughly rinsed afterwards.

Blue.—One ounce of pulverized indigo dissolved in 6 oz. of concentrated oil of vitriol makes what the druggists call sulphate of indigo, and what is known to the old-fashioned dyers as "chymic." If the indigo be good and the acid sufficiently strong, the solution may be made in a glass bottle. For fear of failure in both of these particulars, it is as well to buy the sulphate ready-made from the drugstores. For dyeing 1 lb. yarn, dissolve ¼ lb. alum in sufficient water to cover the yarn, add a little of the sulphate of indigo, put in the yarn, boil for a short time, and rinse well. The depth of color may be graduated by using more or less of the sulphate.

Green.—Prepare a yellow dye of black-oak bark, as directed above, add gradually sulphate of indigo, until the proper shade of green is produced, put in the yarn, stir well, and let it boil.

Lilac or Purple.—For each pound of yarn to be dyed dissolve ½ lb. of alum in sufficient water, and simmer the yarn for 2 or 3 hours. Make a dye of ¼ lb. peach wood for each lb. of yarn by boiling out the wood in sufficient water. Put the yarn from the alum water into this dye and boil from 15 to 20 minutes, remove and drain it, dip in strong lye, and rinse well in cold water. (1864)

Hints About Dyeing Fabric

It is very important in these times of high prices that every possible household expense should be diminished, and if dyeing can be done more economically at home than by sending the stuffs to the dyers, it should by all means be tried. We fear that many will find their attempts at domestic dyeing attended with unsatisfactory results, for the want of a knowledge of a few matters of practical importance.

In the first place every article to be dyed must be thoroughly cleansed, and all streaks and stains removed. Not a mere careless washing, but a thorough scouring of the material is required. This operation will depend upon the stuff and the character of the stains. Boiling in strong soft soapsuds, with a second boiling in fresh suds if the material is very dirty, and afterward a *thorough* rinsing will often be a sufficient preparation. If there are spots of wax, pitch, or similar substances, they must be removed by benzine, and if there are stains of iron-rust, oxalic acid may be used to remove them, washing out the acid completely after the rust is dissolved.

In dyeing goods which already have a color, it must be recollected that it is impossible to dye goods already dark, of a lighter color, without first discharging the dye they already have, and that the existing color, even if light, will modify that which we hope to produce, to a greater or less degree. Boiling with strong soapsuds will discharge a great many light and fugitive colors. Others may be taken out or greatly weakened by putting them into water to which sulphuric acid (oil of vitriol) has been added in sufficient quantity to make it taste unpleasantly sour. In either case the fabric should be repeatedly and thoroughly rinsed before putting it into the dye. Great care is necessary in immersing the stuff in the dye. If thrown in carelessly there will be wrinkles and folds which prevent free contact with the dyeing liquid, and streaks will be formed which no after care will remove. The cloth should be allowed to fall loosely and gradually into the dye in a manner to insure a thorough and equal wetting at once, and while it remains in, it should be frequently stirred in order to insure uniformity of color.

When the desired depth of color has been obtained, the material is to be thoroughly washed until the water runs off tasteless and colorless. Regular dyers give their silks and some other goods a finish by dressing them upon a large cylinder heated by steam. This process can be imitated in a small way by the use of a large tin wash boiler, filled with boiling water. The wet goods are to be laid against the outside, which should be very clean, and stretched with the threads running straight, and smoothed out with a sponge dipped in a *weak* solution of gum arabic. This will give a gloss and stiffness. When the articles are dry they may be removed. (1864)

Something About Rag Carpets

A well-made "hit-or-miss" rag carpet is both durable and pretty, and more wholesome to live upon as it makes less lint than the common wool carpets. Of course I speak of "everyday" or sitting room carpets, not advising the "hit-or-miss" for formal drawing rooms.

It is more work to stripe a rag carpet, and more expensive. The result is not so harmonious and really tasteful as the even mixture of good rags of various colors in a "hit-or-miss" carpet. These are now quite fashionable.

The rags should be evenly cut and sewed with as little bunching as possible. It saves a deal of time and labor to sew the rags on a machine, but this is more easily done when the rags sewed are all of one color as in a striped carpet. To expedite matters in sewing "hit-or-miss" rags, have the rags all cut before beginning to sew. At least have the general tones of the carpet decided. Try to have the gay colors distributed somewhat evenly, and the light and dark rags well-balanced through the whole.

Having decided what proportion of each to use, it is well to parcel them out into a few divisions and then pull rags from each in turn. For instance, put the black and very dark rags together, and white and light neutral tints (all medium grays and browns) in one class, including the various small checks. Place all of the gay colors—yellow, red, light green, and blue—in one division, mixing them up well so that one color will not

be all drawn out long before the rest. It is best not to have too many very gay rags (for instance there may be too much red flannel), but to distribute the bright rags in rather short lengths evenly through the whole carpet.

When you sew the rags, have a quantity from each of the four or five grand divisions placed in regular order. Lap the ends and sew straight across with a firm lock-stitch. Sew another rag in the same way to the end of one of the rags just sewed, and so on, not cutting or breaking the thread until a long line of rags has been sewed together in one seam. It is but a moment's work to cut these short seams apart and wind the ball.

Be sure and have a good strong warp. A carpet with a good homemade warp doubled and twisted, can take at least sixteen years of wear.

In bedrooms the whole floor should not be carpeted. Short pieces of carpeting, or handsome rugs of suitable sizes, are much to be preferred: one before the bed, one at the bureau, wardrobe, or dressing table, one at the washstand, and others before easy chairs, desks, or other places especially used for standing or sitting. These rugs can be shaken out of doors, and the floor can be washed as needed.

No kitchen should be completely carpeted, but a few breadths of rag carpet tacked down lightly so as to be easily and frequently pulled up and shaken, allowing the whole floor to be cleaned, add to the comfort of a much-used kitchen. (1883)

Mending a Rag Carpet

Mrs. H. M. R., of Columbia Co., Pa., suggests the following matter relating to economy in the household:

"One morning last winter as Henry took some hot coals out of the sitting-room stove to start a fire in the kitchen, he dropped nearly half of them on my new rag carpet, and burned seven or eight holes from one to two inches in diameter. At first I did not know what to do, but soon made up my mind to try to mend them, and I think I succeeded admirably, for when they were done they could not be seen half way across the room, and they would never be noticed by any one unless his attention was called to it. I first cut both rags and warp out as far as they were the least bit tender with the heat, then went to the rag drawer and selected rags as near the color of those burned as possible, and carefully joined every rag burned with one of its own size and color. I was lucky enough to have yarn like the warp, for I made the carpet myself.

"Then I served the warp the same way, weaving it in the rags with a darning needle. It is rather difficult getting the warp just right, unless you know how. Begin by putting in every alternate thread; this brings them all over and under the same rags, the first going over. Then commence and put in those skipped, taking every other one left the first time over, and so on until all are in. It is better to pull some of the warp out a little farther than it was burned, so that the knots may not all come in on place. This is easier done while the carpet is tacked on the floor than at any other time. It will be found rather trying work at first, but all that is necessary to accomplish it satisfactorily is a little patience and perseverance. Where there are many holes it is better not to try to mend more than one or two at a time. But I think it decidedly pays on a new carpet. Whether it will on an old one each one must judge for herself after she has tried it." (1868)

Ragbags

Persons who make rag carpets would do well to put every rag picked up which would work into a carpet into some receptacle devoted to miscellaneous carpet rags. These would help toward a carpet faster than one might suppose, and if the rags were stripped up at the time of putting away, a carpet would soon be "well begun"; and "well begun is half done."

The ragbag should hang in some near and convenient place. A closet opening from the sitting room or kitchen is a suitable place for it. When this bag is full, it is heavy and should be hung from two nails. A doubled piece of calico cloth, 5 or 6 inches long, sewed upon one side of the top of the bag, with two buttonholes (*see diagram*) for hanging it upon two separate nails, gives a firm bag that will not be likely to tear away from the nail.

RAG-BAG.

A smaller, ornamental scrap bag hanging near the sewing machine is a great convenience. This can be emptied into the larger bag every day or every week.

Bags for different kinds of pieces—one for pieces of worsted, one for unbleached cotton, one for bleached cotton, one for linen pieces, one for scraps of silk, one for bits of velvet—all help toward order and comfort in housekeeping. These may be large or small, as needed, and may be as tastily made as you please. They can be laid together, labeled if you like, in drawers or trunks, or hung in rows in your closet. Crocheted cotton bags are much in vogue; but, dear girls and women, run up gingham and delaine and calico bags instead and give the time stolen from crocheting to something that will yield a mental or physical gain. Better play ball, or climb the hills, or read history and philosophy, than bend over patchwork embroidery or crocheting when you could be employing yourself in a more healthy manner. So much for ragbags. (1873)

Down Spreads

Objecting to cotton comforters on account of their weight and bulk in washing, and lamb's wool blankets because it takes so many to render a bed comfortable in cold weather, down spreads are recommended both for cheapness and convenience.

Last winter an experiment was made with one down spread containing one pound and a quarter of down, and two cotton comforters, each containing six bunches of cotton batting. The result was that the down spread kept the bed warmer than the *two* comforters.

Lamb's wool blankets enough to make a bed comfortable in extreme cold weather, of course, would cost more than either. A down spread is as easily washed as a single blanket, for when down is wet there seems to be nothing of it. For the benefit of such as may never have seen this article, here are procedures for making one. The reader should determine what size best suits his purpose.

Prepare a piece of calico for the bottom cover, tack this cloth upon a quilt frame, and lay a border of cotton batting around the cover. Now put on the top piece of the same size of cloth and tack it down around the edges. Next quilt a line along the upper edge of the cotton border to keep the down out of the cotton. Finish the border according to your taste, take it off the frame, and bind it. Then baste the mouth of a sack containing down around the space left in one of the seams of the spread, shake the down from the sack into the spread, and when the sack is ripped off and the seam sewed up, the comforter is done.

In spreading it upon the bed, much trouble will be saved by shaking the down all to the front side, then spread it smoothly and put the outside quilt on before shaping the down; then gently pat it to its proper place as in shaping a light feather bed. (1862)

A Hooked Rug

V. Ripley of Pittstown, New Jersey, submits the following:

"When I was looking over Richard's wardrobe, I found a great deal of old flannel—some red, some blue, some gray—and a variety of worn-out clothing. It will make me just such a rug to lay before my kitchen stove as I have been wishing for all winter. I talked with Richard about it, and I determined to devote these rainy days, when I cannot visit and am not likely to have company, to making the rug. I explained what I wanted to Richard, and he made me some frames, and a hook to work it with out of an old fork. Our grocer gave us an old heavy burlap bag, saying that he never sold trifles like that to a regular customer. I ripped it open, hemmed around with strong linen thread, and sewed it

Fig. 1.—RUG PATTERN.

into the frame. It is about 2 yards long and 1 wide. Then I displayed my taste in drawing a pattern. As my variety of colors was limited, black predominating, and I intended it only for the kitchen, I could not expatiate in a brilliant cornucopia, such as I made for a parlor rug before I was married. So I decided to make a wide, variegated border into which everything would work, and have as the centerpiece three diamonds, filled around with black (*figure 1*).

"I worked the diamonds first, using my most brilliant colors. The rags I cut into strips from a ¼ to ½-inch wide and pulled from the underside through the foundation, holding the strip in the left hand and the hook in our right. Richard made us some hooks out of two old-fashioned forks, by breaking off the tines and filing down the shank into the shape of an enormous crochet needle.

"The hook is of this shape (*figure 2*), with the handle on the upper end, of course. When the points of the hook got dull, I sharpened them with the file. I worked pretty steadily, and in less than a week my rug was done, the surface trimmed off evenly, and laid before the stove. Mother has rugs of this sort that have been in use for ten years, and are still serviceable." (1867)

A Quilt—Candlewick Bedspread

Mrs. M. J. G. submits the following:

"I had been saving paper rags all winter, having in view a white spread for my bed. The idea has prevailed that patchwork quilts alone were suitable in rooms that were commonly used. A patchwork quilt is a perpetual annoyance to me. The three that I pieced myself before I was five years old, my only ones indeed, were stored away on a shelf in the upper hall closet.

"However, I totally reliquished my purpose of buying a spread the first time I had an opportunity to price them, but did not renounce my intention of having one nevertheless. We have some coarse, heavy, double-width sheets, which my son Charlie had at college, but which have been used very little since, on account of being so heavy. I thought the groundwork of the spread I was examining in the store was not very unlike Charlie's sheets, barring the price; so I told our storekeeper, "I would not take any to-day," and hastened home to see what could be done with one of them.

FIG. 3.—PATTERN FOR QUILT.

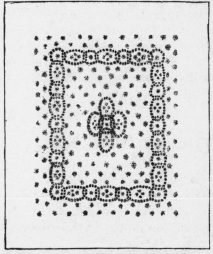

Fig. 4.—THE QUILT COMPLETED.

"After spreading it over the bed, and looking at it from all sides, I removed it to my large work table—the floor—and, bearing in mind the dimensions of the bed, drew a design in dots, and worked in double candlewicking with a darning needle over a smaller table, like that shown in *figure 3*. The wicking is merely drawn once through the cloth at each dot *, and the ends are trimmed off about a third of an inch in length. It was some trouble to make it, and when finished it looked as in *figure 4*.

It took all my leisure time for three or four days; but it pays capitally, because I am so well satisfied with it, and

Fig. 5.—HOW IT LOOKS.

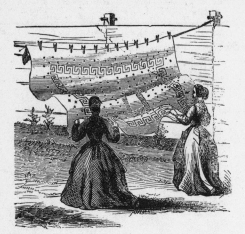

Fig. 6.—WHIPPING IT OUT.

it looks so nicely on my bed, (*figure 5*). Mary says she has seen wick spreads before, and that they will wash. It is only necessary to fasten them strongly with clothes pins to a high line, *figure 6*, and frequently whip them out while drying. Katie and Jennie are thinking of making one for their room, but say they shall improvise a prettier pattern than mine." (1867)

A Carpet or Sofa Rug

The materials used are ends of cloth in five different colors, black twilled woolen tape (½-inch and 1¼-inches wide), yellow woolen braid, black silk thread, and coarse gray linen for lining. To make this rug a sewing

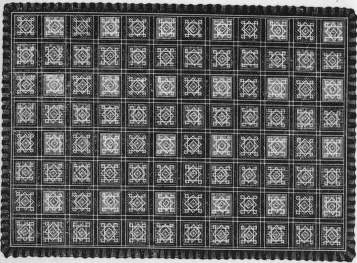

Fig. 68. Carpet or Sofa Rug.

machine is especially called into use as the stitched parts have much to do with the effect of the whole.

The single squares, each 2½ inches large, are of very pretty harmonizing colors, one row being of light gray and green, the other in violet and stone gray, coming alternately. All the squares are somewhat reduced in size, filled up in the middle with arabesque shapes of gold, yellow woolen braid, and stitched on with black silk. The small diamond, exactly in the center of the arabesque, is of a transfer of scarlet cloth ½-inch large, and this is sewn down with black silk. The edges of the decorated squares are basted very evenly together in the before-mentioned colors, and then hidden by black woolen tape ½-inch wide, put on in rows. This tape is stitched on with yellow woolen braid as seen in *figure 68*. At the outer edge the border is only visible for ½-inch. A quilling 1¼ inches wide goes round the carpet. Thick gray linen is required for a lining. (1876)

A Gentleman's Dressing-Case

In traveling, a gentleman, especially, finds it a convenience to have a portable case that will hold in a compact form all the little paraphernalia necessary in performing the offices of the toilet, shaving, combing, etc. The case, as shown in *figure 9*, is a useful, and can be made a handsome, present for a gentleman friend. It is made thus:

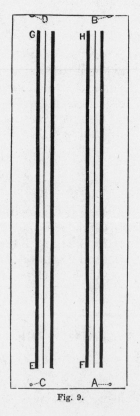

Fig. 9.

Cut a strip of silk velvet, or, if preferred, heavy brown linen, and upon it braid a suitable pattern along the center between *A B C D,* occupying one-half the width. Cut, also, a lining of enameled or elastic cloth upon which, between the space *E F G H,* stitch strips of ½-inch-wide elastic. Make proper divisions for each article it is to contain—brushes, combs, razors and strops, etc., and, at the ends, pockets for various necessary implements. Place the lining and outside together, and bind with galloon or ribbon, fastening strings or straps for holding the case together when rolled. Turn down the side flaps, along the line *A B C D,* and press with a heavy weight.

The proper articles for such a case are: Two razors, a strop, clothes- and hairbrushes in flat boxes, soap box, scissors, penknife, buttonhook, tooth- and nailbrushes, ear probe, nose picker [a nineteenth-century device that has long since disappeared—Ed.], tongue scraper [ditto—Ed.], hand mirror, pincushion, and small housewife [small sewing kit—Ed.], furnished with all necessary implements for sewing on a stray button, or sewing up a rent. The strop, hairbrush, etc., should have short handles, or be of short dimensions in order that the case may not be too long or that the articles protrude from it. The case, when entirely finished, appears like a wallet-shaped roll secured by a strap or strings and occupies but little room. (1876)

Impromptu Handkerchief Night Cap

Night caps should be worn when sleeping in a draft of air, but not otherwise. A very good and effective head-covering may be made in half a minute by any person obliged to sit or sleep in a draft of air in a room, or while traveling in cars, or elsewhere, if he have a fair-size pocket handkerchief, or piece of cloth.

First, spread it flat and fold as shown in *figure 1;* that is, bring two edges together and then turn one edge back

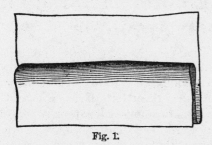

Fig. 1.

even with the fold. Second, seize the folded part in the two hands, and turn the handkerchief directly over from you. Then bring the two upper corners over towards

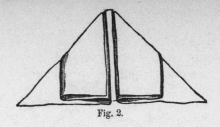

Fig. 2.

you as seen in *figure 2.* Third, commencing at the side next to you, roll up the edge as in *figure 3,* so as to bring in, and fasten the two ends of the fold. Fourth, raise the

Fig. 3.

Fig. 4.

hands up, and a bagging portion will drop down, which is to be placed over the forehead. Bring the rolled part back over the head and around the neck, tying under the chin, as seen in *figure 4.*

Our artist seems to have caught sight of one of the Zouave soldiers in the Park Barracks, while making the sketch. Or more probably he wished especially to attract the attention of soldiers, for they of all others will find this a most convenient arrangement. (1862)

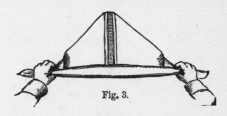

Fig. 2.—MITTEN PATTERN.

Mittens

Comfortably warm mittens are made of old gray flannel, lined and bound with red. It is easy to cut your own

55

pattern. Measure around your hand just above the thumb. Get the length of the whole hand, the length from the base of the thumb to the end of the longest finger, and also the length of the thumb. Then by the aid of the accompanying diagram (*figure 2*), you can cut out a pattern. Be careful and not get the thumb hole too large for the thumb you have made. This is a good way to make mittens for children, and you can make very pretty ones for yourself of fine cloth lined with nice flannel and bound with fur. (1870)

A Fire Screen in Woolwork

The accompanying illustration represents a very pretty design for a fire screen, the result of the united labor of

the cabinetmaker and the lady of the house. Walnut wood is an appropriate material for the frame; and the design of the woolwork, of course, can be varied according to the taste and skill of the worker. The group of flowers and enclosing wreath are appropriate to the character of the frame illustrated; and with tasteful use of the worsted, a beautiful design may be elaborated. The design here illustrated is that of a bouquet in the center, composed of tulips, roses, lilies, primroses, etc., surrounded by a wreath of ornamental grasses. (1876)

Embroidered Flower Stand

This pretty jardiniere or flower stand, *figure 19*, is of Spanish reeds set with zinc, although any stand will do.

Fig. 19. Embroidered Flower Stand.

The medallions which form the upper side of the stand are embroidered on brown cashmere with corn-colored silk in point russe. They contain scenes from "Reynard the Fox." The embroidery is mounted on pasteboard. (1876)

A Flower and Aquarium Stand with Embroidered Lambrequins in Appliqué

This elegant stand, shown in *figure 20*, is suitable for a bay window, though it is so highly ornamental that it will appear as a rich and beautiful elegancy wherever it may be placed. The stand itself may be formed of a table, circular in form, and with a top supported on a pedestal. Upon the top of this stand is placed a deep wooden bowl or small tub, lined with zinc, and furnished with a drain hole which will allow any overabundance of water to be drawn off by removing the stopple each day.

Fig. 20.—Flower and Aquarium Stand.

the holder below of gold thread. Make the tassels between of bright shades of silk or wool.

The fish globe is placed on a stand cut from walnut and bronzed, and is in the shape of a dolphin. (1876)

A Lamp Mat of Embroidery on Cardboard

The model, *figure 93*, is embroidered on a round piece of cardboard, measuring 10¾ inches in diameter, and scalloped all around the edge. It is of a light-brown color, and the embroidery is worked of two darker shades of brown silk. This model is embroidered with colored silks, gold thread and beads. A piece of cloth or pasteboard is pasted to the back to cover the stitches. The whole looks like embroidery on leather. (1876)

Fig. 93. Lamp-Mat.—Embroidery on Card-Board.

The lambrequins are formed of scarlet or green cloth. If of scarlet, the figures must be cut from gray silk and worked upon the edge with silk of a gold color. The wheat is worked in half polka-stitch with various colored silk. If green cloth is preferred, the figures are cut from golden-brown satin, and stitched on with a buttonhole stitch on the edge. The flowers, wheat ears, etc., are in chain stitch, with violet silk. The leaves, stems, tendrils, etc., are worked in green of lighter shades than the ground, with shades of brown in certain parts, such as stems, leaves and grasses. The edges are pinked out in long scalloped points.

If the appropriate fish pattern, seen in the illustration, is used, let the cloth be of a fine blue or sea green. Work the fish in shades of gold and brown, the leaves at the top in bright shades of crimson, purple and green,

A Draped Table or Stand

The standard is such as are used for marble-topped tables, and may be procured of a cabinetmaker, although any used table or even a battered lawn table will do. Instead of a marble top, one of pine is used, which is smoothly covered with green rep, neatly tacked on. A curtain of the same material, a quarter of a yard deep, and made a little full, has a fringe at its lower edge, and is tacked by its upper edge to the table top. Gimp of a color to match is used to cover and hide the edges and

DRAPED CENTER-TABLE.

tacks. The curtain is caught up in plaited festoons every quarter of a yard. Other materials may be used, and other colors to harmonize with the surroundings. By the exercise of proper taste and skill, one may make very pretty chamber sets by draping very rough kinds of furniture. (1870)

An Economical Tablecloth

By the following method a simple, cheap, and yet very pretty cover for a table or stand may be quickly made. The engraving herewith is photographed from one of these covers that was borrowed from a lady who has several of them of her own make which attracted considerable attention.

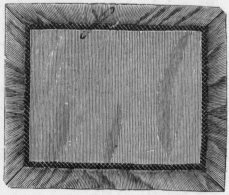

A CHEAP AND PRETTY TABLE COVER.

A heavy double-faced canton flannel is now manufactured, in a variety of colors, having the nap on both sides, and it is on sale generally. Either this or the single-faced can be used, but the double-faced is preferable on account of its extra thickness. The shade can be selected to match the furniture.

When cut to a suitable size, it is bordered with a contrasting shade of the same material of any desired width. But this is best made of the single-nap flannel as the double would be a little clumsy. The border is cut of double width and folded so as to leave the fold for the outside edge, and stitched on. To cover the seam, sew on a strip of velvet or velveteen with cross or feather stitch of filoselle (floss silk), of contrasting shade; gold is preferable. This comes in all colors, and each thread can be split into two or three threads. (1882)

Splasher for the Washstand

The material used in making this splasher is fine white crash or other coarse cotton. The size of the splasher will depend upon the space to be covered. The material must be cut with the selvedge at the top and bottom. The raw edges at each end must be hemmed. Trace the design lightly with lead pencil, and work it in outline stitch with fine cotton. Scarlet is prettiest, and retains the color better when washed. Follow the outline carefully that the design may not be lost in working.

A DESIGN FOR A SPLASHER.

Another pretty kind is made of linen, the design drawn on the cloth with indelible ink. In this case the design is not to be embroidered, as the color of the ink is permanent. The splasher is to be tacked to the wall just above the back of the washstand, thus preventing the wall from being spotted with water. Outline pictures of various designs may be used; flowers, birds, or a combination of both. The Kate Greenaway pictures are favorites as the quaint little figures can be very prettily arranged in a beautiful framework of flowers. (1883)

58

Needlework Christmas Gifts

Christmas is coming with its demand for pretty fancy articles suitable for gifts, and a few suggestions as to new styles of art needlework may be acceptable to those having a number of friends to provide for.

A nice present is a set of half a dozen doilies or small fruit napkins. The latest fashion is to turn down one corner of the linen squares and work upon it an orange, banana, or other fruit, varying the design on each.

Embroidered aprons are now very fashionable for home wear, and may be made of satin, linen, pongee, or muslin, and decorated with silk, wools, or crewels, as the material suggests. A very tasteful apron for a young lady is one of pure white pongee worked with dainty knots of violets, the waistband and strings being of delicate lavender ribbon. They are also made of écru, tied with scarlet, the front decorated with comical looking honeybees, and the motto, in outline stitch, "How doth the little busy bee improve each shining hour!" These are for evening aprons.

A new feature of art needlework is using small worsted or plush balls. These are flattened on one side, and sewed on in groups of three, a shadow being worked beneath each, and when mixed with artistically shaded leaves, are very effective. One thing always to be remembered in embroidery, as well as in painting, is to decide at first on which side of your bunch or spray the light shall fall, and work accordingly, the shades gradually melting into each other, from the deepest to those which are almost white.

It is said the old-fashioned cross-stitch, a double stitch forming an X, on canvas is to be revived; people are bringing out the old screens and pictures worked by their grandmothers, and having them remounted and reframed. Patchwork, too, is quite in vogue, but in a more artistic form than the past generation ever dreamed of. Beautiful sofa pillows are made of curious shaped patches of silk, satin, or velvet, each bearing some dainty bit of embroidery—flowers and fans of different shapes and styles.

An exquisite tidy may be made of a cloth, 10 inches square, on which is sewed patchwork of plush in the form of a wide-spread fan. The corners of the block are of black velvet, and from the top, trailing over the fan, is a spray of moss rosebuds, in Louis XVI style, or ribbon embroidery. The edge is neatly finished with suitable lace.

An effective, though simple, table runner is of dark-green felt, half a yard wide, pinked on the edge, and ornamented with a strip of silk patchwork, about a quarter of a yard deep on each end. Below falls a fringe of the felt, made by slashing it into narrow strips, two or three inches up.

A willow-work basket also makes a very pretty present when the handle is tied with a bow of ribbon, enlivened on one end by a graceful spray in gold-thread couching, which is very easily done.

A new material for working on is chamois, which is nice for portfolios, blotting-books, cigar and shaving-paper cases, and other little conveniences suitable for gentlemen. These are usually ornamented with conventional designs, outlined with gilt tinsel and colored braid, and filled in with pink, yellow, and blue silk or crewels in long stitches. (1883)

LEARNING TO SEW

III. Basketry

Fig. 1.—PREPARING OSIERS FOR MARKET.

Willows and Baskets

The culture and preparation of willows for basketwork is sufficiently easy and profitable to make it worthy of being carried on more systematically than it is at present. There are several varieties of willow which may be made to produce osiers of high quality—the common White Willow (*Salix alba*) and its variety the Yellow or Golden Willow, the twigs of which are used for coarse work, and generally without being peeled, and the Basket Willow (*Salix viminalis*), which furnishes osiers superior to any others in length, flexibility, smoothness, and whiteness, and fitness for the finest kinds of work. These willows are readily grown from cuttings on rich soils or on the banks of ponds and streams. A new plantation should be kept cut closely every year, so as to force out a good annual growth of shoots from the stumps, and the osiers may be gathered after the second or third year.

Fig. 2.—POLLARD WILLOWS.

But osiers may also be grown by cutting off the mature trees a few feet above ground, and thus causing them to throw out numerous small branches, as in *figure 2*. This is called "pollarding," and a willow thus cut off is a pollard or pollarded willow. In one year these shoots will grow several feet in length, and in the fall are cut off close to the tree, and laid away in heaps until the following spring, when at the commencement of the growing season they are placed in water until the buds swell. They are then trimmed and peeled. A boy or girl removes with a sharp knife all the twigs and hands them over to the peeler. This operator sits on a bench or before a log or stump in which is fixed an instrument shaped like that shown in *figure 3*. This is made of two ½-inch iron rods, 18 inches long, welded together at one end, and gradually separating like the prongs of a fork at the other end. A stem welded on serves to retain it in a hole bored to receive it. The osier is drawn through this instrument, which strips off the bark, and it is then laid on one side until a bunch is gathered, when they are tied up, and are ready for use. These operations are shown in *figure 1*. Note that some osiers for coarse work are used without being peeled.

The making of baskets furnishes employment for stormy days or long, dull winter evenings, when otherwise there might be no profitable employment. Weaving osiers into various kinds of baskets is an art which may be easily learned, and once the rougher methods for coarse work, such as barn baskets, or market baskets, or hampers for packing bottles, which in themselves are considerable branches of

Fig.

trade, are well mastered, and facility in them is acquired, the finer sorts of work will come quite handy, and can be easily performed.

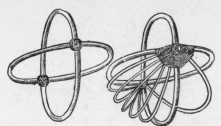

Figs. 4 and 5.—FOUNDATION OF ROUND BASKET.

Fig. 6.—BEGINNING OF BOTTOM.

The commencement of all basket making consists in laying the foundation, and this is shown in *figures 4, 5,* and *6. Figures 4* and *5* show the frame for a round-bottomed basket with handle. *Figure 6* shows the frame for a flat or square-bottomed basket, which consists of three coarse osiers, laid crosswise of three other similar ones.

The weaving commences by passing finer osiers round the coarse ones where they cross each other, and when they are secured together they are spread out until they radiate like the spokes of a wheel, as shown in *figure 7.* The finer osiers are then woven in

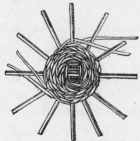

Fig. 7.—WEAVING BOTTOM.

amongst them, and the filling goes on until the bottom *(figure 8)* is finished, when the frame-pieces are bent upwards *(figure 9)*, or fresh osiers are inserted, to form a foundation for the sides. When the sides are carried up sufficiently, the frame-pieces are bent down and woven in amongst the filling, so as to hold

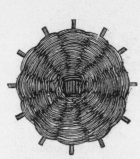

Fig. 8.—BOTTOM FINISHED.

Fig. 9.—WEAVING THE SIDES.

them securely in place for a short piece, when they are cut off, and the top of the basket finished off. *Figures 10* and *11* show how the filling and finishing are done.

The last work of all is to sharpen off the last remaining osiers and thrust their ends through the frame in such a manner that they cannot work out. The basket is trimmed inside, all ends sticking out are smoothly cut off, and the basket is done. (1872)

Fig. 10.—MAKING HANDLE.

Fig. 11.—A FINISHED BASKET.

Homemade Fancy Baskets

A rustic basket made of rude materials can be a useful and decorative object for the home. A basket of this kind would serve for growing a few bulbs in moss, or it may be filled with the plants usually grown in hanging baskets, first lining it with moss. It would not make an inelegant fruit dish.

The round bottom of the basket, *figure 1,* and its cross-shaped base are made of common soft pine. The sides of the basket are thin pieces cut from small branches with the bark upon them. These, which are all of the same size and thickness, are tacked to the bottom,

Fig. 1.—RUSTIC BASKET.

and a hoop made of some flexible twig is put upon the outside at the bottom and another on the inside near the top, and fastened with tacks. The ornamental work around the foot, as well as the feet, is of bent twigs tacked in place while green, and allowed to dry there.

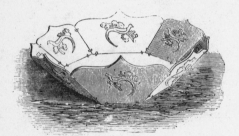

Fig. 2.—CARD BASKET.

In *figure 2* we give one of the imported card baskets of a very simple pattern and easily imitated. They are made of white wood, and each piece has a small, gaily colored bird or flower in its center.

Fig. 3.—BOTTOM OF BASKET.

Another and more elaborate card basket is given in *figure 3*, which represents the bottom, and in *4* and *5*, which show the side pieces of two different patterns. The side pieces are joined to the bottom and to one another by means of small ribbons. Work of this kind, if made of white wood such as the holly, should be left

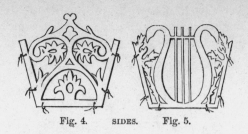

Fig. 4.   SIDES.   Fig. 5.

untouched. But if colored woods are used, they may have a coating of boiled linseed oil to bring out the color and markings. (1869)

A Straw-Work Basket

Straws and wheat heads combined form beautiful baskets and other table articles. If a round basket is desired, it is made thus:

Cut from stiff cardboard a circular piece, as large as is desired for the bottom; also, a circular rim for the top, about one-third larger than the bottom, and ¾-inch wide. The straws are then cut the length of the basket, a sufficient number to extend round the lower circle, ¼-inch apart, and along the inner circle of the rim, ½-inch apart. Introducing the straws into them, press the lower part about ¼-inch through the bottom, and at the top an inch through the holes in the rim, first touching the holes in the cardboard with glue to fasten them securely.

When this is dry, take narrow satin ribbon, or chenille, of a bright shade such as cherry, scarlet, or blue, and pass it in and out between the straws, basket-fashion, until it is entirely covered between the bottom and rim. Split some straws down one side, and after moistening them, press them open. Form these into little loops by cutting pieces ½-inch long and folding the two ends together. Place these around the cardboard rim of the basket by sewing each one on with a needle and thread, first entirely around the outer edge and then a second row of loops over the first, covering the edge of each piece and hiding the stitches. Over this fasten a piece of thick chenille or a quilling of the ribbon. Proceed in the same manner at the bottom, but there place one row of loops down, and the other up, with the ribbon or chenille between them.

Now proceed to finish off the top by cutting the projecting straws in points; finally place a pretty colored picture upon the inner surface of the white cardboard bottom.

Straws of any color may be used for these baskets, and the trimming may be varied to suit the taste. Gold or silver paper, cut into narrow strips, forms a very effective trimming. (1876)

Straw Mosaics

Some fine specimens of straw work have been made by European craftsmen, and having succeeded in imitating a few of these specimens entirely to our satisfaction and the admiration of many who have examined them, it is thought many readers may feel inclined to try this interesting branch of fancywork. This work has been done in two ways—one with the straws cut into figures or blocks, the other forming them by interweaving the straws as in basketwork.

The finest straw is imported from France and Tuscany, the most perfect growing near Florence and other parts of Italy. It is often sold in specialty shops, put up in small bundles. The colors of these straws are brilliantly beautiful, varying from the delicate natural straw shades to the most vivid crimsons, scarlets, greens, etc., and some with a coating of gold and silver foil. A person may easily imagine the capability of such exquisite straws being formed into articles of rare beauty.

It may be, however, that some persons, for various reasons, will prefer using native straw and coloring it themselves. For the benefit of such, a few directions are

Fig. 1. Straw-Mosaic.

added that will enable them to select the best straw, and the kinds adapted to the purpose in question, and also to color them so that they will compare favorably with the imported article. Wheat straw, because of the silica contained in it, is harder and more brilliant than any other, but on this account is not capable of taking the dye in as large quantity as oat and rice straw, which are softer. These are valuable, therefore, for the darker shades.

The straw must be cut just above the knots. This is the best part on account of the protection afforded by the leaves. These, however, must be carefully peeled off. The straws must then be cut into pieces about 6 or 8 inches long, and boiled for an hour or two in clear soft water, then colored with aniline dyes. The foundation for the straw-mosaic designs may be either wood or other material; an ordinary cigar box will answer well for the first example, *figure 1*. This project is made as follows:

Short lengths of straw are split in half with a sharp knife, and those for the groundwork cut of proper widths and lengths suited to the pattern to be formed, placing each different color and size in a separate tray or box to avoid confusion.

That the work may present a uniform appearance, it is important that each band and square should be precisely the same size. To insure this accuracy, paper patterns must be cut, and the straws afterward cut according to them. Each piece, as it is cut, is placed upon a smooth, hard surface and is pressed with a rather hot flatiron, taking the precaution to lay a piece of smooth paper above and below to preserve the straw.

The pattern may be formed by either placing the pieces directly upon the wood or other surface or upon a piece of paper or card to be afterward transferred to its proper place. The figures for this work are, of course, rectilinear, but any embroidery pattern employing *straight lines* will answer for this.

If a design of the proper dimensions is to be formed upon the article, it will not be necessary to draw the figure upon the surface, though a few lines should be ruled to serve as guides. If, however, a sketch is to be delineated, it will be best to draw colored lines of the same width apart as the width of the bands and tesserae (the square pieces in the groundwork intersecting each other at right angles, as shown in *figure 1*). By means of these lines, the colors can be arranged and the figures and other details placed as desired. In making this first example of a straw mosaic, choose a small article. Make a diagram upon the surface, paint each square and block in appropriate colors, and then arrange each straw in its legitimate place.

After arranging the pattern, the next step is to coat the surface of the article to be decorated with a coat of heavy

65

Fig. 2. Straw-Mosaic.

In *figure 3* is given a design with a conventional group of drooping flowers with foliage. The flowers are of a light rose color with yellow in the center; the leaves, shades of green drawn through the groundwork so as to appear as one continuous line. The curious circular flower in the center is of shades of yellow; the stems, brown; the cross buds upon the sides, crimson; the

Fig. 3. Straw-Mosaic.

glue. On this glue foundation the grounding and little square die-shaped pieces (tesserae) must be carefully placed. Use a small stick with glue upon the point, as the small, light pieces of straw cannot be arranged with the fingers. After placing all the pieces, lay a warm flatiron upon them, first shielding the design with paper. *Figures 1* and *2* show designs in perfectly straight lines which will be found pretty for borders. In these, the pieces are cut and arranged in bands and squares, fitted closely together. In *figure 2* is given a design in which the straws are pressed flat, as described, and interwoven for the central cross figure. The four light corner squares are formed of the straws in their light natural color, laid diagonally, the black figures woven in. This operation is performed upon a piece of stiff paper, which is afterward removed, and the entire piece placed upon the face of the article which has received a coat of glue. A weight is then placed upon the surface and allowed to remain for several hours.

The dark and light blocks interwoven in the center are of black and scarlet; those on the four arms of the cross in the center, purple and yellow; the whites are gilded; the shaded bands, dark brown; the border, black and crimson with gold and a lighter crimson in the center. The squares upon the corners of the arms are in two shades of yellow. The corners are not arranged until after the design is placed and affixed to the glue.

leaves below, green and brown in shades. The border is extremely beautiful in crimson and gold, with black strands upon the outside. The groundwork is white. This pattern is also effective, done as previously described, with straws cut and fitted together.

It is difficult, but not impossible, to introduce curved figures in a straw mosaic. The straws must be opened down one side with a sharp-pointed knife, then placed in boiling water until pliable. Then they may be pressed perfectly flat. This will give a broad strip from which petals, leaves, etc., can be cut and placed together in graceful forms. These are put down upon a surface wet with liquid glue. The groundwork is next fitted around it, cutting the straws in long bands, the ends cut to fit each piece to which it comes in contact. Should a small line occasionally remain uncovered, fill it with a little glue upon the point of a knife, and touch with the color of the groundwork. This style is, perhaps, more beautiful than either of the other kinds. (1876)

Fig. 3.—BAG OPEN.

Workbaskets and Bags

Every lady, whether a woman or little girl, should have a convenient receptacle for the implrements which are necessary for her use in sewing. A household workbox, basket, or bag, is a household nuisance.*Each* person should have her own thimble, wax, thread, needles, scissors, etc., and a place to keep them; and the manner in which she keeps the latter is a pretty sure index to her habits of neatness and order in other respects.

So great a variety in the style of these articles lies within the reach of each of us, that our individuality can in no way be better discerned than in the choice we make. Our ministers tell us that copying is a suicidal act, and that the spirit of the aphorism is applicable to the commonest incidents of daily life. Why, then, is it not applicable to our selection of an article which presents so great a variety of forms?—not that the aphorism means, in this case, that we should each have a workbox unlike those we see about us in order to express our individuality, for it would be but another form of the same act, and equally suicidal in its nature. Rather, each of us should sufficiently understand her own needs and preferences, as to have a choice even in so small an item as this.

Grandmother thinks there is nothing quite so convenient as her workbag, *figure 1*, the excellent properties of which are universally acknowledged. It consists of a round piece of boxwood, covered, and surrounded with pockets. Turned wrong side out (*figure 2*) and emptied of its contents, it is easy to see how it is made. The pockets (*figure 3*) are eight in number. These, and the inside of the bottom board are of gray merino. The upper edge of the pocket is scalloped with dark-blue saddler's silk, which is the outside color. A rubber cord holds the gray pockets so tightly drawn up that the bag stands of its own accord, when the strings (*figure 4*) which are run in the outside from opposite directions, are loosened.

Fig. 4.—BAG STRINGS.

Fig. 5.—WORK BASKET.

Fig. 6.—POCKETS.

Fig. 7.—BOTTOM OF POCKETS.

Fig. 1.—GRANDMOTHER'S BAG.

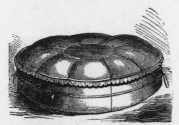

Fig. 2.—BAG REVERSED.

Mother's workbasket is made on the same principle. It is a basket lined with pockets (*figure 5*) instead of a bag. The inside is made separately, and afterwards fastened firmly to the basket at the bottom of the pockets. The top could be simply made fast with coarse thread to the basket, though that would not look so neatly finished as it would wound with ribbon over the top of the basket, and through the material of the lining, with bows tied over between the pockets, where the strain upon the lining is greatest. The pockets (*figure 6*) are made in a straight piece, just long enough to fit the top of the basket. The bottom of the row of pockets (*figure 7*) is slightly gathered to fit a circle of the same material which fits the bottom of the basket.

Katie has a standing workbasket of willow, with three compartments. She has various nice little contrivances to hold her work, among which are "crabs." A crab like this is composed of three pieces of stiff pasteboard of an oval shape, 2 inches in width by 3 in length, neatly covered with silk, and sewed together at two of the edges. By a slight pressure at the ends, if opens and reveals a cozy little room Her needle book (*figure 9*), although large, is appropriate to her basket,

Fig. 9.

Fig. 10.—NEEDLE-BOOK, OPEN.

which is large and roomy. It is of bronze and morocco, bound and lined with blue, with leaves for needles at one end and a place for the thimble in the side of the broad flat cushion at the other end of the case (*figure 10*). There is a morocco pocket between the silk pocket and cushion.

Fig. 11.—NEEDLE-CASE.

Fig. 12.—WORK BOX.

Cora's needle case (*figure 11*) is smaller and is therefore better suited to her workbox (*figure 12*), where every inch of space is precious and accordingly economized. It rolls up quite small and lies under the tray, or sometimes in the tray, beside her button box. Between these and the cushion, is a narrow depressed division for knife, pencil, stiletto, buttons, tape, needle boox, etc. The scissors, tape measure, emery, thimble, shuttle and pin case belong in the division opposite the thread; while under the tray is a ball of welting cord, box of hooks and eyes, case of skeins of silk (*figure 13*), scissors' sharpener, sticks and roll of tape, papers of

floss and French cotton, Afghan needles, a crab or two, and a dozen little bundles of work in various stages of development, besides a thousand and one other articles, which do not legitimately belong to the box, yet are most conveniently kept here.

Fig. 13.—THREAD CASE.

Jennie's workbox (*figure 14*), which is a tidy little affair, is a hexagon of stiff pasteboard covered with silk—gray on the outside and scarlet within. On three of the side pieces are fastened pockets of the same material with which the basket is lined. On one side a covered strip of thin pasteboard (*figure 15*) is fastened for a thimble case, over which hangs an emery (*figure 16*) made from two round pieces of strong linen, stuffed with emery and wool, and covered with scarlet silk. The

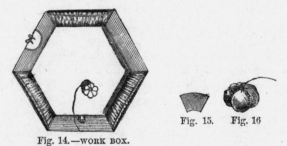

Fig. 14.—WORK BOX.　　Fig. 15.　Fig. 16

tomato shape is produced by drawing a double thread of green silk six times through the center of the emery—each time passing over the surface at an angle of sixty degrees from the last thread. A tuft of green is fastened with the string to the center of one side of the emery to increase its resemblance to a tomato. Jennie made several such boxes for her little friends a few months ago, some of which were very delicate in color—light blue and salmon—sea green and gray—and were prettier than hers, though scarcely as well adapted as hers for daily use. (1867)

Crochet Basket

A pretty "household ornament" is made of an eggshell by breaking off one end carefully, leaving the opening an inch and a half or 2 inches in diameter, according to the size of the egg. Protect the edge with a narrow strip of paper put on with glue. Crochet of any bright wool yarn an openwork basket, just large enough to hold the

CROCHET BASKET.

Fig. 1.—PAPER CARD BASKET.

Each piece is made into a double roll, as shown at *A*, the paper being kept rolled by applying a little glue. The rolls are then glued together by their sides and set up end-wise for the bottom of the basket. The sides are built up in the same manner, laying one roll upon another. By using paper of several colors, a pleasing variety of figures may be wrought into the sides. (1867)

A Gourd Scrap Basket

Large, well-shaped gourds can be made into a number of pretty and useful articles. Among them is the scrap basket shown in the illustration.

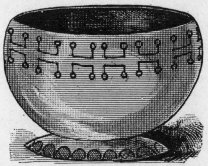

A GOURD SCRAP BASKET.

To make such a basket, select the largest gourd possible, cut off the top, remove the seeds, and scrape and sandpaper the inside surface until it is perfectly smooth. Cut down the smaller piece to the proper size, and glue it to the lower part of the larger one, which forms the basket.

The gourds are often a little irregular in shape, and the best decoration for them is a pattern similar to the one given, an imitation of the designs on the earthen jars made by the Indians of New Mexico and Arizona. The pattern is put on with common paint and a small brush. It may first be traced with a pencil. Red, black, or dark-brown paint should be used, or the pattern may be done in two colors, black and red, or brown and red.

The baskets will be very useful for a variety of purposes but are particularly intended to hold papers

prepared eggshell. Put at the edge of the crochet a stiff cord or small wire, and fasten so that the shell may pass in and out when necessary. Tie cords which will suspend your basket from the center of the top of the window frame.

The basket illustrated is made of single zephyr worsted, and is finished at the bottom with a little tassel of the same, with two or three threads of scarlet in it. If you choose, put tassels at the ends of the hanging string, and crochet a little ruffle over the strong string around the edge of the basket. If you put some rich dirt in the eggshell, and a few kernels of wheat, they will grow and freshen your room long before there is anything green out of doors. But when the spring flowers come, you will want a fresh bouquet in it every day.

The shell of a coconut may be similarly employed; a small two-inch pot, or an egg cup, will answer quite as well as the eggshell, and may be more convenient to those who do not have geese or ducks' eggs. All the grains and grasses look beautifully in these hanging baskets, and trailing plants have a still more pleasing effect. (1868)

A Paper Card Basket

Figure 1 shows a very neat card basket made of paper. The material is cut in pieces from half an inch to an inch square according to the size of the basket wanted.

and magazines or to receive waste papers and scraps. The gourds can also be made into very pretty work-baskets by providing them with a lining. From the smaller sizes, handsome covers for flowerpots can be made, painted in some pretty patterns, ornamented with scrapbook pictures, or in any other tasteful manner. (1883)

A Trimmed Clothes Basket for Bedroom or Nursery

The materials used are an old traveling trunk or large box, gray sailcloth, the same color cambric, round cord, woolen braid, etc. The model shown in *figure 86* is an exceedingly handy thing in a bedroom or nursery; it is a pretty piece of furniture and an excellent way of putting to use an old trunk that cannot be used for traveling any more.

Fig. 86.   Trimmed Clothes-Basket for Bedroom or Nursery.

The side walls are covered with gray cambric, laid into even box plaits, while a covering of strong linen secures the bottom. A lambrequin of sailcloth surrounds the upper margin. The border on the lambrequin also decorates the rim all around the cover. The latter is covered smoothly with sailcloth, edged with a border of arabesques, and is decorated with an oval rosette of cambric, having in its center a handle braided of crochet cord. The points of the lambrequin are each cut into five scallops and finished off with red or white ball fringe. The rim of the cover is to be decorated with a border as wide as itself. The rosette on the cover is of gray cambric, scalloped all around, buttonhole-stitched and decorated with single balls.

Fig. 87.

The inner space of the trunk is divided into compartments by walls of cardboard covered with cambric, as shown in *figure 87*. Three pockets with laps are affixed to the cover. All the edges are bound with red braid and are further elaborated by narrow embroidery or white lace. (1876)

Coconut-Shell Hanging Basket

A very pretty hanging basket can be made by sawing off about three inches from the smaller end of a coconut, removing the meat, and covering the outside with wood mosses. These may be fastened to the shell with glue. Then plant within the shell itself some such creeping herb as moneywort which droops gracefully over the sides and a verbena. These cups or baskets are very easily and quickly made, and they are very beautiful.

The shell is of course suspended upon a string which may be attached to the upper rim of the cup by means of small holes. Small vines or moss may be trained up the strings. These ornaments cost little or nothing, and they add much to the cheerfulness of a room. They are as good as medicine in the room of an invalid. (1862)

IV. Paper Crafts

Wall Panels for Home Decoration

The use of decorative panels allows those who can not afford costly pictures to produce a pleasing, cheerful effect in their rooms at a moderate outlay. The panels are used to break up the bare spaces between windows and in other parts of the room, and the size may be proportioned to the space they are to occupy.

The material is usually well-seasoned wood, and for some purposes, heavy bookbinder's board or very stiff pasteboard may be employed. These are first painted with two or more coats of some warm gray or other neutral tint, mixed with much turpentine, so that, when dry, they will present a dead surface without any gloss.

The decoration of the panel is usually a vine or a branch which will allow of the introduction of bright colors for the flowers and pleasing tints of green and brown for the foliage and stems. Bright-colored insects may also be introduced.

TWO STYLES OF PANELS.

The engravings from panels that have been executed will give hints as to this kind of decoration which is, of course, only possible for those who have some skill in the use of the brush. The edges may be finished by neat lines of some dark color. Another method is to decorate the panels with real objects. A cluster of nicely dried grasses, a group of graceful ferns, or a tasteful arrangement of brilliant autumn leaves may be made very effective. We have seen pleasing panels, in which birds, made up by gumming real feathers to a cardboard form, were introduced with a branch upon which they were resting, painted in. Lichens, mosses, cones, and other handsome objects may be used to decorate panels with very pleasing results. (1883)

A Book Cover in Cardboard Fretwork

It frequently happens that many valuable and costly volumes become so shabby by long or hard usage that they appear a "disgrace" on the table or shelves. In such a case, it becomes a matter of importance to be able to renew them.

There are various methods of doing this, but here is one that is not only elegant, but easily done. First go through the book page by page, and clean the margins with a clean eraser or with bread crumbs. The edges, if gilded, can be renewed with liquid paint gilding, first putting a heavy weight on the volume, then, with a flat brush, going entirely over the edges. Next take a piece of purple, crimson, or blue velvet or velveteen. Cut it sufficiently large to cover the entire binding, with a narrow piece over each side to secure it on the inside of the covers. Paint these edges with sizing made with glue and flour paste, and cover the whole binding with great care.

Next measure the cover and back, and take a piece of cardboard that will cover the entire back and a second piece for the front. Draw upon these pieces the design shown in the illustration, *figure 35.* Place the two boards upon a smooth cutting-board, and with a very sharp knife, cut out the design. For the front, mark out a central space for a label giving the name of the volume, etc.

When entirely cut, proceed to color the boards with brown stain, and lay them under a press to dry. Then, if necessary, give a second coat. If a light, bright binding is desired, gilding may be used. When the coats of paint are dry, give them a fine varnish, and, while a little sticky, decorate them with gilding or colors, as the taste dictates. Or the whole may be painted in the illuminated style. When done, paint the inside of the boards with glue, and place them directly in proper position on the velvet. The effect will be found very beautiful. (1876)

RACK.FOR NEWSPAPERS.

It is easily made of heavy cardboard. Cut two pieces 18 inches long and 12 inches wide for the back, and two pieces the same length and 10 inches wide for the front. The back pieces are covered with gray linen and sewed bound together. The inner piece is covered with bronze-green felt, with corners of a darker shade, worked on with feather stitch in black silk floss.

The bands are of darker shade, worked with bright colored silks in various hues. The band is fastened on the front with "blind stitch." The long stitches which go across from one edge of the band to the other are of bright yellow brown; the shorter stitches which cross them are of dark red and light blue. The stitches which extend outwards from the edge of the band are of black and pink silk. The bands are put on before the felt is attached to the pasteboard. After the two front pieces are put together, the back and front are sewed together along the bottom, and a cord is attached to the front piece near the top, taken through two holes in the back, and fastened. Three brass rings are very firmly sewed to the upper edge of the back, by which the rack is hung against the wall.

A very pretty rack can be made by using linen throughout, omitting the corner-pieces, and making the bands of velvet, of knot-work, or of canvas, worked with bright wool and silk. The shape may be changed by slightly rounding the upper corners of the front, or both the front and back. (1883)

Fig. 35. Book-Cover.

Rack for Newspapers

In a family where a number of papers are taken it is almost a necessity to have some accessible place besides a table in which to keep them. A rack like the one given in the engraving can be hung beside the table, or on an out-of-the-way bit of wall space, and answers the purpose admirably.

Cheap File for Newspapers

A file for holding papers is the neatest arrangement for the purpose we have seen; but many who do not care to go to the expense of purchasing such a one, will like an arrangement described as follows. It is not new, but is nontheless useful for that:

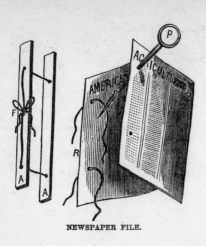

NEWSPAPER FILE.

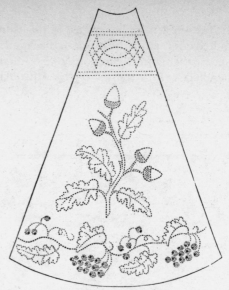

PERFORATED LAMP SHADE.

Take two pieces of stiff pasteboard, each the size of the paper when properly folded. These are for the covers. Make of hardwood, two strips, *A, A, figure 1,* about ¾ of an inch wide, and ³/₁₆ of an inch thick, and as long as the covers. Through these bore two holes with a small awl, each hole about 3 inches from the end. Take a piece of narrow tape or good stout small cord, about 2½ feet long, and put it through the holes in one of the sticks. Make holes in the pasteboard covers to correspond with the sticks, and put the string through one of the covers, and you are ready to put in papers.

F, represents the sticks and strings without either covers or papers. At *R,* is seen one stick and cover, and the manner of putting in a paper. To do this properly, lay one of the sticks on the back margin of the paper and make the holes by that, so that they will all agree. Then run the awl through the paper, draw the string into the slot in the awl, pull the awl back out of the paper and you have the string drawn through. Then put on cover and stick, draw the strings up tightly and tie them, and you have the whole thing complete. The awl, *P,* can easily be made out of a wire, such as is used for bails of pails, with the aid of a sharp cold chisel and good file. (1864)

Perforated Lampshade

While Brother Henry was home during vacation, our store-bought lampshade gave out, and, for his temporary convenience, he begged some pasteboard and cut out and sewed up a piece the size and shape of the old shade. This, indeed, was a *shade.* The board was so thick it permitted no rays of light to pass through it, and the reflection only served to make "darkness visible" throughout the rest of the room.

Such gloom was not to be borne; so four oblong openings were cut in the shade. Next colored tissue paper was pasted on the outside, and the edges of the openings were finished with gilt paper. Pictures were then inserted on the underside as transparencies. Two of them were scenes from Central Park; one, the head of Washington; and the last, but not the least attractive, a gay young lady, fairly dazzling at night with diamonds, caused by the lamplight shining through the holes pricked for that purpose. White tissue paper was pasted on the underside of the shade, and the lower edge bound around with gilt paper. In the four alternate spaces, flowers were then pricked. But this one is not the *chef d'oeuvre.*

I have just finished one for the college brothers which, though simple, is really quite elegant. This last I made out of six equal-sized pieces of Bristol board of the shape shown in the engraving. These pieces are to be joined near the top and the bottom by ribbon passed through holes stamped for the purpose.

Around the lower edge, I traced by means of impression paper a wreath, vine, tendrils, leaves, and clusters of grapes, and at the top a plain narrow braiding pattern. In the center of each piece, I traced some design such as a butterfly, oak branch, leaves and acorns, ivy vine, a full-blown rose with stem and leaves, a grape vine, and lastly a bouquet of various kinds of flowers and leaves.

Then, with the Bristol board resting on a cushion, began the slow and tedious work, prick, prick, prick, with various-sized needles, using occasionally a knitting needle and even a stiletto, until all was completed. Upon holding the paper up to the light, the various designs were developed in unsuspected beauty. The pieces are to be lined on the inside with white tissue paper, and then joined together. (1869)

A Picture Frame

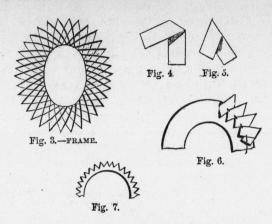

Fig. 3.—FRAME.

Fig. 4.

Fig. 5.

Fig. 6.

Fig. 7.

This frame is made of gilt paper, cut in large sheets, one of which is sufficient for three frames like one in *figure 3*. The outer row of points is made from strips half an inch in width, cut into pieces 2 inches in length. The strips used for each of the other rows are a trifle narrower and shorter than for the row immediately outside. Double the paper down first from the left, as in *figure 4*, and then from the right, as in *figure 5*. Sew each row of points, beginning with the outer one, upon an oval cut from an old box cover, *figure 6*. The inner row of points is a piece of the gilt paper upon which points are cut *neatly*, and pasted over the last row of stitches, *figure 7*. (1868)

A Screen of Cigar-Box Wood with Paper Applications

The materials used are a cigar box, black glazed paper, glue, and narrow brown silk ribbon. This pretty screen is particularly serviceable in shielding the light of a lamp. The screen, as *figure 96* shows, consists of five equal parts, each 11¼ inches high and 4¾ inches wide, cut smoothly of cigar-box wood. The upper curved parts must be cut exactly according to the design. The decoration on the parts is cut of black glazed paper, and pasted on with glue in the manner indicated in the engraving. The parts are connected by narrow silk ribbon of the color of the wood that are passed through holes bored at the top and bottom, one inch distant from the edges, and tied into small bows. (1876)

Sunflower Fan for Decorating Walls

Cut yellow paper into strips 6 inches wide and 30 inches long, one strip for each fan. Color the paper a dark brown along one edge for a depth of 3 inches, and notch the other edge with the scissors into deep points. For coloring the paper, dye or paint may be used, as happens to be most convenient.

After the paper is dry, fold it very carefully, creasing each fold well. After it is all folded, make a small hole through the brown part, half an inch from the edge, and put through it a fine wire or waxed thread. By this thread or wire, the paper is fastened to thin wood. A piece of wood half an inch wide which has been sandpapered, answers the purpose. A hole is made at one end of the handle, the wire or thread is tied through it, and the edges of the paper fastened down along the edge of the handle with mucilage. When done, the fan will look as shown in the engraving.

Any room which has a corner too dark to hang a picture in, can be brightened wonderfully by putting there a group of bright-colored fans. The thoughtful housewife will find many other means of making the home neat and attractive. (1883)

Fig. 96. Screen of Cigar-Box Wood with Paper Applications.

Screen For a Night Lamp

A screen for a small night lamp may be made by taking a piece of pasteboard 12 inches wide by 20 long, and covering it with material on which a neat pattern has been worked. Draw a line through the center so as to make two leaves, each 10 by 12 inches, and, with a sharp penknife cut along this line, taking care to cut only about half way through the board. The leaves will fold easily but still remain firmly together. Take a few stitches with a needle and stout thread from one leaf to the other to strengthen them

SCREEN FOR LAMP.

The cover may be made of silk, embroidered, or of linen with a pattern on it in outline. Java canvas worked with some simple pattern in cross-stitch makes a pretty cover. The cover and a lining are basted smoothly on each side of the pasteboard, and the edges bound with narrow ribbon.

Small blocks of wood, with a groove cut in the top to hold the screen, may be used as holders. They may either be painted a color to harmonize with that of the screen, or stained a dark brown or black, and oiled or varnished. (1883)

A Harp Card Stand

Take a piece of heavy pasteboard, 12 or 14 inches square, draw on it the figure of a harp, and with a sharp penknife cut it out, leaving narrow strips in imitation of the strings of a harp and leaving also one cross-bar near the top to hold it firmly together. To form the *rack*,

Fig. 3.—CARD-RACK.

cut out of pasteboard, not so heavy as the first, scalloped or fan-shaped pieces, 1½ inches across, 16 or 18 in number. Cover these and the whole harp, except the strings, with delicately tinted paper pasted on. Cover the strings with strips of gilt paper. Paste a narrow binding of gilt around each scallop and around the margin of the harp. Now, sew these scalloped pieces on either side of the harp, from the top downward, lapping partly on each other as seen in the engraving. Cover the stitches of the last two put on by a small rosette or bow of ribbon. A bouquet of gilt flowers may be pasted on the vacant space at the bottom, and a sprig on either side at the top. To produce a richer effect, scallop shells, readily obtained near the sea, might be used in lieu of the paper scallops. (1868)

Uses of Crêpe and Tissue Paper

The social and domestic duties of the housewife are often so exacting that she has very little leisure in which to construct the numerous dainty receptacles and decorations that play so important a part in the furnishing and adornment of the modern home. All women take delight in beautiful surroundings, and those whose time is largely occupied with weightier matters and whose means are limited will be glad to learn of any method by which really artistic results in fancywork may be produced with a small outlay of time and money.

With the aid of the exquisite crêpe and tissue papers now sold by stationers and dealers in art materials generally, a great variety of pretty and useful household treasures, such as candle and lampshades, photograph cases and frames, boxes and bags of all kinds, and handkerchief and glove sachets, may be produced with little trouble and expense. The crêpe papers are offered in all the popular shades and, being very pliable, they can easily be ruffled, shirred, and shaped over almost any surface. In fact, the number of ways in which they can be disposed is a constant source of surprise to the ingenious and tasteful worker, who will be able to utilize even the smallest pieces. These papers can almost invariably be used as substitutes for satin, silk and plush, which have heretofore been deemed quite indispensable for fancywork; and when decorated with skilfully arranged ribbons and with the charming flowers that can be easily made of the plain tissue papers, they produce effects that can scarcely be surpassed by the richer and far more costly fabrics. Both the plain and the crêpe papers will be found very useful in making favors for luncheons and cotillions, and prizes for card parties. (1895)

A Gift Bag of Crêpe and Tissue Papers

The little bag illustrated at *figure 1,* which is a fair example of what can be done in this work, is not at all difficult to make and may be used for a variety of practical and ornamental purposes. It would make a decidedly appropriate receptacle in which to present some commonplace gift, such as gloves, handkerchiefs or bonbons.

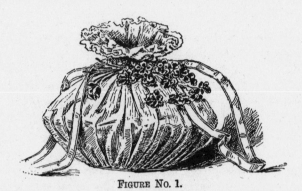

FIGURE NO. 1.

The materials required for its construction are two strips of crêpe paper, one white and one violet, and each 25 inches long by 7 inches wide; three sheets of tissue paper, one green, one light-violet and the other dark-violet; three-quarters of a yard of No. 3 violet satin ribbon; and a suitable quantity of dextrine and pasteboard. In adhesive qualities dextrine is far superior to both paste and mucilage, and it is especially satisfactory for paper work because it dries very quickly. It may be procured in small quantities at any drug store. It must be moistened with hot water until a thick paste is formed, which should be applied with a palette knife. The paste should not be made too wet, nor should it be too plentifully applied, as in either case it would discolor the paper. [Note that, although dextrine is still readily available, any twentiety-century paper cement will suffice.—Ed.]

Cut lengthwise of the white crêpe paper a section 20 inches long and 7 wide, and a similar section of the violet crêpe paper. Great care must be exercised in this part of the work, as the beauty of the effect depends largely on the manner in which the paper is cut. A good plan for beginners is to experiment with a small piece of the material and thus familiarize themselves with its elasticity before beginning the actual cutting.

To make the bag, first join the narrow sides of the white crêpe paper by laying one edge over the other and pasting it carefully, thus forming a flat seam. Connect the edges of the violet paper in the same manner, and place it inside the white as a lining. Then, with a needle and thread, make a row of stitching through both papers about 1/16-inch from the lower edge, and draw it up, thus forming the bottom of the bag. Cut two circular pieces of pasteboard, 2 inches in diameter; cover one of them with violet crêpe paper, drawing it well over the edges and fastening it underneath; and cover the other piece in the same way, first adding a little cotton and sachet powder. Apply dextrine to the underside of the unpadded circle near the edge, place the gathered edge of the bag evenly upon it, and press with the hand until the bag adheres firmly all round. This arranges the base of the receptacle, and the padded circle placed over the stitches on the inside provides a neat finish for the lining.

Now make two rows of stitching through both papers, one about 1 inch from the top, and the other ½-inch lower; and in the casing thus formed insert drawstrings of violet ribbon, passing them through an opening at each side, the same as in an ordinary shopping bag, and allowing the loops to hang as pictured. The loose, fluffy appearance at the top is produced by carefully pulling the edges of both the outside and lining.

The violets which decorate the bag are extensively used in connection with this kind of work. They are often made up in pink or yellow and are very effective, particularly when chosen to harmonize with the lining or trimming of the article upon which they are placed. Cut from the two shades of violet tissue paper sections the exact size and shape of *figure 2.* Take one dark and two light sections, place their centers together, and fold them into quarters without having their edges uniform. When folded they should resemble *figure 3.* Hold them firmly in the hand, twist the point once, and then open the flower so as to produce the full appearance shown at *figures 4* and *5.*

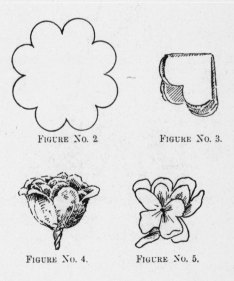

FIGURE NO. 2.　　FIGURE NO. 3.

FIGURE NO. 4.　　FIGURE NO. 5.

From the stem cut a strip from the green paper 1/16-inch wide and 5 inches long. Beginning at one end, twist the strip tightly between the first finger and thumb, leaving ⅛-inch plain, which attach to the back of the flower with dextrine. Stems made in this way are much lighter and more flexible than wire; and although they may appear rather difficult to prepare at first, a few attempts will develop the requisite amount of skill.

About twelve of the little flowers will be needed to decorate the bag. They should be arranged in a small cluster and fastened with a piece of stemming, which should then be pasted to the bag in such a manner that it will not interfere with the working of the drawstrings. (1895)

A Box for Playing Cards

At *figure 13* is displayed a little box designed as a receptacle for a pack of playing cards. It will be found both convenient and attractive, and very little material will be needed for its construction. Indeed, any small pieces of crêpe paper that have been left after completing a larger article may be utilized in making this ornament, as it is not necessary to have the puffing and sides of the same color. Any prettily contrasting shades may be combined, and flowers and ribbons judiciously placed will add much to the harmonious effect.

FIGURE NO. 13.

In making the box there will be needed two pieces of strong cardboard each 3 inches long by 2½ inches wide, two pieces each 3 inches long by 1 inch wide, and one piece 2½ inches long by 1 inch wide. Cover each of these pieces with tissue paper, either in the same shade as that chosen for the exterior of the box or in a prettily contrasting tint; then glue or sew these parts together so as to make the case, the covered sides being turned inward.

The puff which trims the box is made from a piece of crêpe paper 2 inches wide by 10 inches long, the full effect being produced by rubbing the finger carefully through the center, leaving the sides untouched. Arrange the puffing completely around the sides and bottom of the box, as illustrated, fulling it well at the corners, and gluing the edges just over the front and back of the case. Now cut two pieces of cardboard each 3 inches long by 2½ inches wide, cover them with crêpe paper, and affix them carefully and firmly to the back and front of the box so as to conceal all the edges of the puffing.

The flowers used for trimming are the same as those ornamenting the bag illustrated at *figure 1*, except that four pieces are used the size of *figure 2*, thus giving the flowers a fuller appearance. When so profuse a decoration of these blossoms as that pictured at *figure 13* is to be arranged, about one-half the flowers should be made without stems. These may be tastefully disposed among the others and will be found most effectual in concealing the ends of the narrow ribbon loops which appear so daintily among them. Four slips of ribbon or paper about ¼-inch wide must now be fastened under the flowers and decorated respectively with a heart, a diamond, a club, and a spade, cut from heavy paper in a color that will harmonize with the rest of the box, and pasted on. A narrow ribbon fastened at each side supplies the means of suspending the box, which will be handsome enough for the drawing room or boudoir. (1895)

A Banana Sachet of Crêpe Paper

A sachet of crêpe paper is at once novel and effective, and with ordinary care it will be found quite as durable as one made of silk or satin. Most of the general directions for constructing sachet cases of ornamental fabrics can be easily adapted to suit the requirements of crêpe paper.

Let us make the banana sachet shown at *figure 118*. Cut a piece of plain, lightweight wrapping paper or

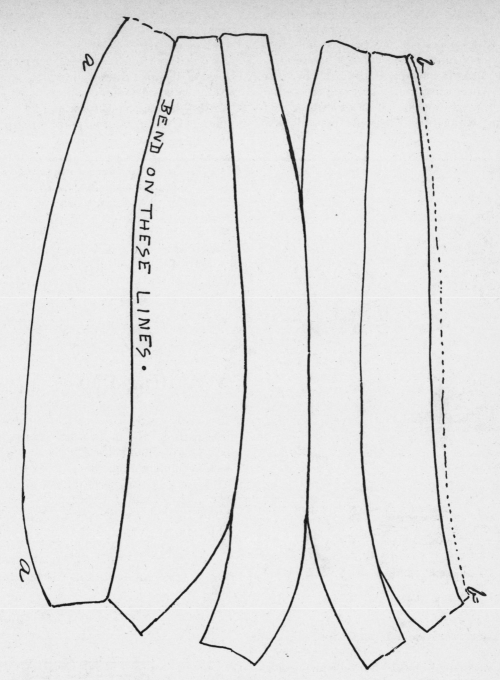

FIGURE NO. 114.

very thin note paper exactly the size and shape of *figure 114*. Turn down the edge at the solid line next to the dotted line *bb,* and glue the turned-down portions securely to the edge *aa*. This will form a casing for the filling, which should be of fine white cotton plentifully sprinkled with sachet powder. The perfume will be more lasting if the cotton is first pulled into small pieces and the powder worked evenly through it. The top or stem end is open (see *figure 115*), and before putting in the filling, crease the paper on the solid lines to form the faces or sides noticed in the natural fruit. With the blunt end of a lead pencil push the perfumed cotton through the opening at the top, being careful not to pack it too tightly, as the object is to provide sufficient support to keep the case in shape, not to make a hard filling.

Cut a piece of gold crêpe paper exactly the length of the banana, and wide enough to go once around it without a lap; and hang the paper in the sunlight for a day or until it has faded to the shade of a yellow banana. Stretch it slightly through the center and to within an inch of each end, and arrange it about the form, shaping it at the ends so as to cover them smoothly. At the stem end insert a gathering string, using a needle and straw-colored sewing silk. A neat finish may be easily arranged, for as the paper will not ravel or fray, it is possible to trim it quite close to the gathering. The completed stem end is shown at *figure 116*. The other end of the banana is finished by covering the casing with a very thin coating of glue or good paste (not mucilage), and shaping the crêpe paper smoothly over it. (See *figure 117*.) Both ends should be carefully trimmed with a sharp scissors, that there may be no rough edges.

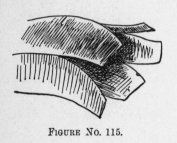

Figure No. 115.

Figure No. 116.

Figure No. 117.

Figure No. 118.

Color the edges with Vandyke-brown or sepia oil paint, applying it in quite lavish touches with either a palette knife or a small bristle brush, and using a banana as a model. The slight tinge of green on the sides along the little ridges or seams should also be done with oil paint, as watercolors, owing to their very thin consistency, would be certain to run and make it impossible to obtain the clear decisive lines seen on the real fruit. As a ripe banana generally has one or more bruised spots, it will heighten the effect to paint these upon the paper imitation with burnt sienna and sepia. Watercolors will be found best for this purpose, but too much must not be taken upon the brush. If oil paints are more convenient, they may be applied quite satisfactorily with a bristle brush, the strokes being made with the crinkles. Do not take up too much paint on the brush, or the effect will be streaked instead of even and soft.

Of course, turpentine and oil paints have a more or less unpleasant odor, and the oil is apt to spread, for both of which reasons watercolors are to be preferred for use on either French tissue or crêpe paper. Good results may be obtained by experimenting on a piece of crêpe paper with watercolors, using what is termed a "dry" brush—that is, a brush that has been thoroughly wet and then shaken until its point is sharp and shows less than half a drop of moisture. If too much water is shaken off, the hairs will separate, and there will not be enough liquid to dissolve the paint; but if there is a slight amount of water left (approximately half a drop), the brush will retain its sharp point after being rubbed over the cake of paint, and it will be easy to draw a clear line with it. With care and a little practice, watercolors may be used much more effectively than oil paints in "touching up" the banana (shown complete at *figure 118*), except at the sharp end, which needs the rough finish already described. (1895)

A Writing Pad

The writing pad pictured at *figure 151* is very simple of construction. For it procure a piece of the stiffest pasteboard obtainable—at least $^3/_{16}$-inch thick. Cut a section 14 inches long and 10 inches wide, cover neatly with crêpe paper, and either turn all the edges in, having first creased them or else trim them off very carefully, and cover them with a band of ribbon or with crêpe paper twisted loosely. Cut four straps of flat silk elastic in a narrow width and arrange them as shown, sewing their ends in place under the edge finish; beneath these straps slip a sheet of blotting paper. (1895)

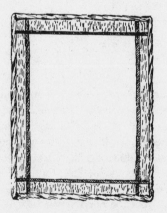

Figure No. 151.

A Portfolio

FIGURE NO. 152.

To construct the portfolio displayed at *figure 152*, cut two pieces of heavy cardboard each 14 inches long and 10 inches wide. After trimming the edges smoothly, cover each section on the outside with a split sheet of cotton wadding, sprinkle with sachet powder, and secure the wadding in place by winding it loosely with sewing cotton, which can be easily removed after the crêpe paper cover is put in place. This cover should be double, as the wear on it will be greater than it would be if the cotton were not used. Finish the inside smoothly with crêpe paper, and connect the two boards at each end with a strip of silk the exact shade of the crêpe paper, plaiting the silk at the back of the portfolio, and

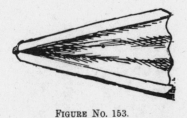

FIGURE NO. 153.

gluing or sewing the side edges neatly to the boards. Bind the back with firm ribbon or double silk, and finish the edges like those of the writing pad described above. An end view of the portfolio is given at *figure 153*. (1895)

A Rocking Blotter

Figure 154 illustrates a unique blotting pad. For its foundation use a piece of heavy pasteboard, curving it with a hot iron as follows: Heat the iron moderately, carefully marking the cardboard to show exactly how far the outward curve should extend, and then iron it as though it were a shirt collar—that is, pass the iron briskly over the cardboard, bearing gently upon its broad end. The cardboard will curl slightly, and may be easily handled and shaped while warm. Neatly cover it in the inside with crêpe paper and on the outside with blotting paper, and connect the ends under a bow of heavy satin ribbon the exact shade of the crêpe paper. If it is impossible to exactly duplicate the tint of the crêpe paper in the blotting paper, it is best to have the latter white. It will not be practical to make the bow of crêpe paper, as the wear and strain upon this ornament necessitates the use of a firm material. (1895)

FIGURE NO. 154.

An Ornamental Desk Candle-stick

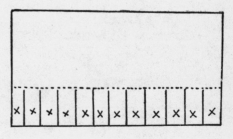

FIGURE NO. 162.

A tiny candlestick of paper makes a very pretty ornament for a desk, and may be constructed thus: Cut a circular piece of cardboard 3 inches in diameter, and also a section like *figure 162*, slashing the latter at the solid lines, bending the little tabs marked *X* to stand at right angles to the remainder of the section, and forming a hollow cylinder, with the tabs projecting at the bottom (see *figure 163*). Then paste the cylinder upon the center of the circular piece.

Cut a strip of crêpe paper 1 inch wide, across the crinkles, stretch one edge carefully to produce a fluted effect, gather 4 inches of the unstretched edge on a fine drawing thread, paste this edge inside the little cylinder, and bend the frill outward when the paste is dry.

Use a plain lengthwise strip to cover the cardboard cylinder, and also the bottom of the little stand; and cover the upper side of the base with a gathered strip, stretching the outer edge and applying the paper as smoothly as possible. Add a narrow ruffle of paper at the outer edge, and conceal the joining with a cord of paper pasted firmly to position.

Place in the candlestick a small colored wax candle, choosing it to match the paper if possible. The base may be cut square or the shape of a heart, spade, club or diamond. A very unique ornament may be produced by using a playing card for the foundation, allowing the face and back to remain uncovered, and trimming with crêpe paper around the candle holder and with a cord at the edge of the base. (See *figure 164*.) (1895)

FIGURE NO. 164.

A Bureau Cover

A novel bureau cover may be arranged in the following manner: First cover the top of the bureau with a piece of ordinary Canton flannel, securing the material *under the edges* of the top by means of four tacks, which will not disfigure the bureau in any way and will keep the cover from being easily displaced. Over the flannel fasten pale blue crêpe paper with a few pins; and then make a spread of fine dotted Swiss exactly the size of the top, and trim its front edges and ends with a ruffle of the Swiss or with a fall of lace 3 or 4 inches deep and half as long again as the edges to which it is applied. The gathered edge of the ruffle or lace may be concealed by a strip of lace braid, beneath which a ribbon may be run in such a manner that it can be easily removed when the cover is to be laundered. (1895)

Picture Frames

We all enjoy having pictures of our friends and favorites about us, not always out of sight in albums, etc. but prettily framed and scattered about our rooms, that we may gaze upon the familiar features without an effort. Some of us, however, are obliged from reasons of economy to deny ourselves the pleasure of possessing frames for these little treasures, although the desire to be surrounded by such pretty ornaments is constantly presenting itself. By careful observation we will find that some of the most exquisite of the picture frames now offered in the shops are constructed of the inexpensive materials, and that taste and judgment are the chief contributors toward producing the effects which we admire so much.

FIGURE NO. 14.

The little heart-shaped frame pictured at *figure 14* is very popular at present. It makes a pretty and appropriate favor to use at a bridal breakfast or luncheon, each of the bridesmaids being presented with a photograph of the bride enclosed in this suggestive form; and a suitable number of frames joined at the sides, and each containing a picture of a bridesmaid, would form a suitable souvenir for the bride. White frames would, of course, be most appropriate for the purpose just mentioned, although any of the dainty shades of pink, yellow, or green, now so much used to convey a distinctive idea of harmony at such affairs will also be found attractive.

To make the frame, proceed as follows: Procure a pattern the size desired, and cut two pieces of cardboard exactly like it. Make a round or square opening in one piece, to form an aperture for the picture, and cover this section with yellow crêpe paper, sticking it at the back. Then paste the edges of the three sides of the other piece of cardboard to the corresponding edges of the covered piece, leaving the upper edges open for inserting the photograph; and fasten an inch-wide strip of cardboard at the back to form an easel.

The little daisies used in decorating the frame are made of white tissue paper, and are a study of the natural flower cultivated in many gardens. The process of making them will be much facilitated by folding and cutting according to directions: Take a piece of white tissue paper having one side square, and fold it as represented at *figure 15*. Fold in the same manner three times until the paper looks as at *figure 16*. Cut off at *A-A*, and slit down four times about ⅛-inch. When unfolded the petals should resemble *figure 17*. It is not necessary to have all the little petals exactly the same size (as uniformity is not the practice of Nature), but they should be as much alike as possible. Three pieces like *figure 17* will be needed to form one flower. They are placed together and bent downward in the center, with the point of a lead pencil, the bent part being tightly twisted to form the inside of the calyx. Then a piece of green tissue paper, cut the shape of *figure 18*, but left the length desired for the stem, is placed over the twisted part, with the points extending at the back of the flower, and securely glued. The remainder of the green is twisted between the first finger and thumb for a stem. When the glue dries, the flower should be opened to appear as natural as possible.

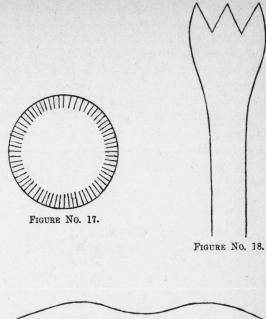

FIGURE NO. 17.

FIGURE NO. 18.

FIGURE NO. 19.

The leaves accompanying the flower are shaped like *figure 19*, but a little variation in size and color will be found an improvement. They are fastened to the stem as shown in the complete flower, represented at *figure 20*. The flowers and leaves may be arranged in any way directed by one's taste. A very pleasing effect may be produced by trimming in some graceful way with baby ribbon.

FIGURE NO. 20.

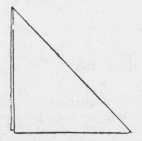

FIGURE NO. 15.

A   A

FIGURE NO. 16.

The process of folding and cutting described must be followed in making nearly all the flowers hereafter mentioned, so the method should be very carefully studied, that errors may be avoided. The shaping will be found somewhat awkward at first, but after a few attempts the worker will become familiar with the system and will feel amply repaid for the time bestowed by the rapidity with which she is able to make the different parts of a flower as well as stems and appropriate foliage.

FIGURE NO. 21.

Figure 21 represents a unique frame 6 inches long by 5 wide. It is cut from cardboard and is covered with apple-green crêpe paper in the same manner as the heart-shaped frame just described. The little projections on each side of the opening are made of light-weight cardboard, covered on one side with the green crêpe and glued on as shown in the illustration. The frame is further embellished at the edge by the addition of a cord made of green and white crêpe paper. The idea of making cord out of these materials is certainly a great stride toward perfection in their use, as we all know how much beauty and finish is added to any piece of fancywork by the judicious use of cord. Plain tissue paper can be used for the purpose, but it is not so easily managed as crêpe paper and, when finished, does not present the smooth appearance which is the chief beauty of the trimming.

For the cord decorating the frame under consideration, cut four crosswise strips of green and four of white crêpe paper about 1 inch wide. Join the green strips neatly end to end, and also the white ones; and then fasten the two shades together. Secure one end of the resulting strip to a table with a thumbtack, and, beginning at this end, twist the whole length until the paper assumes a tight, round appearance. Loosen the tack, tie the ends together, and allow the two strands to twist themselves together. If the result is not satisfactory, a little shaking and adjusting will doubtless have the

desired effect. Rubbing the cord one way with the hand over a hard cushion will flatten any rough surfaces that may appear. Fasten the cord to the edge of the frame with good glue, joining it at the corner, where any little decoration may be used to conceal the junction. The bowknots are made of cord tied in the usual way, and are stuck on. This cord can be made of any desired thickness by simply cutting the strips wider or narrower.

Small field daisies are grouped on this frame. It requires a piece of white tissue paper 1 inch square to make a daisy. Fold in the same way as illustrated at *figures 15* and *16*, but cut according to the dotted lines at *figure 22*. When opened the paper should present all the points of the daisy. Take a piece of yellow tissue paper ¼-inch square, and cut it into fine strips, leaving just enough space on one side to hold the parts together. Crush these into round shape, and glue the piece directly in the center of the flower. Now fold a piece of paper 1 inch square one time less than directed for *figures 15* and *16*, so as to form eight points instead of sixteen; and cut like the dotted lines at *figure 23*. This imitation of a calyx is fastened in the center to the back of the flower, and then a strip of tissue paper in the same shade is twisted and fastened to the back for a stem.

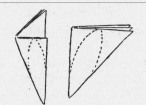

FIGURE NO. 22.   FIGURE NO. 23.

FIGURE NO. 24.

Cut the leaves like *figure 24*, and secure them to the stem as previously described. This flower may be varied to suit the taste; it may be given the appearance of a fully opened flower or, by simply closing the petals together, of a bud. (1895)

A Photograph Case

A very pretty design for a photograph case is shown open at *figure 25*. Such a case can be made to contain as

many pictures as required, by simply increasing the number of parts. It is also easily folded into the compact form represented at *figure 26*, thus securing the photographs from dust and at the same time providing a pretty ornament for cabinet or table. This sort of case will be found particularly suitable for holding any set of pictures of which the entire number is necessary to convey the impression desired. The one here pictured is made of white crêpe paper, with puffings of similar paper in a dainty shade of apple green, and over all are painted delicate tracings in watercolor gold. When the case is closed the sprays of oats, and the cord, combining the prevailing colors of the ornament, form a very effective and complete decoration.

FIGURE NO. 26.

These together form the back of the case, which is entirely covered on one side with white crêpe paper. Cut a strip of green crêpe paper 5½ inches wide, and form it into a puff by drawing the finger through the center. Place the puff entirely around the back, fulling it over the edge and fastening it on the opposite side. Conceal the cloth hinges, which appear inside, with strips of white crêpe paper, and then place the different sections forming the interior directly over the corresponding pieces of cardboard, being careful to cover all rough edges of puffing, etc., and leaving a small space at the top for inserting the photograph.

The oats ornamenting this case may be made of brown, yellow, or green tissue paper, to harmonize with the rest of the work; and they will be particularly effective when used in combination with flowers. Olive-green paper was chosen in this instance. The oats are formed thus: Roll small pieces of tissue paper into a soft ball, place the ball in the top of a piece of green tissue paper shaped like *figure 27*, and twist the points and

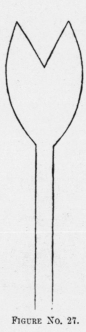

FIGURE NO. 27.

For a case of the proportions represented, a roll of white crêpe paper, a smaller roll of apple-green paper, a sheet of olive-green tissue paper and some cardboard will be required. Cut six pieces of cardboard (ordinary pasteboard may be used) each 5¾ inches long by 4 inches wide. In three of these make an oblong opening, and cover them smoothly with white crêpe paper. Join the other pieces of cardboard together with strips of white cotton cloth, leaving spaces of ¾-inch between them.

stem tightly in opposite directions over the ball. The first kernel is made with a long stem to serve as a support for the whole spray, the other stems being cut much shorter and glued to the longer one in a manner imitating nature as closely as possible. Three of these sprays are glued to the exterior of the case, and when they are properly disposed, with the addition of a cord and bowknot, the article is complete.

Three or four of the paper-covered frames, placed so one will hang directly over another and joined together with cotton cloth or strong paper, as above described, will form a very pretty panel to hang in the narrow space between two windows, brightening and apparently shortening that part of the wall in a most satisfactory way. Portraits of our favorite authors or composers may be attractively displayed in this way, and when hung beside one's escritoire or piano, testify in a most graceful manner to our appreciation of the originals. (1895)

FIGURE NO. 29.

A Photograph Box

The handsome photograph box pictured at *figure 28* is very easy to make; and glove, tie, and handkerchief boxes may be constructed in the same manner, a little variation in size being all that is necessary. The foundation of this receptacle is an ordinary shoe box. The box is covered with yellow crêpe paper, lined with plain tissue paper in the same shade and decorated with white morning-glories and yellow-and-white cord. The materials required in the making are a roll of the yellow crêpe paper, a smaller roll of the white crêpe paper and two sheets of the green tissue paper.

FIGURE NO. 28.

To form the tufted lining which decorates the interior of the box, shown at *figure 29*, cut six various parts, two for the ends, two for the sides, one for the bottom and one for the cover. Cover one side of each piece with perfumed cotton wadding about 1 inch thick, and over this place the tissue paper, drawing it well over the edges and securing it to the opposite side. With a strong needle and thread tuft the wadding and paper evenly, using a small piece of crushed white paper to accentuate each indentation.

When the parts have all been covered in this way, glue them tightly and evenly into the box. Cut the crêpe paper two inches higher than the side of the box, and sufficiently long to cover one side and two ends. Draw the finger through the center to form fullness, place the paper in position, and glue one edge to the top of the side and ends, allowing an inch of paper to extend above for a ruffle, and turning the other edge under and securing it to the bottom of the box. Fasten the lid to the box with a cloth hinge securing the latter to the back, and cover with good glue. Cover the back with yellow crêpe paper, allowing it to extend about an inch over the cover; and then cover with crêpe paper a piece of cardboard the exact size of the top, and glue it in position, thus concealing all the unsightly ends and edges.

The morning-glories illustrated are among the simplest and most effective flowers that can be made. Cut a piece of crêpe paper, lengthwise of the roll, 3 inches long and 2 inches wide, and glue the narrow sides together. Form stamens by twisting narrow strips of white paper. Place these in the center of the flower, and twist all together tightly at the base. Then pull the crêpe paper at the top and bend it over as seen in the natural flower. The calyx and stem are shaped like *figure 30*, and are glued on as previously described. The leaves are fashioned like *figures 31* and *32*, the smaller ones being placed at the bottom of the calyx. The tendrils appearing among the foliage are formed by twisting narrow strips of green tissue paper and curling them over a pencil. Sixteen morning-glories will be needed for this box. The size may be varied by increasing or diminishing the length and width of the sections forming them. These flowers are pretty when produced in shades of pink, purple, and heliotrope; and the white variety is very delicate when tinted with watercolor paints.

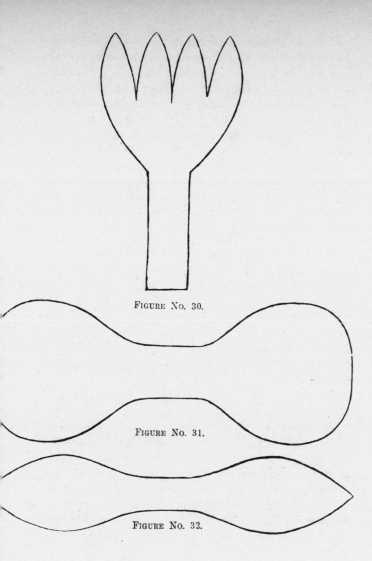

FIGURE No. 30.

FIGURE No. 31.

FIGURE No. 32.

The cord decorating the box is composed of yellow and white crêpe paper and finishes the edge of the cover, the bowknot forming the means of opening the box. A strip of No. 3 white ribbon may be secured to each side between the lining and exterior to prevent the cover falling back. A box of this kind covered with heliotrope crêpe paper, lined with white paper and ornamented with white morning-glories having heliotrope-tinted edges would be highly artistic. (1895)

A Stamp Box

Figure 35 represents a very dainty and attractive stamp box. The box is shown made of white crêpe paper, lined with blush-pink tissue paper, and decorated with small pink flowers made in the same manner as the violets previously described (*see directions for a gift bag*).

FIGURE No. 35.

Cut six pieces of cardboard in the following sizes: two pieces 3¼ inches long by 2 inches wide, two pieces 3¼ inches long by 1 inch wide, and two pieces 2 inches long by 1 inch wide. Cover each piece on one side with a thin layer of cotton wadding, and over this place pink paper, drawing the latter well over the edges and gluing it to the opposite side. Fasten these parts together, with the pink paper inside: the result should be a box 3¼ inches long, 2 inches wide and 1 inch deep. The cover should, of course, be fastened at one side only with a narrow strip of cloth or paper.

Cover the sides of the box with a strip of white crêpe paper 2 inches wide pulled to form a puff and ruffle. Secure one edge to the bottom of the box, and fasten the other to the top, allowing a ruffle about ½-inch deep to extend above. Cut a piece of cardboard the exact size of the lid, cover it with white crêpe paper, and fasten it securely to the lid, concealing the cloth or paper hinge and all rough edges. From white cardboard cut one piece 2 inches long by 1 inch wide, and two pieces each 1⅜ inches long by 2 inches wide. The first piece is to be glued exactly in the center of the box, dividing it into two equal parts. The others are to be placed one on each side, slanting from top to bottom and fastened at one end.

About fifteen little flowers are needed to decorate the cover, and a few loops of narrow ribbon are placed among them.

A very good glue for this work, that is not so liable to discolor the paper as the dextrine previously mentioned, is prepared by pouring boiling water on gum tragacanth and allowing it to stand until the gum is thoroughly softened. This will be found particularly satisfactory for joining cord in constructing boxes, etc.

In preparing these pretty boxes for special gifts or for special rooms, the prevailing tint in the furnishing of such rooms should be considered and a harmony of color maintained. (1895)

A Handsome Lampshade

Beyond a doubt one of the most pleasing and artistic uses to which crêpe and tissue paper can be put is the making of the candle and lampshades now in such general vogue. The beautiful colors in which the papers are produced and their wonderful flexibility and gracefulness offer possibilities for the development of exquisite effects that could not be attained with any of the other fabrics used for such work. Besides, the cost of shades constructed of crêpe and tissue papers is very small when compared with that of similar creations in silk, lace, and flowers, and the amount of time and patience required in making is much less. When crêpe paper is used, the foundation of a shade is secured to the frame with glue, while silk used for the same purpose needs to be stitched tightly and evenly to position. Nor are these advantages counterbalanced by inferior durability on the part of the paper shades, as they withstand the ravages of sunlight and dust fully as well as those constructed of the more expensive materials.

Wire foundations are required in making lampshades. Most dealers in lamps have these frames for sale, but they can readily be made at home by anyone possessing a little ingenuity. They are composed entirely of strong wire, which is bent with pincers into the required shape, and then soldered securely in place.

Figure 36 represents a handsome lampshade. The foundation which is known as the "20-inch Chinese square," is pictured at *figure 37.* [A more contemporary wire lamp frame may be used to better advantage.—Ed.] It is covered with Nile-green crêpe paper and decorated with pink chrysanthemums and buds. The materials needed in making this shade are:

1 roll of Nile-green crêpe paper.
2 sheets of light olive-green tissue paper.
2 sheets of dark olive-green tissue paper.
7 sheets of light-pink tissue paper.
7 sheets of white tissue paper.
3 sheets of Nile-green tissue paper.
4 yards of florist's stemming.
1 cake of wax.
1 spool of wire.

The wax should be slightly heated while being used.

The wires of the frame may be wound with narrow strips of Nile-green tissue paper, glued at short intervals to keep the paper in place; or they may be painted, if preferred. The collar of the frame should be covered on the inside with asbestos fabric, and over this Nile-green tissue paper should be neatly and tightly drawn, the edges being fastened on the outside of the frame. The asbestos is necessary to protect the frame from the heat of the lamp.

Now trim both edges of the roll of crêpe paper; gather the paper with strong linen thread, leaving a heading of about 5 inches; and tie the paper tightly about the collar of the frame. Arrange the paper so that it falls evenly all round the frame, and glue the edges together carefully. Next secure the crêpe paper to the curves of the frame with good glue, drawing it down tightly. Pull out the heading at the top, and ruffle the lower edge with the finger and thumb to produce a full appearance. The foundation will then be complete and ready to receive the decoration.

FIGURE NO. 36.

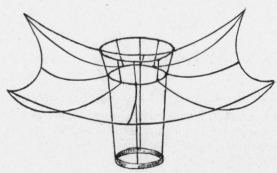

FIGURE NO. 37.

Any of the large flowers previously described would form a pretty trimming for this shade; but the chrysanthemum is, without doubt, the handsomest and most effective blossom for the purpose. The endless variety of tints in which this flower is produced adapt it for the ornamentation of foundations of nearly all colors; and the gracefulness of the pretty buds, and of the full-blown blossoms with their wealth of curling petals, afford many opportunities for artistic arrangements.

The chrysanthemums decorating the shade illustrated are of the variety known as the "Ceres," and have green centers and pink-and-white petals. The petals are formed thus: Place together a piece of white and a piece of pink tissue paper each 6 inches square, with the white inside, and fold as described in the directions for the heart-shaped frame. When the folding is completed, the paper should appear as represented at *figure 38;* and it should be cut according to the dotted lines. Sixteen petals should be the result when the paper is opened

nesses of curled paper. Often these parts of the chrysanthemum are curled without creasing, to form only two thicknesses. This process is much easier than the other, but it does not give the flower the waxen appearance when finished which is one of its chief beauties. If only a few petals are creased and curled at a time, the paper will be found much more manageable. Five leaves are curled to form one flower, pink being substituted for white in two of them, to supply the deepness of color required for the outside petals.

Three 1-inch squares of the two shades of green tissue paper are now folded and cut to form fringed circles, which are strung through their centers upon a piece of wire that is bent over at one end to prevent the papers falling off, the lighter shade being placed inside. These circles form the pistil of the flower; and the curled leaves are now placed upon the wire in the same manner, pushed together tightly, and held in place by a piece of wax squeezed about the wire.

The calyx is composed of a piece of green tissue paper 4 inches square, which is folded and cut to form eight pointed petals, and is then placed upon the wire and glued to the back of the flower, concealing the wax.

The bud is made by arranging one leaf of curled petals upon a wire, closing the parts together, and securing them in place with a small piece of wax. The calyx is cut and set quite deeply about the bud, being arranged to cover the wax. The wire stemming is cut four inches long and is attached to the calyx with a little glue.

FIGURE No. 38.

FIGURE No. 39.

A complete flower is pictured at *figure 39.* Fifteen flowers and eight buds will be required to decorate the shade; and when they are all completed, arrange them on the foundation as gracefully as possible, placing stemming upon all buds, and upon as many flowers as may be deemed necessary. The decorations are all secured to the foundation with good glue. A frame of any shape may be covered in the manner just described.

Each one should be creased lengthwise through the center, the white being inside, and should be curled over a hard cushion with the back of a buttonhook or the blunt side of a vegetable peeler, rolled from center to end and then back again. This gives each petal four thick-

91

In another very beautiful shade the foundation is composed of white crêpe paper, the edges of which are tinted with yellow watercolor paints; and large bunches of yellow chrysanthemums supply the decoration. These flowers are made in the same way as the pink ones described above, except that the pistils are yellow, and six leaves of petals instead of five are used for each flower, which is thus given a much fuller appearance. Different shades of yellow may be used, the darkest being chosen for the center petals. The "Moonlight" chrysanthemum will combine very charmingly with the yellow variety. It is exquisitely delicate, the two inner leaves of petals being white, while the other four are in the lightest shade of yellow.

The "Lillian B. Bird" is another member of the popular chrysanthemum family and is very beautiful when reproduced in paper, its delicate, quill-like petals contrasting in a marked degree with the gracefully curling ones of the other varieties. Two of the lightest shades of shrimp-pink are united in this flower. Fold eight double pieces of paper in the lighter shade, each 5 inches square, to form thirty-two petals, cutting the same as for other chrysanthemums. Fold and cut three double pieces, each 3 inches square, making them exactly the same shape as the larger ones. Twist each petal loosely between the finger and thumb. Now place three small circles of yellow tissue paper upon a wire, and string on the twisted petals, placing the smaller ones inside. When all are on, push them up closely and secure them in place with a small piece of wax. These chrysanthemums form quite as attractive a decoration as the other varieties, and are not quite so difficult to make. (1895)

Candle Shades

Supports for candle shades may be procured at any art store and are quite inexpensive. [With the renewed interest in things antique, candle shade holders are once again available through specialty lighting suppliers.—Ed.] They are attached to the candles, and may be raised or lowered at pleasure. Small mica shields are also obtainable and afford excellent protection if the candles are to be lighted. A pretty yet simple design is illustrated at *figure 44*. The shade is made of yellow tissue paper, lined with white tissue paper and decorated with white violets. Cut crosswise of the material a strip of each color 5 inches wide, and 33 inches long. Place the strips together, and shirr them about an inch from each side by folding the paper over a knitting needle or hatpin, and then pressing it with the right hand toward the left

FIGURE NO. 44.

in fine plaits. Cut a strip of cardboard ⅛-inch wide and sufficiently long to extend around the collar of the holder; cover it on one side with a thin coating of glue, and full one shirred edge of the paper evenly upon it. This forms a ruffle for the top of the shade. Secure the ends of the cardboard together, and place it upon the support. Pull out the shirring at the bottom of the shade, shaping as illustrated; and then glue the ends of the paper together. The violets are made as in the directions for the gift bag.

Another attractive little shade is made of white crêpe paper, and may be decorated with violets or any preferred variety of small flowers. One roll of crêpe paper will be required to make this shade. Cut lengthwise of the roll a piece of paper 25 inches long and 5 inches wide. Full the paper evenly upon a strip of cardboard, the same as directed for making the preceding shade; and when the glue is dry, pull out the heading, secure the ends of the cardboard firmly, and glue the loose ends of the paper together. Carefully ruffle the other edge of the paper with the finger and thumb, pressing down until the shade extends outward the desired distance, and bend the edge irregularly. Next fasten a circle of cardboard ⅛-inch wide and 4 inches in diameter to the underside. If a color is used for the foundation of the shade, the strip of cardboard should be covered with tissue paper to correspond.

Four-leaf clovers cut from heavy green paper will form very pretty trimmings for such shades, and small butterflies of lightweight cardboard covered with tissue paper and decorated with gold paint and some glitter will add to the brilliance of the general effect.

Many odd designs for candle shades will suggest themselves. The chrysanthemum shade is particularly pretty for decorating candelabra. The foundation is formed of white tissue paper after the design illustrated at *figure 44*, and the edges are glued over a circle of cardboard ½-inch wide and 4 inches in diameter. Tissue paper in the desired shade is cut in strips 2½ inches wide, which are curled in the same manner as petals for chrysanthemums and are secured close and full to the foundation. (1895)

Candy Boxes

Candy boxes may always be made ornamental, and they provide a simple and pleasing mode of offering the candy, which would not be nearly so tempting if displayed in a bowl or other large receptacle. Boxes covered with crêpe paper can be made for very little, and they should be of white pasteboard, with or without hinged lids, and unfinished both inside and outside. Cut a piece of crêpe paper as wide as the bottom and two ends of a box, and long enough to cover the inside and outside of the lid and the back, bottom, and front of the box. Using good flour paste, neatly fasten the paper in place, folding the extra fullness over the ends as shown at *figure 45*, and turning in the paper that extends beyond the lid, so the edges will have a neat appearance and will require no other finish. If the box has a cover with sides, instead of a hinged lid, arrange the paper upon the ends of the cover the same as upon the ends of the box.

FIGURE No. 45.

Finish the upper edge, if the box has a hinged lid, or the lower edge of the cover, if the box is of the ordinary kind, with a cord of crêpe paper. To make the cord, shape a strip of paper 2 inches wide, cutting parallel with the crinkles, and twist it tightly as shown at *figure 46*. An equally satisfactory completion may be arranged

FIGURE No. 46.

by using small braids formed by plaiting three narrow strips of paper, and pasting a flat bow on the front or top of the box. A tiny loop should be neatly secured to the front edge of the hinged lid. Inside the box paste a ruffle 1 inch wide all round the upper edge, as illustrated at *figure 47*. This completes the box, which is pictured at *figure 48*.

FIGURE No. 47.

FIGURE No. 48.

Of course a box of this kind may be made much more elaborate by the addition of paper flowers (directions for which have been previously given), and bows of narrow satin ribbon matching the flowers or in the dainty shade of bright green often seen in growing flower stems. A many-looped knot of the ribbon should be arranged to conceal the fastening of the flowers to the box. Such dainty boxes may be used in many ways. They may be made to harmonize with the bureau ornamentations, and may be employed as receptacles for the countless stray buttons, pins, and odd articles of jewelry that so frequently give the bureau or dressing table a most disorderly appearance. (1895)

A Match-Scratcher

A very useful and decidedly unique match-scratcher is made of crêpe paper cut in strips 3½ inches wide and as long as the width of the paper. Form these strips into loops and ends to imitate a stylish bow of ribbon, as represented at *figure 49;* and on one of the longest loops, which should be not less than 6 inches in length, fasten a piece of sandpaper, sewing it securely through the double fold of paper, as at *figure 50.* Hang the completed article from a strong brass screw-hook secured in the side of the dressing table or bureau or under the gas jet. A spray of pinks, bluets or some other dainty flowers slipped under the tying loop would greatly increase the beauty of this useful novelty without greatly augmenting its cost. (1895)

FIGURE NO. 49.

FIGURE NO. 50.

Pincushions

Small pincushions are now in very general favor, two being usually seen on my lady's dressing table. Round, square, and long narrow cushions are equally fashionable, but they are invariably small. Square cushions are most easily made to wear the "milliner" smartness, but cushions measuring 7 inches in length and 3½ inches wide may be trimmed with flowers or lace.

In dressing a cushion, first cover it with crêpe paper, sewing the paper in such a way that all the joinings or seams will come at the sides where they will be concealed by the decorations. (See *figure 51.*) Cut a strip of paper across the crinkles 1½ inches wide as long as the circumference of the cushion. Carefully stretch out one side of it to form a ruffle, and gather the other side with a small needle and silk or fine cotton, being very careful not to tear the paper. Sew this ruffle to the cushion half an inch above the side seams, apply a cord of paper to hide the gathers, and finish the corners with stiff pompadour bows made thus:

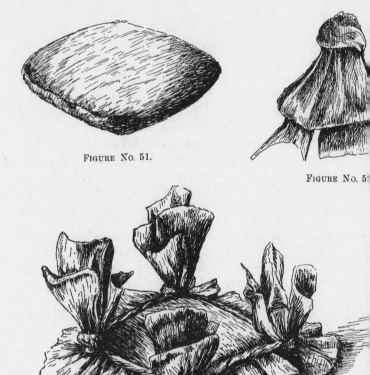

FIGURE NO. 51.

FIGURE NO. 5?

FIGURE NO. 53

Cut a strip of paper 11 inches long, running the way of the crinkles. Mark a point 4½ inches from one end, and a second point 4 inches from the first. Double the paper so as to join these points of division, thus forming two loops; and twist a loose knot to cover the ends of the loops, as seen at *figure 52.* Shape the remainder of the strip (2½ inches) into a pointed end; and the bow, with its two upright loops and pert end, will then be ready to sew upon the cushion, as pictured at *figure 53.* Four of these bows complete the unique decoration, although lace could be gathered loosely about the bows or arranged in a sort of jabot from one corner to the one diagonally opposite. (1895)

A Hairpin Holder

Another novelty is a hairpin holder in the shape of a candlestick. The supplies needed to make this holder are a sheet of medium-weight cardboard, crêpe paper, some curled horsehair and a candle and shade holder. Cut a piece of cardboard the shape shown at *figure 54*, making it 6 inches wide and 7½ inches from the point to the tip of the handle. Cover it smoothly with crêpe paper and finish the edge with cord. Shape a piece of cardboard 4 inches wide and 5 inches long, as at *figure 55*, and cover it with crêpe paper as far as the dotted line, and with plain white glazed paper above. Cut incisions ½-inch deep from the lower edge of the end covered with crêpe paper. Curve this piece carefully to imitate a candle, spread the small square tabs formed by the incisions at the bottom, and glue them firmly to the stand or base, as depicted at *figure 56*. Ruffle a piece of crêpe paper 10 inches long, and paste it round the candle at the joining of the white and crêpe paper, arranging the frill so it will stand out stiffly. Fill the hollow candle with curled hair [absorbent cotton will do.—Ed.], pushing the latter down half an inch below the top of the candle. This forms a convenient cushion for the hairpins. (See *figure 57*.)

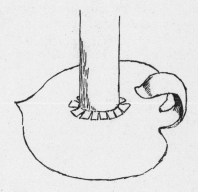

FIGURE NO. 56.

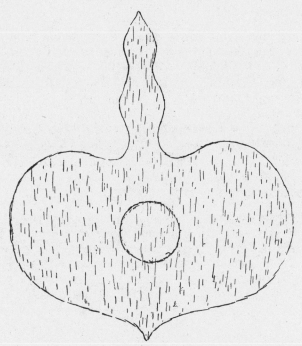

FIGURE NO. 54.

FIGURE NO. 57.

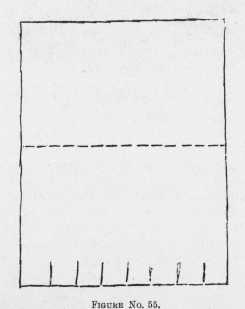

FIGURE NO. 55.

To complete the semblance, a candle shade should be attached. A holder may be purchased at any lamp shop, and upon it a shade may be made to match the candlestick. Cut a piece of crêpe paper 14 inches long and 3 inches wide, gather it to fit the ring at the top of the holder, and glue or sew it firmly to the ring. Carefully stretch the lower edge of the paper, giving the shade the admired "spring." Finish it with a fringe 1 inch deep,

95

cut across the crinkles (see *figure 58*), and pasted neatly inside the shade so that only the fringed portions show. Complete the top with a double ruffle formed by gathering a strip 14 inches long cut across the crinkles. The arrangement of the ruffle is shown on the shade seen at *figure 59*. (1895)

FIGURE NO 58.

FIGURE No. 59.

Easter Egg Nests

The giving of presents at Easter has become very general, and as some difficulty in selecting appropriate gifts is often experienced, here are a few suggestions to show the availability of crêpe and tissue papers for making dainty articles suited to the occasion. It is far more desirable to construct a present with one's own

hands than to simply purchase it, for in this way the donor is able to more fully express the kindly sentiments by which she is inspired.

There should be some especial reference to the season in an Easter gift, and this fact naturally limits the range of selection. The egg has from time immemorial been regarded as the symbol of the resurrection, having been used before the Christian religion was preached to typify the after existence so firmly believed in by most of the civilized world at that time. Eggs have in consequence been given a prominent place in the decoration of Easter cards and gifts, and each year they are more lavishly used by the younger generation. In the South, the annual "egg-rolling" is an event that is looked forward to with the keenest anticipation by the children from the beginning of Lent, and no child is too poor to have half a dozen dyed eggs.

The dyeing of Easter eggs is a very simple matter nowadays, but not many years ago the only process followed, in addition to the use of indigo blue, consisted in sewing a strip of chintz securely about each egg and boiling the latter for nearly an hour. The result of this primitive treatment was always uncertain, and the colors were seldom transferred in a wholly satisfactory manner; but occasionally an egg would be obtained with a prettily tinted spray or blossom perfectly reproduced upon it, and this would incite the patient decorator to renewed efforts.

When eggs are given as presents at Easter, it is highly important to have a suitable receptacle for them. A pretty nest that will hold four or five eggs can be easily made of white and grass-green crêpe paper. Cut the paper into strips four inches wide, with the crinkles running lengthwise; and either twist them tightly or

FIGURE No. 60.

plait them in braids of three. Then carefully arrange the cord or braid to shape a nest 7 inches in diameter and about 1 inch deep, as shown at *figure 60*, securing each round with paste. Tiny yellow or pink flowers may be made and fastened about the upper edge, and strips of green paper cut the shape and size of blades of grass may be arranged naturally between the blossoms. To make the flowers, cut from ordinary French tissue paper pieces the shape of *figure 61* and measuring ¾-inch each way, and twist each piece exactly at the center to produce the effect shown at *figure 62*. (1895)

careful to have the crinkles in the paper run as illustrated. Slightly stretch or shape each petal so it will present a rounded appearance, as shown at *figure 66;* and also stretch the upper edge, as at *figure 67*, until the effect pictured at *figure 68* is obtained. These petals should be 1½-inches long and 1 inch wide at the broadest part, and enough of them should be made to cover the shell as directed in the instructions given below.

FIGURE NO. 61.

FIGURE NO. 62.

FIGURE NO. 66.

FIGURE NO. 67.

An Easter Egg "Rose"

A very pretty and delicate Easter offering can be made by using an eggshell that has been emptied from one end. Having prepared the shell, paint small pink flowers around the edge with oil colors; and when the paint is thoroughly dry, further decorate the shell with crêpe paper in the shade known as light-coral, proceeding as follows: First prepare a small quantity of paste, and then cut a number of petals the shape of *figure 65*, being

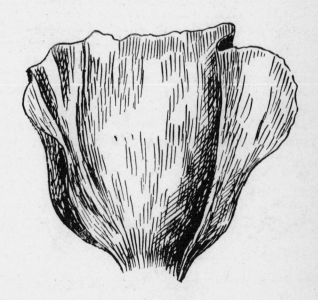

FIGURE NO. 68.

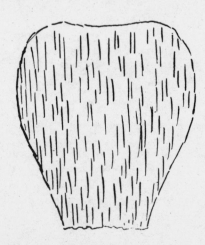

FIGURE NO. 65.

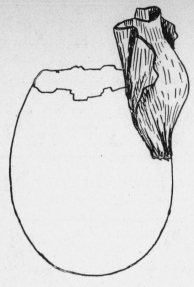

FIGURE No. 69.

FIGURE No. 71.

Begin at the top and paste a row of petals about the shell so that their upper edges will extend ½-inch above the top of the shell, as seen at *figure 69*. Five or six petals will be needed for this row, as their side edges must overlap quite ½-inch to produce the full effect of a rose. After the petals are pasted on, shape them again, for they will very likely have partially lost their "spring" during the handling which was required to fasten them to the shell. Now attach a second row of petals so that their tips will come ½-inch below those of the first row, and arrange a third and a fourth row in the same manner. This done, cut larger petals the shape of *figure 65*, making them 4 inches long by 3 broad before the paper is stretched. Arrange a small plait in each petal after it has been shaped (see *figure 70*), and paste a row of these petals to the bottom of the egg to represent the outer petals of the rose. Cut two circular pieces of cardboard 1½ inches in diameter, and neatly cover one side of each with green crêpe paper. Paste them together with the rough sides inward, paste the covered eggshell firmly to this foundation, and the little receptacle will appear as pictured at *figure 71*. (1895)

Flowerpot Decorations

Flowers always make appropriate Easter gifts, but the cost of a box of handsome cut flowers places such a present beyond the reach of many donors. A pot of growing ferns, however, or a small palm or short thick-growing azalea may usually be purchased for a very reasonable sum and will be a lasting delight to the recipient. When a growing plant is chosen, the red earthenware pot may be easily and attractively covered with paper. Encircle the pot with a strip of cotton batting, as at *figure 72*; cover this with another strip 2

FIGURE No. 72.

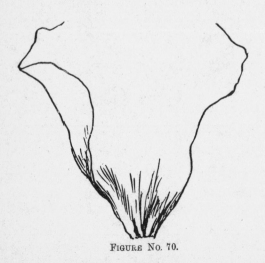

FIGURE No. 70.

inches wider and at least 2 inches longer, and continue to add strips, each 2 inches larger each way than the one beneath, until the pot is wholly covered with cotton. This gives the pot a bulging appearance, disguising its original shape (see *figure 73*).

Gift Box for Cut Flowers

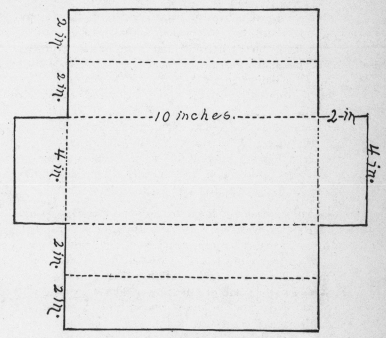

FIGURE NO. 73.

Cut a strip of crêpe paper with the crinkles running crosswise, making it long enough to go twice round the largest part of the pot, and as wide as the distance from the upper edge of the pot to the center of the bottom. Using No. 36 sewing cotton or fine twine, gather the upper edge of thé paper to fit the top of the pot, and secure it with a band of satin or pretty brocaded ribbon. If the ribbon is considered too expensive, sew a strip of white cambric tightly round the top of the pot, over this sew a strip of paper just long enough to meet, and conceal the joining with a stylish bow of paper. The strip and bow should not be less than 3 inches in width. The other edge of the cover should be gathered, drawn in tightly and sewed securely, care being taken to leave considerable space about the hole in the bottom of the

FIGURE NO. 76.

FIGURE NO. 74.

FIGURE NO. 77.

FIGURE NO. 75.

pot. The upper edge of the pot may be covered with the strip, as depicted at *figure 74;* or the effect illustrated at *figure 75* may be obtained by ruffling a shorter piece of paper cut lengthwise of the roll, sewing the ruffle upon the cover, and concealing the joining with a tightly twisted cord. The latter finish is prettier than the former, but not so durable. (1895)

A box for cut flowers may be made of cardboard shaped according to *figure 76,* the dimensions being proportionately increased to produce the desired size. Cut the cardboard half through along the dotted lines, and bend it at those lines to form the box. Cover it with crêpe paper before fastening it into shape, and then carefully sew the upper corners together, and conceal the necessary stitches with tiny bows of the paper. Line the box with white or green paper, and when it is ready for use, put in a piece of waxed paper, and fill with small flowers. Make a stiff bow of crêpe paper with very long ends, as shown at *figure 77;* fasten it to one lap of the top, and let it extend over upon the other. The top opens at the center, and all decorations must be arranged with this fact in mind. (1895)

A Lampshade of Crêpe Paper

A shade may be made for a standing lamp in the following manner: First construct a full skirt of crêpe paper, using the entire length of the roll and all but 4 inches of the width. Having cut off the 4-inch strip, gather the balance of the paper on fine binding wire; and after the skirt is adjusted to the lamp, carefully stretch the lower edge of the paper to simulate a ruffle. This completes the first skirt or layer of the shade. Select the next darker shade of paper, cut a second skirt 2 inches shorter than the first, and gather and arrange it on the lamp in the same way. The strips cut from the skirts must be reserved for making a full ruff at the top of the shade. Make two more skirts, each two inches shorter than the preceding one, and attach them as above described. Then with a needle and No. 36 cotton sew the four skirts firmly together at the top.

Gather separately the four strips for the ruff, having first cut the three wider ones to be the same width as the first—4 inches; and join them to the top of the shade, sewing them to the frame only where it is necessary, as the effect will be much better if the ruffles are allowed to stand like the petals of a full flower. The lower edges of all the skirts and the upper edges of the ruff must be ruffled like the edge of the first skirt. The manner of

FIGURE No. 79.

Lampshade "Addenda"

The most fashionable tints for lampshades are grass green, moss green and apple green; but if the bluish tinge of Nile green is preferred, use apple green, Nile green and sea green. The first-mentioned combination will usually be found to harmonize more satisfactorily with the china and wall decorations, and will have a more charitable effect upon the complexion.

Despotic Fashion just now insists that green shall be universally used for ornamental purposes, and the giver of a luncheon who desires to follow the latest mode must study how she can introduce that beautiful but rather difficult color to the best advantage. The shades must be green, but made in such a manner that the light will be reflected rather than softened. (1895)

FIGURE No. 78.

Gentleman's Toilet Tray

To a man few minor mishaps are more annoying than the loss or temporary disappearance of his collar buttons, and he is always glad to have a safe and convenient receptacle for them when not in use. A small ornamental tray may be easily made for this purpose and may be placed upon the right side of the bureau or dressing table far enough back to prevent its being brushed aside by the collar and scarf, which are generally hastily thrown down.

ruffling it is clearly displayed at *figure 78*, which shows a strip of paper with its edge stretched or ruffled. *Figure 79* depicts the completed shade. In forming the ruffles, stretch the paper from 1½ inches to 2 inches above the lower edge, according to the size of the shade. (1895)

FIGURE No. 93.

For such a tray use as a foundation the top of a jewelry box about 2 inches wide and 3½ inches long; and cover it with a piece of crêpe paper, turning all the edges inside as neatly as possible. (See *figure 93.*) If this is not deemed sufficiently elaborate, use twisted paper, applying it as shown at *figure 94*, and finishing the upper edge with a plait formed of three twisted strands. The cords of paper must be arranged so closely that it will be impossible for any very small article placed in the tray to slip between them.

For the supports of the tray take four empty spools on which No. 90 or 100 sewing cotton has been wound. Cover these with crêpe paper gathered and arranged in the manner shown at *figure 95*, and tie each at the center with a piece of satin ribbon. If the room is decorated in pale blue, which is just now a very fashionable color for the purpose, choose bright magenta ribbon. Glue each support to place, being very careful that all ends of paper are turned in and held out of sight by the glue. (1895)

taking care to preserve the proper proportion between the various parts of the figure. Being assured that the pattern is accurate, cut four pieces of cotton wadding like it, two for the top of the case and two for the bottom; and sprinkle heliotrope sachet powder between the layers. If the powder were placed on top of the wadding, it would discolor the paper.

Cover the inside of the case with white crêpe paper and the outside with pale blue; about the outer edge carefully sew white silk lace in a delicate pattern; and conceal the inner edge of the lace with a row of small flowers made according to the directions given at *figures 61* and *62* (See instructions for Easter egg nests.) Procure a half pan of magenta-purple watercolor, which is an entirely new tint showing an aniline brilliancy. Tinge the edges of the tiny petals with a medium shade of this paint, and then secure each flower in its proper place with a very little glue. Form two many-looped bows of bright green and pale blue ribbons, making one a little larger than the other; and dispose them gracefully on top of the case, as pictured at *figure 103*. (1895)

FIGURE No. 94.

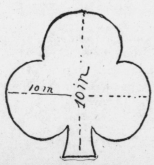

FIGURE No. 95.

A Handkerchief Case

A handkerchief case may be made in the shape of a heart, or it may be in the form of a "club" on a playing card. For the latter shape cut a paper pattern according to the outline and measurements given at *figure 102*,

FIGURE No. 103.

Cottage Decorations

Few materials are better adapted for cottage decoration than crêpe paper. For a bed chamber done in pink, pretty and serviceable sash curtains may be made of white and pink crêpe paper as illustrated at *figures 194* and *195*. The window glass will protect the paper from

FIGURE No. 102.

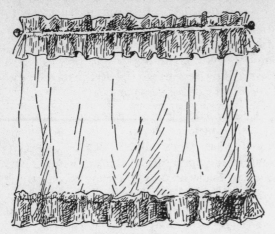

FIGURE No. 194.

FIGURE No. 196.

FIGURE No. 195.

the outer dampness, and the decoration, which may be executed in green and pink watercolors, will show to excellent advantage against the light. Care must be taken not to lay one color over another in using the paints, and the decoration must be painted on broadly with a large brush. Each curtain must be gathered at the top upon a string, tape or, better still, a small brass or wooden rod. If preferred, the curtain may be made of thin muslin, with paper for the ruffles at the top and bottom.

Long curtains are not desirable in summer, because the windows are left open and the wind and moisture allowed to enter without hindrance. The top of the window frame, however, admits of many pleasing effects in decoration, and crêpe paper will be found excellent for the purpose, as it sheds dust much more readily than woven materials. At *figures 196, 197* and *198* are pictured three artistic styles of window draping, all of which may be easily arranged with the help of a few tacks. At *figure 198*, tarlatan is represented in conjunction with crêpe paper.

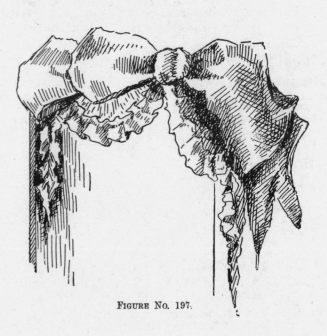

FIGURE No. 197.

Mantel decoration is quite simple just at present, and some dainty designs are shown at *figures 199, 200, 201* and *202*. It will be seen that sprays of flowers attached to the mantelpiece or placed in vases materially improve the plainer styles of covering.

102

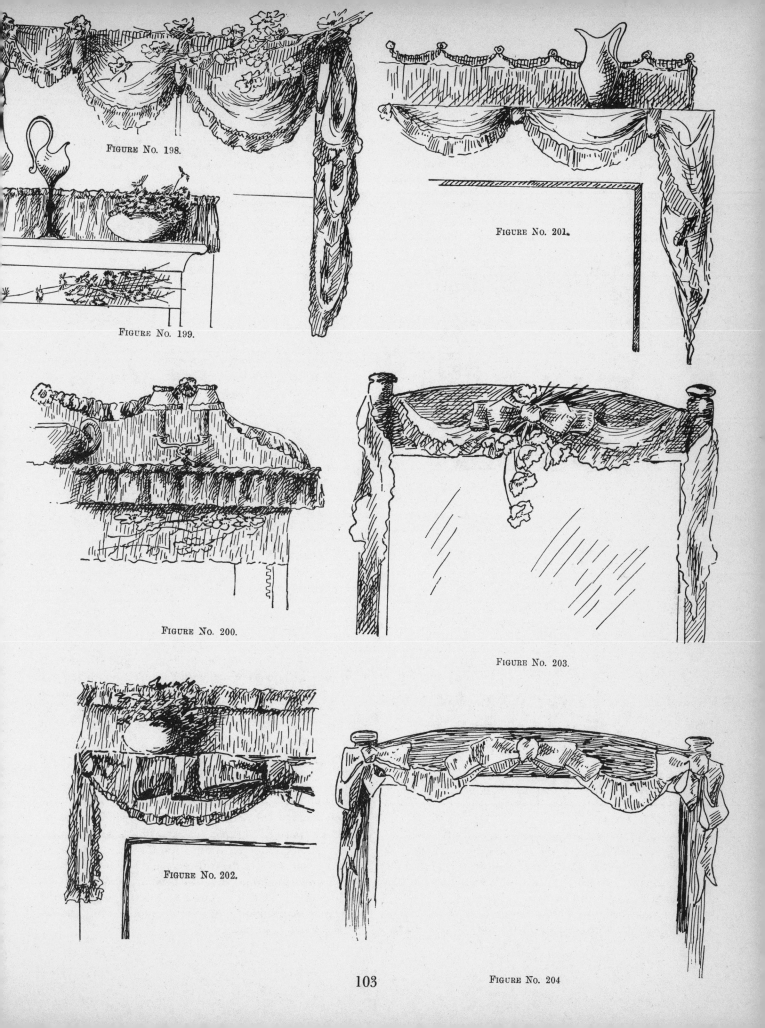

FIGURE No. 198.

FIGURE No. 199.

FIGURE No. 201.

FIGURE No. 200.

FIGURE No. 203.

FIGURE No. 202.

FIGURE No. 204

Ornaments for the bureau have already been described, and only the drapery now remains to be considered. For the decoration pictured at *figure 203* use white tarlatan, edged with crêpe paper cut across the crinkles and pulled or stretched at the edge to form a fluted ruffle. Drape the tarlatan as represented, and arrange long stemmed blossoms in the bow at the center, allowing some of them to fall over the mirror. *Figure 204* illustrates strips of crêpe paper disposed in bows and festoons.

FIGURE No. 207.

FIGURE No. 205.

FIGURE No. 208.

FIGURE No. 206.

Exquisite dressing for the bed may be easily arranged with crêpe paper. The pillow sham shown at *figure 205* has a center of white paper, bordered with a colored ruffle, the joining of which is concealed by a row of narrow lace edging; and that seen at *figure 206* has also a white center which is edged with lace and relieved by a

spray of tinted flowers made of crêpe paper. *Figure 207* depicts a sham decorated with a contrasting ruffle and a monogram. The monogram may be cut from white or colored plain paper and either sewed or pasted to the smooth circle of crêpe paper. The charming decoration displayed at *figure 208* is contributed by tiny clusters of baby ribbon and half wreaths of flowers painted with watercolors. The ribbons may be of any harmonizing tint, and the flowers may show many different colors or several shades of one color. Thus, for a blue room the bowknots could be made of pale-blue ribbon and the flowers painted in three shades of blue ranging from a soft grayish tone to indigo for the darkest touches. Whenever possible the ruffles should be cut with frayed edges. Cards should never be used upon any part of a sheet or pillow sham, as they are too stiff to yield to the weight of the paper and would produce a decidedly ungraceful appearance.

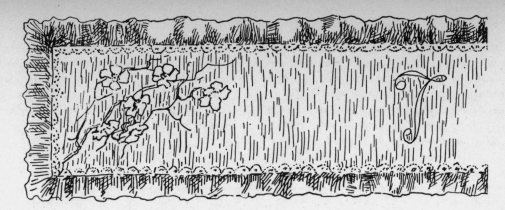

Part of a very pretty sheet sham may be seen at *figure 209*. This ornament should, of course, correspond with the pillow shams with which it is used. It may extend to the edges of the bed or may reach the floor at each side, but in the latter case, owing to its lightness, it will require a lining of heavy, white muslin to make it hang gracefully and keep it in place. A paper pillow sham looks best when basted to a square of thick muslin and pinned to the pillow at each corner. When thus arranged, the dainty creation will last a long time.

A spread may be made by joining three, or, if necessary, four strips of crêpe paper the length of the bed and the full width of the roll. Each joining may be covered with ribbon, or a simple seam may be run on the sewing machine by placing the right side of the ribbon to the right side of the paper and taking a ½-inch seam. If preferred, insertion may be used instead of ribbon. One edge may be laid upon the paper and stitched by machine, but the other edge will have to be fastened by hand, as the crêpe paper will be too bulky to pass under the arm of the machine. If a second person aids the operator by moving the mass of material as it is sewed by the machine, the crinkles will remain intact and an even effect will be secured. Such a spread will, with ordinary care, last an entire season. At night it should be folded smoothly at the seams, that the paper may retain its original surface.

FIGURE NO. 210.

The dressing table may have two or three covers harmonizing with the chosen decoration of the bed, and the glass above it may be draped as at *figure 210*, white cotton tulle or tarlatan being associated with the paper to produce a cool and airy effect. The tulle or tarlatan will last quite as long as the paper, and it should be of the sheerest and thinnest quality obtainable.

which is merely nominal in price. The edges should be trimmed with a frill of paper stretched at the outer edge to look like *figure 211*, and securely sewed by machine to the selvedge of the tarlatan, a heading being arranged to conceal the row of stitching. *Figure 212* shows the completed canopy.

FIGURE No. 211.

FIGURE No. 212.

A sofa cushion can be made very ornamental by the use of crêpe paper. A square of embroidered linen or duck may be used for the practical center, and the corners may be arranged as at *figure 213*. The center can be removed and laundered, and as this receives the most of the wear, the paper will last a long time, unless the cushion is intended for very hard usage, in which event it should have a severely plain cover of crêpe paper finished with a cord made by twisting together three or four smaller cords of the paper.

When long curtains are desired to hang from the canopy over a bed, crêpe paper pulled or stretched out of the "crimp" will be found very artistic, and much more healthful than heavy brocades or other heavy materials of similar texture, which are likely to retain poisonous gases and the germs of disease in spite of the most thorough airing. A very pretty and inexpensive decoration for a canopy may be arranged with white tarlatan,

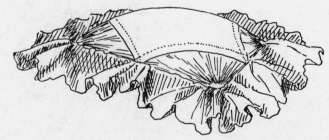

FIGURE No. 213.

Strips of crêpe paper folded several times and passed through the open designs of wicker or bamboo furniture give a pleasing touch of color that must be seen to be appreciated.

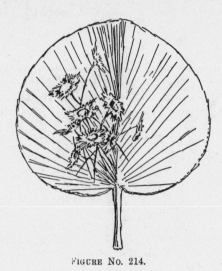

FIGURE NO. 214.

A palm-leaf fan decorated on one side with a large flat bow of paper is much more alluring than a plain one, and if the other side is adorned with big "splatched" flowers done with oil paints, the fan will assume a character and standing that is all the more attractive because of its association with the artist. The spray of paper flowers used on one of the pillow shams described above, or any other pretty cluster of paper blossoms may be applied to a large palm-leaf fan as shown at *figure 214*. Every flower or petal should be securely attached to the fan so that the light paper will not be too much disturbed by its passage through the air.

Figure 215 shows several styles of covers that are for light use. Such a group of cushions will make a most delightful corner in the cool, shady drawing room of a summer cottage. (1895)

FIGURE NO. 215.

V. Shellwork, Beading & Other Household Elegancies

Collecting and Preparing Shells

The many elegant articles adorned with shells which are brought to this country from the Mediterranean have induced persons of taste to endeavor to copy some of these beautiful but costly elegancies.

Those who can enjoy the pleasure of a trip to the seaside will have but little trouble in collecting many beautiful specimens of shells. The ways and means of collecting them are numerous: Some are secured by dredging the deep waters; others are tossed or washed on the beach by the waves. When the tide is low, the collector should be arrayed in stout rubber boots and waterproof leggings. With a long-hooked staff or rake with close teeth, a light hatchet, and a strong sharp knife, he should wade out amongst the rocks and pools and search the crevices and ledges of overhanging rocks. Every loose stone must be turned over; every collection of leaves and seaweed dragged up and examined for the treasures hidden beneath and through them. Chitons and limpets, which are to be found on rocky coasts, may be detached by the use of the knife, and in case of the former, if living, placed between two boards and left there to die. There are some—the ormers, for instance—which may be detached from the rock to which they cling by the use of warm water and a sudden push with the side of the foot; if violence is used, the delicate shell would be broken. As all species of mollusca harbor in great quantities under the loose fragments of rock and in the basins and crannies, these places should be closely inspected, as frequently very elegant and uncommon specimens are found there.

When it is possible to examine coral reefs, quantities of the most beautiful shellfish will be found. By washing seaweed, various tiny shells of rare beauty may be secured, and these are invaluable for groundwork and minute flowers. By using fresh water, the marine treasures will fall to the bottom of the vessel. Bivalves may be taken on sandy shore by digging with the rake or a spade or fork. Among rocks others may be found which have buried themselves so deeply that recourse must be had to the hatchet and drill in order to excavate them. Cockles may be easily gathered with the rake or a common garden hoe. The marks in the sand will always point out the spot upon which to dig, and, by using the hoe expertly and industriously, a bushel or two of cockleshells may be gathered in a few hours.

After securing the shells and other marine treasures, the collection is washed in vessels of sea water and finally passed through sieves of various sizes, from ½-inch mesh to 1/32-inch or through ¼-inch and 1/32-inch

Basket of Shell-Flowers.

sizes. The residue of the fine sieve should be dried and closely examined for minute shells.

When the shells contain fish that are alive, they may be plunged into scalding water. Univalves are cleared by extracting the fish with a crochet needle or hooked wire. From bivalves the animal may be taken with a knife, tying together those desired closed, and allowing those wanted open to remain and dry, gaping, as they always do.

All shells should be soaked in fresh water for a few hours to prevent further chemical action of the salt water upon the carbonate of lime of which they are composed. If the shells retain an unpleasant odor for any length of time, they may be washed upon the inside with a weak solution of chloride of lime which will speedily deodorize them; but such a solution must be applied with great caution. Delicate shells required to be cleansed with a soft brush in order to avoid marring the beauty and delicacy of the markings and of the epidermis, which, in some species, is as delicate as a gossamer work. It is so exquisitely lovely that one might imagine it to be the fairy sheen from which the mermaids weave their misty robes.

Many shells naturally possess a fine polish and require no preparation, either for display or for ornamental purposes. In general, however, it happens that when shells become dry they lose their natural and fine luster. This may be easily restored by washing them with clear water in which a little glue has been dissolved. There are some, shells however, which appear exceedingly dull upon the outer surface on account of the epidermis with which they are covered. This may be removed by steeping the shell in warm water and then rubbing hard with a brush. When the epidermis is thick, it will be found necessary to mingle a little nitric acid with the water. This, however, must be used with great caution since it destroys the luster of every part it touches, and the water should be only impregnated sufficiently to remove the thick skin without acting upon the shell beneath. The new surface must now be polished with a chamois skin and finely pulverized chalk. When these are ineffectual, pumice stone must be applied to rub off the coarse external layers and disclose the hidden beauties beneath. (1876)

General Directions for Arranging Shell Ornaments

The ornamental arrangements of shells are of several classes, and success in any of the modes of applying them depends to a great degree upon the taste displayed in their selection and handling.

Whatever the purpose to which the shells are to be applied, it is always advisable to sort them into their several species, classes, and colors, placing each kind in a box or tray fastened upon a light board so as to avoid overturning and confusion. A few general rules will apply to work of all kinds in this department, viz., that contrasting colors must be arranged with an artistic eye. In using shells in mosaic patterns, light delicate tints display to greater advantage the gorgeous hues of crimson, brown, and purple. Long borders or flat surfaces must be adorned with oval, oblong, or triangular figures, with beaded edges of tiny bivalves. Large figures must stand out upon the surface in bold relief, and made prominent by a groundwork of silvery, glittering opaline shells.

Never crowd a mass of incongrous designs upon one article. And in arranging figures, place every shell first upon a design marked out upon cardboard, and from thence transfer it to the article to be ornamented. (1876)

A Clock Ornamented with Shells

A common clock, such as can be procured for a comparatively small sum, can be changed into an elegant and ornamental article suitable for a handsomely furnished room by being tastefully ornamented with shells. Supposing the case to be one of the wooden Gothic style, paint the entire case with glue. Then with the halves of pretty colored bivalves form a set of ornaments

for the upper part of the arch, a large one for the center and smaller ones extending down the sides. Cover the ornamental turrets with small shells artistically arranged or with a long spiral shell. Arrange flowers or mosaic figures upon the prominent parts, and fill in with small shells so that even the smallest possible space is covered, the delicate rice shells answering well for little crannies.

Upon the front, below the door, fasten a handsome bivalve in such a manner that it forms a receiver for the key. The edging should be of black snail shells, with an inner border of bivalves placed closely side by side. (1876)

Fig. 1. A Shell Bracket.

A Shell Bracket

A very pretty bracket is made of common scallop shells and arranged as seen in the illustration, *figure 1*. A piece of stout pasteboard forms the back, on which are glued three shells to cover the upper part of the bracket, and six to cover the lower part. The shelf is made of pasteboard, with its back edge bent down ½-inch to enable it to be securely sewed to the back piece before any shells are put on. This shelf is covered with three scallop shells and bordered with a row of spiral shells. The shells project just enough over the pasteboard to hide it; they are fastened on with glue, and spiral shells fill up the spaces between the larger ones. If a black bracket is desired, the whole may be given a coat of black varnish. It is in better taste, however, to use a transparent varnish that merely brightens the natural colors of the shells (1876)

Dressing Table Ornaments

The manufacture of shell toilet boxes for handkerchiefs, brush and comb, etc.; baskets for hairpins; stands for pincushions; powder and jewel boxes; and catchalls—all made to match or correspond—is exceedingly interesting. The boxes must be formed of heavy pasteboard; the little basket for hairpins may be made of any cunning little handled basket. All of them are to be lined with velvet or silk of bright color with soft interlining of absorbent cotton. Broken or marred china ornaments, bottles, etc., may be covered with shells to form beautiful toilet articles.

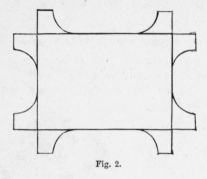

Fig. 2.

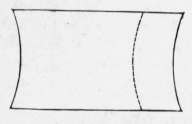

Fig. 3.

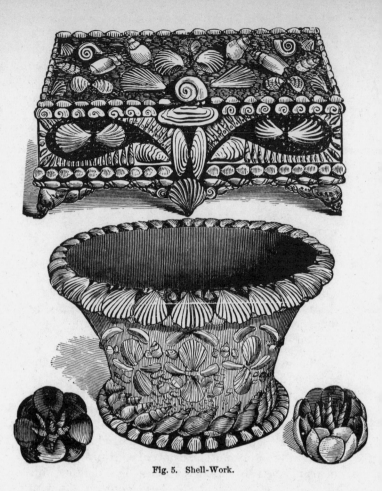

Fig. 5. Shell-Work.

The diagrams, *figures 2* and *3*, show the shapes of the pasteboard for the handkerchief box, and the same will answer, elongated, for the brush box or tray. A somewhat higher shape will do for the jewel box with a pincushion on the lid. The catch-all—for various articles removed at night, such as collar, cuffs, ribbons, etc.,—is made of similar shape, but with a back to hang against the wall, as in *figure 4*.

Fig. 4.

Having cut out the various parts, line them, and sew together with strong thread. Over the seams paste muslin, and bind the edges of each piece with the same. Fasten the lids on with strips of strong muslin, using for all the fastening strong glue. The cushion should then be made and fastened upon the top of the box with glue and strips of card or muslin across the ends and sides, which will be afterward covered with shells.

The work box in *figure 5* has for its basis a plain pine box, lined with velvet or silk and divided into compartments for the accommodation of sewing paraphernalia. For the lid, after covering the entire surface with glue, proceed to arrange the shells in various patterns. In the center fasten a large pointed univalve with rich-colored and pearl markings. This will be used as a knob whereby to raise it. The shells for such a box may be beautifully marked by pouring wine on certain parts. This will so change the commonest snails, limpets, periwinkles, and even the common mussel shells, that they will appear like rare and choice tropical shells. A handsome cowrie for the center of the front, with four flat shells of the kind with holes along one side, would look well, and smaller ones of the same kind can be used for the ends. (1876)

A Window Box Decorated with Shells

A beautiful window box is made by this mode of decoration, the basis of which is a plain wooden box upon which glue is applied and the shells arranged in a mosaic pattern with a large figure in the center. Small shells arranged in diminutive patterns are used at each side and at the corners. The groundwork is filled with rice shells. The whole may be varnished, as the water used upon the plants can then be readily wiped off and the dust brushed away from day to day.

Flowers in Shells.

Fig. 6. Shell-Work.

For large work like this, common shells will be found useful, and large flowers may be formed in the different natural colors of the shells—white, yellow, pink, and orange. The snail shells in black, brown, and stone colors form beautiful centers for figures, and by using black and dark-colored snail shells with oblong shells and bleached mussel shells, good designs may be formed. The bright little orange-colored snail shells are very effective as groundwork. Other arrangements with limpets for center and corner pieces, and flowers of the bright-colored shells with limpets for centers, are a pretty change. Edgings of limpets, set closely, with a groundwork of powdered shells, or small rice shells thickly studded over the surface with small, black snail shells, and tiny white cockles, or the little "fingernail" shells form another beautiful design. Old stands, baskets, small tables, flowerpot covers, and various other plain or disfigured pieces of furniture may be entirely covered and made quite ornamental by the tasteful use of even common shells. (1876)

Flowers in Shells

Shells, bearing plants, are certainly as graceful, if not more so than the hanging flowerpots of bronze, terra cotta, etc. Considering the high price of the latter, while so many shells lie buried under dust in closets and garrets as useless things, this little discovery will be welcome to many friends of flowers—especially their *human sisters.*

The cuts will give a sufficiently clear idea of the manner in which they are to be used. The places where they are to be suspended will depend upon individual convenience and taste. Regard should, of course, be had to proper position for light and heat. For attaching the cords it may be necessary to drill a few small holes in the shell, into which wires can be inserted, and the cords attached to them.

Some hints to those not much acquainted with floriculture may be useful. To these should also be added a list of botanical names, by which to obtain seeds of plants best adapted for planting in shells. The seeds may be found at most garden stores.

The impracticability of draining holes in shells seems the first obstacle; but three years' experience has proved it of no serious consequence. Into large shells (over 6 inches), put first a handful or more, according to the size of the shell, of coarse clean sand, or better still, coarse powdered charcoal, and upon this the light soil, to receive the seeds or plants. It is also well to mix a little powdered charcoal with this soil. In a large shell four or five plants of different kinds may be grown, and if there is among them a semi-aquatic plant, for example a *Mimulus*, the soil will more frequently be found too dry than too wet.

Small shells need hardly any sand or charcoal, as the moisture in the limited quantity of soil is quickly exhausted by the roots. Careful watering when dry is, of

course, a matter of importance with these as with every potted plant. Many persons think that there is not room or soil enough in a shell to support plants; this is a common error. In pots, plants succeed and bloom generally better in little soil than in too much, and consequently more are killed by too large vessels than by small ones. Three years ago an acquaintance planted a Lobelia in a shell, holding not quite two tablespoonfuls of soil, and it is still growing in it, flowering exuberantly every summer!

Here is a list of plants, successfully grown in shells; those marked with * are only for larger shells:

*Anagallis Monelli
*Campanula speculum
Cenia turbinata
Cochlearia or Jonopsidium acaulis
Grammanthus gentian
Gypsophylla muralis
Linaria cymbalaria
Lobelia ramosa
Mimulus moschatus
*Mimulus speciosus, and others
*Manulea violacea
Mesembrianthemum tricolor
Nemesia floribunda
Oxalis rosea
Portulacca grandiflora
Silene alpestris
Saxifraga sarmentosa
Sedum coeruleum

Tradescantia caudata
Tradescantia discolor
Isolepis tenella, Agrostis

Climbing plants for large shells:

Ipomea nil and quamoclit
Maurandias
Orobus coccinous
Thunbergias

For garnishing: mosses (Musci and Lichens), and Lycopodia. (1859)

Decorative Beadwork

Various elegant articles for the adornment of the house and person can be formed of beads of different colors and sizes upon frames of wire. These frames, in case of large articles, must be soldered together by a professional, but in forming small pieces, such as ornaments for the hair, earrings, brooches, etc., the amateur worker can fashion the wire into appropriate forms and bind them together with fine flexible wire.

Flowers, clusters of leaves, butterflies, and geometrical figures are most appropriate for this work, and may be fastened to a framework of brass or copper wire. With small pliers, a pair of cutting nippers, and a coil of the finest wire thread, the craftsman may fasten beautiful figures in beads of various kinds.

Beadwork and Bead Mosaic

Persons who are partial to working with beads will find this mode of applying them a most interesting and useful one, inasmuch as by it various articles of furniture and ornament that have become disfigured by age may be so embellished and renewed as to appear even more elegant than when fresh and new.

The patterns most easily delineated in this work are those of a geometrical character; therefore, any pattern employing straight lines (as in Berlin work) may, with ease in working and beads of proper color, be used for this. For old-fashioned conventional figures, monograms, and heraldic devices, beadwork is peculiarly well adapted. But where skill is required by practice, any pictorial design may be worked in this bead mosaic with fine effect. It is well worth all the time and patience a person is willing to devote to it. By applying this work to blocks of stone, brick, or porcelain, tiles of the richest character may be made.

The materials, etc., used for this work are beads of the colors required, a handle with a needle inserted in the end for taking up the beads, small plates or saucers for holding the beads, sewing-silk or thread, and glue. The smooth round beads, used for ornamenting parts of Berlin zephyr-work, are most appropriate for these mosaics, but the "bugles" and a few sparkling cut beads may be introduced with fine effect in parts of the works. Gilded beads should be of the finest quality. Steel beads, though affording a brilliant goundwork and rich, sparkling additions to various parts, must never be applied to work that is in danger of becoming wet or damp, on account of the liability to rust. Avoid using mottled or figured beads, and let the entire work be done with those of like size, except in those cases in which it is necessary to make a part specially prominent.

The groundwork, whether of wood or other material, should first be painted white and the pattern traced upon it. For a beginner, this may be a simple pattern in regular mosaic; for instance, a cross and monogram in the center are formed of gilded beads, surrounded by the shield-shaped groundwork in bright garnet beads. After tracing the design upon the white-painted surface, a portion of the glue is spread with a soft brush over the surface. The black lines of the design will still show through distinctly. Then with a small brush, touch a spot on the design, and while this is sticky, the beads are taken up upon the point of the "lifter" and placed upon the design in proper position. In case of a spot of some size on the groundwork where a number of beads of the same kind are required, the beads may be strung upon silk, and several laid on at the same time. In some cases where a large space is to be covered, quite a large string may be fastened on, or the strand may be turned backward and forward until the whole surface is covered. It is best to form the outline of a figure first, and, when practice gives a little skill, the pattern may be carried out by copying the little squares on the design, and stringing beads to the glued surface. Thus the beads are applied and more glue added from time to time until the entire figure is filled in.

For mosaic figures and lozenge-shaped designs, an outline of black beads produces a fine effect, appearing to throw the figure out from the surface. The background, or groundwork, is then filled in by laying first a single row, following the outline of that part of the design with which it comes in contact, and then filling up the remainder with either curved or straight lines, according to the character of the article. The glue must be brushed on gradually and with even touches so that it may not be thin in some places and raised in uneven irregular patches. While the work is still damp, it must be gently but firmly pressed with a hard roller or pad, and a heavy book or other weight laid upon any finished parts will improve the appearance of the work.

When entirely finished, a soft paper must be placed over the whole piece and a hot iron held upon it, firmly but not sufficiently hard to crush the beads. After this is done, and the glue dry, the interstices must be gone over with a brush dipped in linseed oil until the divisions are entirely filled with it. Then dust over it some finely-pulverized whiting, taking a stiff brush, such as is used for oil painting, called "bristle-brushes," and work this pretty well into the interstices. This will not only remove any of the glue that may remain to impair the beauty of the beads, but will form a solid groundwork around the beads which will, when dry, become a compact mass so firm and hard that any reasonable amount of rough usage will fail to break or crack it. The face of the beadwork must be wiped off with a clean soft cloth and gently polished with a chamois skin or old piece of silk. In fastening in the panels of this mosaic, a molding or band of wood, either gilded or carved, should secure them around the edges, and where this is of dark color, the surface next to it should be covered with gold beads, and vice versa.

Beadwork can be used as elegant enrichments for the top of fancy tables, brackets, étagères, etc.; also, for covers of books and other light articles, panels of screens, doors and cabinets, upon frames for pictures or mirrors, and as wall decorations around a mantel. (1876)

Mosaic Screen and Panel

Two designs for these mosaics are given. The pole screen, *figure 1*, is embellished with a design representing one of Aesop's fables, "The Fox and the Crow," with letters and borders of flowers which are to be delineated in their own appropriate colors. As will be seen, the back of the fox is dark and shaded, three of the darkest shades of brown being required for it. A light yellowish shade is used upon the side and down one leg, as well as on the hind leg and tail. The trunk of the tree is also in browns of different shades. The foliage should be in apple-greens; the apples, yellow and scarlet; grass, yellow, greens, and browns; fence, stone-colors; background, bluish-gray; crow, black, shaded with dark grays; and the letters in gold. The framework is made up of crimson and yellow flowers in the corners, with yellow centers. The lower ones upon the lambrequins are purple. The rose is shaded pink. The outside border is to be black and gold.

Figure 2 is a panel containing a rich border and heraldic device suitable for various purposes. (1876)

A Beadwork Butterfly

One of the simplest ornaments is the butterfly. The skeleton for these butterflies is given in *figure 6* and is formed of a single piece of wire bent according to the diagram. These decorative objects are effective as dress ornaments. The finest seed beads are used for the butterfly's antennae and as an edging. The colors may be adapted to the dress. One can make an elegant and complete set of butterflies composed of cut jet beads, with gold beads and spangles introduced on the figures. Earrings, composed of small butterflies upon a spray of leaves, are particularly beautiful. (1876)

Fig. 6.

Fig. 7. Butterfly.

A Beadwork Flower Basket

Figures 11 and 13 are designs for a beadwork basket used for holding flowers. The handle of this is very pretty. A wire ring, *figure 11*, easily and quickly made, forms the frame for the bottom of the basket. To this other small rings, put on at regular distances, serve as feet. On the crossed rods in the middle rests one ring; seven more such rings of the same size joined together and united at the bottom make the shallow sides of the basket, after they are turned up. Each ring is filled up in the middle

Fig. 1. Bead-Mosaic. The Fox and the Crow.

Fig. 2. Bead-Mosaic Panel.

A Beadwork Frame for Photographs

The materials used are white glass and chalk-white beads and fine wire. *Figure 18* represents a pretty frame

![Fig. 11. Bead Flower-Basket.]

Fig. 11.   Bead Flower-Basket.

with a rosette crocheted in gold thread, and another one made in well-known double *en relief* circles, which show a calyx—similar to a dew drop—of a Roman pearl.

To wind over the outer edge of the basket, the feet, or the handle, single gold beads are intermixed with the white crystal ones. The two wire rods of the curved handle are wound over together at the ends, while towards the middle, three small rings separate them from each other. (1876)

Fig. 18.   Bead-Frame for Photographs.

Fig. 13.   Design for Bead Flower-Basket.

made of loops of beads lying over each other like scales. It may be made of any color beads, either square or oval in shape according to taste. The figure indicates the easy manner in which the frame is made.

Eighteen to twenty-two beads are strung on fine wire, bent into a longish loop. The wire is then tightly twisted beneath it. These loops are fastened to an oval of white cardboard cut as large as it is desired the frame should be. The wire stems are covered always by the succeeding loop, the beads on the latter being alternately four glass and four chalk-white. The rosette at the bottom is formed of several loops arranged in a circle, the stems in the center covered by rows of beads laid crosswise.

The frame may be finished by pasting a pressed paper mat corresponding to the size of the photograph in the center of the cardboard, and pushing the photograph in through an opening left at the top and bottom of the border. The border surrounds the picture. (1876)

A Flower Stand of Beadwork

This flower stand, *figure 82*, is constructed of bronzed cane and is furnished with an inside dish in which to arrange the flowers—although any similar piece of furniture will do. The height of the stand is 6 inches; its diameter, 10 inches. The margin is surrounded by a border of bead mosaic; the place where this is set is

Fig. 82. Flower-Stand.

covered by a cord twisted with gold beads. The border is worked crosswise. For the foundation milk-white beads are used; blue and gold beads form the forget-me-nots; for the upper scallops, black beads are taken; and for the edging, gold beads, of which also the small tassels and the fringe are made.

To construct the mosaic border, string two black, one gold, and two milk-white beads for the first row; then turn, string one milk-white bead, run your needle through the second following one, string another white bead, run your needle through the gold bead, and so on. For the long, hanging ornaments, take twelve white beads on thread for the foundation, and add the fringes of gold beads. (1876)

Beadwork Star

In forming stars for a tiara, the beads are all placed in this manner, as shown in *figure 10*. The framework of the design forms two stars, the inner one held at the points to the outer. The circle in the center is of small beads around a large central one. Seven of these stars upon a band form an elegant tiara for the head. These are also fine for elegancies. (1876)

Fig. 10. Star.

Embroidery of Feathers and Beads for a Sofa Cushion

The materials used are red cloth, small black and white feathers, and black and white beads of various sizes and shapes. This new way of putting feathers to use is strongly to be recommended on account of its splendid appearance and simple and quick execution. Those who take pleasure in exercising their skill and ingenuity in inventing patterns for themselves will find a wide field for their efforts.

The engraving (*figure 23*), which is full size, clearly indicates the manner in which it is executed. The feathers must be chosen as even as possible, sewed down at the stems, and finished off at the center with beads. The twigs, tendrils and stems are constructed of black and white beads of various sizes as shown in the illustration. (1876)

Hair Work

Brooches, Lockets, etc.

As the hair is the only part of our beloved friends which can be kept *in memoriam*, it is natural that we should desire to preserve the treasure in some way that will testify to our appreciation of its value. And when this can be done in a manner that is both pleasing to the taste and that will insure its prolonged or lasting preservation, it becomes a work which all may desire to be able to successfully practice.

The most simple mode of preserving hair is within the case of gold and glass, of which we have so many beautiful and elegant articles in jewelry. The locket or

other article being obtained, the hair to be manufactured must be cleansed by washing with tepid water in which soda and borax have been dissolved, and then rinsing in clear water.

The tools necessary are small, sharp scissors; a sharp-pointed knife; a pointed instrument like a darning needle fastened in a handle; small pliers; spatula; a half-dozen camel's-hair brushes; a small curling-iron; and a piece of glass upon which to work the hair.

The materials required are fine annealed wire of two or three sizes; gold and steel beads; pearl beads of best quality; gold wire thread; glue; India ink; a collar stay; knitting needles of several sizes; and gold-beater's skin [gold leaf—Ed.].

The Single Plait.

The most simple form of hair work is the old single plait of three or four strands which we see in the lockets and brooches handed down to us by our grandmothers. Still this form of preserving hair presents so many valuable recommendations, that we recommend it as the first achievement of beginners.

The manner of making it is this: Soften a piece of gold-beater's skin by moistening it with tepid water, and with glue on the edges, secure it to the glass palette. When it is dry, proceed to arrange the hair upon it. Make the hair into three or more strands, as desired. Take one of them in the left hand, and with the right smooth out all the hairs, passing the strand between the fingers until flat and glossy. Then with a camel's-hair brush make a line longitudinally, with glue, along one edge of the gold-beater's skin. Lay the strand upon it, and, with the point of the knife and the needle, arrange the hair into a long, smooth band. This strip prepared, proceed to the others, and so arrange one after another until all of them are prepared. The hairs must lie side by side, smoothly, and no one must overlap the other. Cut off the ends smoothly and evenly, and when dry, slip the edge of the thin spatula beneath the gold-beater's skin and remove it from the glass, placing it between the leaves of a book or folds of paper. Lay this beneath a weight until perfectly dry.

When several of these plaits are made and dry, place them upon a firm cushion or on a board, and secure each one by wrapping the ends with fine wire, and fastening close together with a pin in each one. Then weave them together as in any ordinary braid. When finished, secure each end as before directed, and running a thread of wire through each end, twist together firmly. As this plait should cover the entire surface beneath the glass of the locket, the ends are merely cut off smoothly after the plait is fastened to the card or other foundation with clear glue, card or paper answering in this instance as well as glass. When dry and pressed, the plait can be cut to suit any article, whether large or small. Fine braids may be used in answering rings or in tiny lockets, etc., or may be used as charms, and there is really no more simple and appropriate mode for preserving a memento of a friend.

Tasteful Designs.

Various devices such as crosses, hearts, birds and monograms, may be formed in a manner somewhat similar. In these the bands are first fastened upon the gold-beater's skin, dried, and pressed, and then placed upon the tablet upon which the design has been sketched.

In some devices the hair of several persons, and of different colors, may be beautifully arranged, so that the contrasting colors will produce an artistic effect. In the design, *figure 1,* the cross may be of black hair, the anchor of a brown, and the heart of light flaxen or gray; or these colors may be reversed, or others substituted. Various other devices may be formed of hair fastened upon gold-beater's skin. In *figure 2,* the shield is

Fig. 1. Hair Cross.

Fig. 2. Design for Shield.

composed of gray hair, with a narrow band of dark hair, and the monogram in the center of two shades of hair, while the scallops around the edge are also of dark hair, with pearls set in each of the connecting points. Where bands of pearls are required, a piece of thin card, such as visiting-cards are made of, should be cut to fit the space, and the pearls set on it. Where really fine pearl or wax beads can be procured, they answer extremely well for ordinary work. They are fastened by forcing pins into the holes through the center and fastening with glue.

Where leaves or flowers are desired, they are made by a different process. Instead of being affixed to gold-beater's skin, the hair is simply wet with glue and, while moist, twined around thin wire for the stem. Then thin strands of the hair are drawn into the form of leaves and secured with gold thread. The introduction of gold or pearls produces fine effects when judiciously arranged. The devices may be altered or others designed to suit the requirements of the case according to the materials to be used: flowers, feathers, etc. (1876)

Hair Flowers

Flowers for brooches or other personal ornaments are made by laying wide flat bands of suitable size upon pieces of cardboard covered with gold-beater's skin. Where the shape of the flower is cupped, the card is dampened and pressed into molds such as are used for wax flowers, and the hair fastened to these. For instance, suppose the flower to be a cluster of convolvuli, *figure 6,* which we have seen exquisitely formed in hair. For these flowers the hair must be of two shades, strongly contrasted. The dark hair is laid in a broad flat band upon the gold-beater's skin, after being stiffened with glue. When dry, a circular piece, with a section cut from it as in *figure 4,* is fastened upon a similar piece of cardboard which has been shaped in a convolvulus mold. At the lower part, to imitate the light part in the center of the cup, the very light hair is put as in *figure 5,* and fastened within upon the dark hair. The outside is then covered with dark hair only, fastened on carefully with glue and held in place until dry, by thread, which is afterward removed. The edge of each flower is finished with a fine plait made with a few long even hairs, or, if preferred, with seed pearl beads set close together with glue.

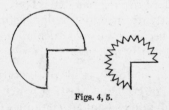

Figs. 4, 5.

Fig. 6. Cluster of Convolvulus.

The wire is then fastened to a wire stem covered with brown tissue paper. Through the opening within the wire, stamens and pistil are passed and secured to the stem, and a calyx of fine paper muslin or stiff silk of proper shade is fastened around with glue so that all is finished off neatly and the fastening of the parts to the stem hidden.

Flowers of various sizes may be made in this way, some clustered together, others of larger size used singly. In forming small flowers, the strand of hair must of course be less. The convolvulus is made in a similar manner, the wire being small in comparison to the ring, and the hair shaped into the bell form with the fingers while moist. When dry it will retain the proper form.

Besides the encasing of hair in jewelry, the formation of wreaths, bouquets, etc., for framing as house ornaments has become exceedingly popular in the past few years. This mode of preserving the hair possesses many advantages, inasmuch as thereby a large collection may be made, and the hair of families thus preserved in a form not only pleasing and appropriate, but so lasting, as well, that it may be handed down from generation to generation as one of those "heirlooms" always valued and sacred as a *memento mori* of those gone before.

The instruments, etc., required for this branch of hair work are similar to those used in the former. The hair must be assorted and tied in bunches, with different colors and lengths in separate coils or strands. Hair should be tied in such a manner as to prevent any tangling or knotting. Have some fine clear glue, fine annealed wire, round gold and pearl beads, a few gold spangles, some stamens in black and brown shades, and a few wire rings of different sizes (such as are used for curtains).

To form *a simple whorl-shaped flower,* take one of the rings of desired size, and a piece of fine wire an inch or 2 long. Then take a strand of hair about ¼-inch wide, brush out flat and smooth, and moisten upon the underside with a little glue. Fasten the end neatly to the wire with a strand of silk thread, and holding the ring between the fingers, pass the band of hair over the ring and then down to the wire. Push it up closely to the tied end and fasten with the silk and then turn it up again over the ring next to the former part covered and down to the wire as before. Continue this until the entire ring is covered, when the flower will appear as in *figure 9.*

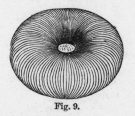

Fig. 9.

Fig. 19. Roses.

To form a *rose, figure 19,* take a piece of covered wire of the proper color, and rather fine, and upon it form a number of loops of different sizes carefully graduated. The loops are made thus: For the central ones, use a fine knitting needle. With the wire held between the thumb and finger of the left hand, and the knitting needle above it between the middle finger and back of the forefinger, take a strand of hair. Fasten it by the end to the wire and, passing it over the needle, fasten it to the wire by making a twist around it. Then pass it again over the needle in the same manner and fasten just below the last, continuing this until eight or ten loops have been made. Then slip the needle out and with the next largest needle make another series of loops, then the next, until a sufficient number have been formed for a rose of the desired size. The loops should be of uniform size of each series and regularly increased, looking as if woven upon a strand of wire from 2 to any number of inches in length.

Then take a piece of stem wire, covered with black or brown paper or cotton, and turning over one end proceed to arrange the loops, commencing with the small ones, which are coiled round upon the wire in close circles. Continue this until the large outer loops are carefully arranged upon the rounded edge of the rose. Form a calyx with five long loops of hair fastened around the stem with wire, and finished with an ovary of wax made of the proper shade with fine umber or sienna, or for light yellow hair or flaxen shades a little chrome may be added or other tints to correspond with the color of the hair.

Fig. 23. Form of Leaf.

Leaves are formed in several ways. For one kind, double a piece of wire and twist an inch or two, as a sort of handle; then holding this between the thumb and finger of the left hand, fasten to it a thin strand of hair, making it smooth and flat by passing it between the fingers. Bend the ends of the wire to the right and left, and, holding the end of a knitting needle horizontally over the twist of the wire, pass the strand of hair around the needle and fasten it by crossing the wires below to the right and left. This will form a loop. Make several of these, and then slip them from the needle and arrange them into the form of a leaf. A cluster of leaves is formed by making three or four such leaves and fastening them together. A compound leaf, *figure 23*, is made by using a very small-sized needle, making only one loop at a time upon a fine wire and arranging them naturally upon a long piece of wire, then fastening five such clusters on a stem wire.

16 D.   Asters.

Asters, figure 16D, and other circular flowers of like form, are made by turning this looped wire round and round to form a flat surface, then fastening beneath with wire or calyx of silk or other material.

The smoothness and regularity of hair work is its greatest beauty, and there is no branch of fancywork which requires so few rules or which may be so readily acquired by practice. A dextrous use of the fingers, neatness of finish, and that skill in manipulating called "nimble fingering," are the great requisites in forming perfect leaves and flowers of hair.

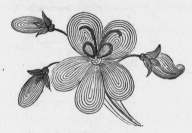

Fig. 12.   Pansies.

Take nature for your guide, and with hair of various colors and lengths, you will be able to form almost any flower you desire. *Pansies, figure 12*, are beautiful formed from two shades of hair. With the pliers turn over a piece of stem wire. Then take a piece of smooth, short hair of dark shade, fasten one end to it, and with a collar stay of the width of the upper petals, held close to the wire, pass the hair over it, and fasten it to the wire just below the first tie. Remove the collar stay, and by bending the wire, shape the petal properly. Make two of these; then make three upon a smaller collar stay of light colored hair, the more golden the prettier.

Then with two or three hairs of jet black, make long loops and form marks upon the hair to imitate the markings on the natural petals. Set the two large dark petals on the wire, turning them upward, and the three light ones below with a pearl bead in the center. These may be made to look very beautiful, especially if the marks upon the light-colored petals are well put on, which should be done so skillfully that they appear as if embroidered in various shades of black and brown.

The *forget-me-not, figure 18*, is very lovely formed in hair. The shortest possible pieces answer for the tiny loops which compose the separate blossoms, and must be clustered around a small gold bead.

Fig. 18.   Forget-me-not.

Bell-shaped flowers are pretty and graceful, and may be either large upon a slender pendulous stem, or a cluster of small ones drooping from one stem as in the *lily of the valley, figure 27.* The nodding blossoms are composed of three loops, fastened upon a thread-like wire with a small bead slipped on and fastened just at the base of the petals, like a continuation of the corolla.

Fig. 27. Lilies-of-the-Valley.

16 B. Fuchsia.

Buds of roses and other flowers are easily made of elongated loops and cut hair. A *fuchsia, figure 16B,* is formed by making the stamens and pistils of black feather strands and jet beads. The petals folded around them are made of loops of light hair. The stiff leaves of the calyx are formed of wire, bent into the desired form and covered with a flat band of dark hair, made smooth and glossy and wound round this support and then fastened around the corolla. The hair from one of them is folded around the lower part, forming the full part of the calyx and surrounding the ovary. This is fastened off at the stem with fine thread-wire or silk thread.

Tendrils are formed by rolling a few hairs upon a knitting needle, moistening with mucilage, drying, and then drawing carefully from the needle. The loops of various length, width, and thickness form the foundation for almost every flower and leaf. To form these with the nicety and precision of silk gimp is to gain the most difficult point, and to form these loops into various beautiful and graceful forms is to overcome the chief difficulties in making hair flowers. These loops are covered with the flat bands of hair, arranged upon petals of very thin cardboard, folded one over another, with a circle of light hair at the center where a single bead finishes each one.

Leaves are made of locks of hair, wet with mucilage and flattened between the fingers, then laid upon the palette and shaped with the point of the knife and wet camel's-hair brush into the waving, graceful leaves accompanying the flowers. The fine sprays are made either with India ink, upon the foundation of soft, flexible strands of hair, or shaped with the brush and pointed instrument. Hair from the nape of the neck, or the soft hair of children is best for the fine tracery upon the outer parts. The tie holding the sprays together is made of gold thread or a little gold band may be procured from a jeweler and fastened as a bouquet holder.

16 A. Orange Flowers.

Figure 16A is a cluster of *orange blossoms* and should be made of snow-white hair. The loops are formed, as previously described, and fastened to a stem in clusters together with a spray of leaves and long oval buds made of a number of loops wound closely and held in place with mucilage. The center of each flower is formed of a cluster of six seed-pearl beads surrounding a gold one.

Fig. 21.

Figure 21 is a pretty flower and made rather differently, the center being composed of loops with one on the margin of each petal. A little distant between these, a strand of three or four long hairs is wound and fastened with thread-wire or silk at each turn back and forth. The centers are chalk-white beads with a jet one in the middle. The hair should be of two contrasting colors. The leaves are small and delicate and are made of little loops of hair.

16 C. Clover Leaves.

Figure 16C is simply *clover leaves* formed of loops of several sides, fastened one in another, and then grouped in triplets with a round smooth bead at the base of each three.

Fig. 24.

Figure 24 is an *oxalis blossom* which is made of five loops of hair joined with a center of pearl beads and leaves like the clover.

Fig. 22. Double Marguerite.

Figure 22 will be found very effective. It is a *double marguerite* and is composed of an infinite number of tiny loops fastened on a round ball, covered with net of suitable color. These are prettiest made of all shades of red or golden hair. The leaves should be of dark brown with markings of gold color. Neatness, taste, and patience alone will make perfect hair work, with practice. (1876)

Fish Scale Embroidery

Fish scales, sewn upon silk or satin, may be arranged so as to form flowers, leaves, ornamental borders, and also birds to enrich many of those small articles of taste which always conduce to throw an air of refinement over a home, and give the visitor a favorable opinion of the occupants. The effect produced by the employment of a material generally so little regarded as the scales of fishes is one which will much surprise and gratify those who have never seen it employed in this manner.

The scales of various fishes may be used, but those of the perch are much to be preferred on account of their beautiful serrations. When taken from the fish they should first be thoroughly cleaned, and, before they have become dry and hard, two holes should be pierced through each with an instrument made of a stout darning needle fixed in a wooden handle. These holes should be made near the roots or bottoms of the fish scales, which will then be quite ready for use in the embroidery.

The best ground, and that usually chosen, is one of blue or pink silk, or, still better, satin of either of these colors. The pattern should first be drawn to the required size upon white paper, and its outline then carefully pricked through with a needle. Through the holes thus made, powdered vermilion must be rubbed and this will transfer the pattern to the ground. If the ground is of a dark color, whiting should be substituted. [These interesting directions were of course written before the invention of modern transfer paper.—Ed.]

When the paper is removed the pattern will be seen clearly indicated on the silk by small dots. As these are in dry powdered color and are easily obliterated, it is necessary to make the outline more permanent by going over the line with a fine brush and vermilion or white watercolor according as the ground may require a dark or light outline. This method of tracing will also be found useful in many other kinds of embroidery. The lines drawn should always be well within the dots so that they may be easily covered and hidden by the work.

After the pattern has been traced in this manner on the satin, a rose or some similar flower has to be worked in the fish scales. A row of these is neatly and carefully sewn through the two holes spoken of previously, round the circumference, to represent the outer circle of petals, and within these a second circle is stitched, overlapping the former, so as to conceal the threads by which they are attached. This is repeated till the center of the flower is reached. The center is formed in a large flower by a cluster of beads, and in a small one by a single bead. Yellow or gold beads look remarkably well as centers as these most nearly resemble the pollen of the natural flower. Small leaves, or leaves which consist of a number of separate leaflets, may be well made in fish scales, but larger ones may require to be worked in ordinary embroidery. Stems may also be worked in embroidery, very quickly and effectively, too, by using chenille.

Trefoil and the maidenhair fern are among the best leaf forms for representation in fish scale embroidery. The fish scales may be combined with small flowers, leaves, dots, and other ornaments. The accompanying illustrations represent various modes in which this style of decoration may be employed to adorn articles of the toilet, screens, etc., which will readily suggest themselves to the clever designer. (1876)

Fish Scale Screen

Fig. 17. Banner.

The screen, *figure 17*, is made of pink silk; the border, which is shown of a darker shade in the engraving, is

green. The whole work is bound with gold-colored braid. The effect of the fish scales upon the contrasting colors, pink and green, is very fine, and, indeed, it would be difficult to name a method of ornamenting screens and other articles which produces a more beautiful effect. The brilliant tints of hummingbirds, peacocks, parrots, and other gay and resplendent natural objects can be imitated with great fidelity and success. (1876)

Fish Scale Pincushion

Figure 15 is intended for the top of a pincushion, the ground being of a light-colored satin. The stems may be worked either in gold thread or maroon-colored silk, and the petals of the flowers and the leaflets are each composed of one fish scale. In a case like the present, where single scales are used, it is of course impossible to hide the stitch by which they are fastened to the background, but this may be rendered decorative by carrying the thread across the scale from its root to its edge, so as to resemble the center rib of the natural leaf. The flowers in this design are single, and have five petals with a bead in the center. (1876)

Fig. 15. Pincushion.

A Matchbox

Figure 3 shows a bony scale or plate from a sturgeon. The edges are serrated and afford conveniences for

125

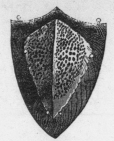

Fig. 3.—MATCH BOX.

fastening the box by means of two screws or tacks directly to the wall. It also can be placed on a neat shield of black walnut or other wood as shown in the figure. The surface is just rough enough for lighting a match, which suggests its appropriate use as a matchbox. It is most convenient and durable. (1868)

Bird Design of Fish Scales

The design given in *figure 16* is one which may be applied to almost any article and in combination with flowers or an ornamental border if desired. The eye of the bird is formed by a single bead, and the beak, legs, claws, and some of the feathers should be worked in silk embroidery. If, in this or any other design for fish-scale embroidery, brilliant color be desired, it may be obtained by using the scales of various kinds of fishes, or, more conveniently still, by tinting the scales before they are sewn on with bright transparent varnish-colors. (1876)

Fig. 16. Bird.

Feather Fashions

What fashion is or who decides what the fashions shall be, we do not pretend to discuss. A thing is "the fashion" and that is the end of it. The matter is alluded to now to show one particular phase of the prevailing taste. Stuffed birds and wings and breasts with feathers on them have long been used for decorating the things ladies call hats. This season the style has broken out in a new quarter, and the most curious combinations are seen.

Some college boys, wishing to play a trick on the professor of natural history, took the body of a beetle, fastened some grasshoppers' legs and butterflies' wings to it, and placed it on his desk. When the professor came in, he gravely took it up and said: "Gentlemen, I have here a remarkable specimen of a humbug." The ornaments to which we refer as being at present popular are of some such construction as this "humbug."

Fig. 1.—ORNAMENT OF CEDAR-BIRD, ETC.

The head of one bird, the wings of another, and the tail of a third is no unusual combination, provided marked and brilliant contrasts can be secured. *Figure 1* shows the stuffed body of a cedar bird, its wing feathers being tipped with bright scarlet and finished off with the long, sickle feathers of a black Spanish cock. These tail feathers are not drawn of their proper length to save room.

The desire seems to be to get strong colors, and it is said that a great many of the parrots kept by the bird dealers have been bought up and slaughtered by these makers of feather ornaments. Birds of brilliant plumage, such as the scarlet tanager and the oriole, which formerly sold to the bird stuffers at 20 cents, now sell to the feather workers for $1.

Feather Dusters

Small feather dusters are most convenient to have in the household, and are much preferable for most purposes to the turkey wing which is so frequently used. Larger ones are made of various kinds of imported feathers, while for the small ones the feathers of the barnyard fowls will answer a good purpose. When fowls are killed, preserve the longer feathers with care, especially the tail feathers of the male birds.

Fig. 2.—FEATHER ORNAMENT.

Individual feathers are worked up in the form shown in *figure 2*. A pasteboard form is made and feathers of different kinds and strongly contrasting colors are sewed on in successive layers. Feathers of fowls and geese are worked in and we doubt not some of the brilliant plumage of the pigeon and turkey may come into play. What may be called the tail of this artificial bird is furnished with some long feathers, and what should be the head is finished off with a velvet bow.

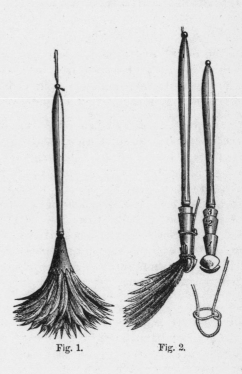

Fig. 1.   Fig. 2.

Fig. 3.—ORNAMENT OF BLUE JAY, ETC.

The *outré* ornament in *figure 3* is made of a yellow bird with expanded wings, and furnished with a tail made up of cock's feathers from which the plume has been stripped, except at the tips. This is worn upon the hat directly in front.

We do not approve of shooting useful birds for such purposes, but if any of our readers have showy feathers, we give them this hint for making them up according to the prevailing custom. (1869)

The peculiar form of the duster, *figure 1*, is given to it by the shape of the lower part of the handle to which the feathers are attached. The shape of this handle is shown at the right hand in *figure 2*.

There are at the bottom three cones terminated by a knob, which last has a groove to hold the string. One handy with the jackknife can readily whittle out such a stick, and by the aid of sandpaper make the handle part smooth enough to be painted.

In attaching the feathers, the shortest ones are put on first. A knot is made in the binding string like that shown in the lower part of *figure 2*, and the manner of putting it on is shown in the same figure. A row of short feathers is put on, and then the string is carried to the notch above, a row of longer feathers put on, and then again, when the longest and handsomest feathers are used.

When all are securely bound and tied, a conical cap is put over to conceal the fastenings and give a finish to the work. This cap may be of thin leather or of some brightly colored fabric. We have seen red flannel used with good effect. The whole is made to look more workmanlike by clipping off the ends of any feathers that protrude too much. (1869)

A Popcorn Picture Frame

A neat little frame, suitable for a small picture, makes a pleasing and useful article for a present. The one we have in mind is called a popcorn frame because that grain is largely used in making it, but a variety of other grains and seeds may be employed in the same manner.

The frame in question is first cut out of thin board, but in the absence of that, stiff pasteboard will answer. A row of cherry stones is fastened on both the outer and inner edge of the frame with strong glue. Then a hazelnut is put at each scallop. Some plum stones are placed here and there, and the remaining space filled with popcorn of the red variety (if possible), all fastened with glue. The fruit stones should be well cleaned, and the frame will look all the better if these have a coat of varnish before the corn is put on, that being sufficiently bright without varnish.

This manner of covering a frame is given as a suggestion, but it may be varied according to the materials one has at hand. Beans of different colors and other seeds—such as those of the castor-oil plant, beechnuts, chinquapins, very small acorns, and other things—will answer for the larger objects, while the pearly rich popcorn, as well as the little bright yellow variety, will answer if the red kind is not at hand. One with a little ingenuity will find no difficulty in producing a pleasing effect.

[Purists will be interested in the following:—Ed.]Glue for such uses should be very strong. It is easily made thus: Place in a tin cup some pieces of good cabinet-maker's glue, and pour on enough cold water to well cover them. Set in a cool place (away from the fire) over night, or long enough for the pieces to swell up and become limber. Then pour off all the water that will drain away and set the cup in another dish in which is some water. Set the whole on the stove and allow it to heat gradually. The pieces of glue will dissolve in the water they have taken up; the solution or made glue will be very strong and must be kept hot while using by placing the cup in a larger vessel containing hot water. If more water should be needed, it may be added hot and a very little at a time. (1882)

A POP-CORN PICTURE FRAME.

Homemade Photograph Frames

Fig. 1.—THREAD PHOTOGRAPH FRAME.

Here is a very pretty frame, enclosing a photograph, which is made by winding colored thread upon a piece of very thick pasteboard in the manner shown in the engraving. The star is 8 inches across from point to point. Rich brown thread, or other colors, the coarser the better, is selected, and ten rows of threads wound around two notches opposite to each other, say from 1 to 4; then ten threads from 2 to 5; then ten from 3 to 6; and so on round and round until the whole pasteboard is covered. A pin thrust into each outer point, holds the threads from slipping off, and they are held securely in the inner angles by sewing a few times through the board, with a needle. The whole is simple, easily made, costs but a trifle for the thread, and is quite pretty. The open space in the center is an octagon just large enough for an ordinary photograph. They may be smaller.

Fig. 2. STRAW FRAME.

A pretty frame may be constructed wholly of wheat or rye straw, cut and joined in the manner shown in *figure 2*. The straws should of course be large and firm. They are easily shaped with a sharp knife, and then fastened with glue, or strong gum arabic, or other adhesive material. By applying black or other color to portions of the straw a very neat variegated frame is produced. The one shown in the engraving is 6 inches high, and 4 inches wide, on the outside, but they may be of smaller size if desired. (1868)

To Make Gold Spangles (Glitter)

There are some kinds of ornamentation in which spangles and other brilliant ornamentation are very effective, and as all persons may not have it in their power to procure these "sparkling aids" just when they are required, here is a process by which they may be easily made, and be found as brilliantly beautiful as those purchased.

Take a glass bottle, and with a soft brush paint the outside surface with thin glue. While the surface is still moist, cover with gold leaf by lifting the sheet carefully upon a "gilder's-tip," and throwing it lightly upon the bottle. If a person is dextrous, the fingers and breath will be sufficient. After the leaf is applied and made smooth, burnish it lightly with a wad of cotton. Go over the leaf carefully with thin copal varnish, using a soft brush. Add a very little linseed oil to the varnish to prevent rapid drying.

Place in a cool cellar for a few days, and then with a sharp-pointed knife cut off the spangles in any shape desired. The gold leaf will chip off in bright, glittering flakes that will be found very fine for many purposes. (1876)

Summer Fancywork

Those who live near or expect to visit the sea during the summer will find many uses for the graceful seaweeds thrown up by the waves. The simplest way to mount them is to float them upon panels of cardboard.

First soak the seaweed thoroughly in a basin of water. Then have ready a flat dish, also filled with water, into which place the piece to be mounted, and let it spread out. Slip the cardboard under it, and raise it quickly out of the dish. Let the water drain off, and with a fine needle arrange the tiny branches. Lay the cards out to dry, and the seaweed will be found as firmly fastened to the paper as though glued. A beautiful album can be made of these "flowers of the sea." (1883)

Home Decorations for Thanksgiving

At Thanksgiving a few wreaths and other decorations, put up in places where they will show to the best advantage, will do much toward giving the room a holiday look. The work of making these wreaths affords much pleasure, equal to the satisfaction felt when viewing the completed work.

Golden wheat, and autumn leaves, and berries belong to Thanksgiving as fitly as holly and mistletoe to Christmas. The bright berries of the mountain ash can sometimes be kept until Thanksgiving, but not always so, and it does not always do to depend on them. Sumach, if gathered before it looks dried and brown, will keep its lovely dark-red color. Climbing bittersweet or waxwork berries are most effective. If they are brought in from the woods on long stems, they can be easily trained over pictures and along the wall.

Substitutes for berries may be made in various ways. Cranberries can be arranged in bunches with little trouble. Each berry is strung on a fine wire *(figure 1)*, the ends of which are then doubled and twisted together. Six or eight berries are tied into a bunch *(figure 2)*. The wire must be cut into pieces about 5 inches long,

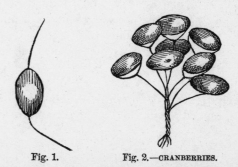

Fig. 1.   Fig. 2.—CRANBERRIES.

and should be the fine kind used for wiring cut flowers. Peas and beans softened by boiling can be put on wire in the same manner and, before making into bunches, given a scarlet coat by dipping in sealing wax dissolved in alcohol.

Fig. 3.—AN EVERGREEN WREATH.

One of the easiest methods of making wreaths is to tie small bunches of evergreen to hoops of the desired size. These *(figure 3)* may be made out of strips of heavy pasteboard, or barrel hoops cut the right length and securely tied. Ropings are made by tying small bits of evergreen to rope with fine cord. For some places, laths covered with evergreen *(figure 4)* are more useful and more easily managed than the limber roping.

Fig. 4.—EVERGREENS ON A LATH.

If the front hall is wide and roomy, as every hall should be, it should have a full share of the decorations. Large, round wreaths may be placed over each picture. A group of flags of different sizes, in the most conspicuous place on the wall, and laths, well covered with evergreen, mixed with bright berries, can be used over the doors. Place a small stand beside the door leading into the diningroom; arrange a wreath of box or clubmoss around the edge of the top, and a vine of bittersweet, mixed with evergreen, around the standard. After the seeds are removed from a large, yellow pumpkin, fill it half full of damp sand, place on the stand, and fill with dark green box, bittersweet berries, sumach, long heads of wheat, a few bunches of bright fall leaves, heads of millet, one or two ears of corn, and small red or other bright apples, stuck on twigs.

Over the mantel in the parlor, make an inverted V-shaped arch *(figure 5)*, by joining laths covered thickly with evergreen. At the top of the arch place a cluster of

Fig. 5.—MANTEL DECORATIONS.

berries and some green to trail downward. Instead of a wreath over the pictures in the parlor, put vines of bittersweet with which evergreen or trailing clubmoss has been mixed. If bittersweet vines can not be procured, use any graceful vine-wild grapevines and Virginia creeper answer well-and decorate it with clubmoss, or evergreen and berries made as described. Beneath small pictures a cluster of green may be tacked, and a vine extended from it up over the picture, as shown in *figure 6.*

Fig. 6.—PICTURE DECORATIONS.

The decorations over the diningroom mantel may be quite different. A large bunch of evergreen, mixed with wheat, millet, and berries, should be tacked up near the ceiling, and vines or ropings of green may hang down and be fastened out at each side. Beneath the arch should be placed a cornucopia filled with autumn fruits and vines.

Vases, even if choice, and treasures of art are removed from the mantel to make room for two vases manufactured, like the one in the hall, from the plebeian pumpkin and filled with autumn fruits and vegetables. These various suggestions given above can be easily carried out from the illustrations. They may be changed to suit the different places to be decorated. (1883)

130

Table Decoration

Within the past few years great advance has been made in the art of table decoration, and the horticultural societies abroad offer prizes for the best specimens of this department of the florist's art. Stands usually of glass are made for the purpose of holding flowers for the table, and where living plants are used the pot is placed beneath the surface of the table. The regular leaves of an extension table are replaced by common boards cut so as to allow the stem of the plant to pass through, while the pot stands upon a stool or something provided for the purpose. Several tablecloths are used and are lapped around the stems of the plants that come through the table.

Here is an illustration from the garden of one of these prize decorations to show to what refinement the art is carried, and to be suggestive to those who would like to undertake something of the kind.

For the family table a simpler decoration is more appropriate. A few flowers put loosely into a glass are in much better taste than a large, heavy, crowded bouquet. In any decoration, whether for a private or a public table, heaviness must be avoided, and lightness and grace should characterize every design, whether large or small. The matter of home decoration is easily managed, and may be dismissed by saying—the simpler the better.

It often happens that parties, festivals, and other social gatherings take place during the season of flowers, at which refreshments are served. Those having charge of the table arrangements naturally desire to decorate with flowers, and usually make the mistake of having these in great quantity without bestowing any care upon the arrangement. A crowded bouquet in any place is less pleasing than a loose and graceful one, and this is especially the case in table decorations. Where persons are to be seated at the table, it is especially important that the decorations should not be so heavy as to obstruct the view from one side to the other. Light, feathery foliage and delicate vines should form the chief material of all table decoration, and flowers may come in for color, but not, as is too often the case, to make up the mass.

One with a little ingenuity and skill can make up tasteful decorations from very ordinary materials. If elevated stands like those shown in the engraving are wanted, and glass ones cannot be procured, let the tinman make the portions to hold the flowers (to be filled with wet moss), and support them on glass rods. Even wooden supports may be used if quite clothed with vines.

In the country an abundance of ferns may be had for the searching, and they can be largely used in such work. The leaves of carrots, parsley, and the common yarrow are not to be rejected. The young growth of grape and hop vines, with the spray of asparagus, will, under a skillful hand, work into pleasing forms, and the common greebrier may be turned to good account.

The green groundwork being secured, then flowers may be sparingly worked in. If no flowering vines are at hand, those that do not bear flowers may be made to do so by binding to them carnations and other flowers that hold well without water by means of a very fine iron wire. By the exercise of a little ingenuity a table for a summer festival can be made beautiful by the use of common and inexpensive materials. (1873)

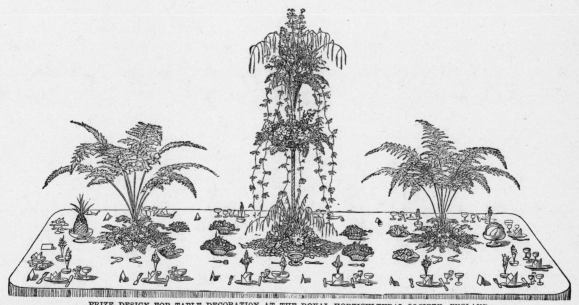

PRIZE DESIGN FOR TABLE DECORATION AT THE ROYAL HORTICULTURAL SOCIETY, ENGLAND.

131

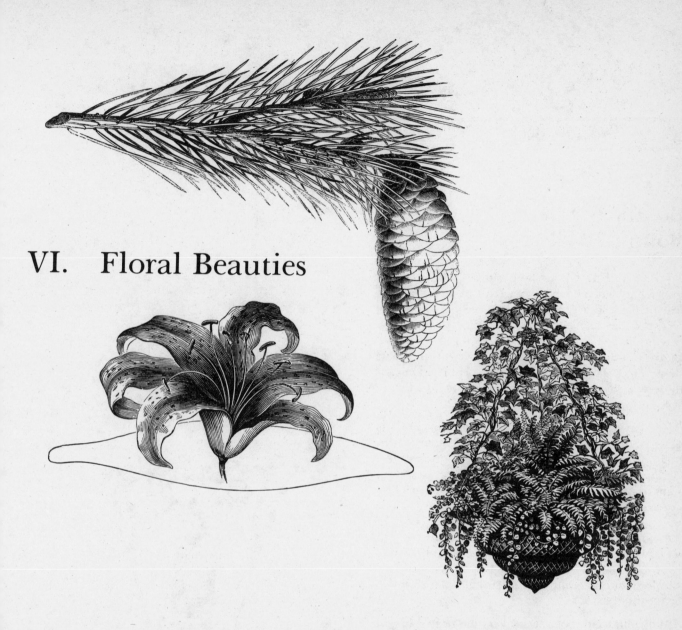

VI. Floral Beauties

Bouquets and Bouquet Making

To a lover of flowers nothing can be more beautiful than a bunch of them bound together in such a careless way that each flower has sufficient freedom to show its own peculiar habit. Such a bouquet is to be prized, whether culled in our own garden or the gift of a friend. Placed in water, its beauty can be enjoyed until the last flower fades. This is the bouquet found in the homes of those who have flowers in plenty. Among all flower lovers in the country, it is the real thing.

The city bouquet from the florists is no more like this than a Fifth Avenue residence is like a country farmhouse. In one of these natural lovable bouquets there are flowers enough wasted, by being covered and out of sight, or in their yet undeveloped buds, to make a half dozen of the fashionable sort. The city florist, when he sells flowers, is very careful not to sell buds and stems at the same time. In the free way of cutting flowers with their own stems, there is involved a loss of future bloom which he can ill afford, so the flowers are gathered stemless, and the want of their natural stalks supplied by means of art.

With most city bouquet makers the next thing in importance to flowers is a *broom*—a regular corn broom, and this, both brush and handle, is worked up into the most costly bouquets. The broom splints are broken apart and each separate flower if mounted on a broom-corn stem by means of a few turns of a thread-like annealed iron wire as in *figure 1*. Sometimes strong elastic grass stems are employed, or pine is split into slivers and used instead of broom-corn. A coarse wire may also be used for the stem and this is attached to the flower by running it through the lower part or the flower cup, and twisting it below, as seen in *figure 2*.

A sufficient number of flowers being prepared in this way, the bouquet is then to be made up, and here is where the broom-handle comes into play. A piece of the

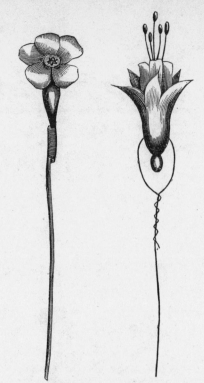

Fig. 1.   Fig. 2.
ARTIFICIAL STEMS FOR FLOWERS.

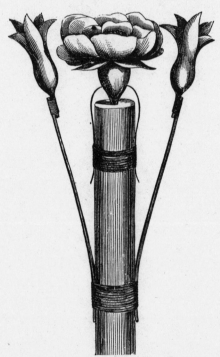

Fig. 3.—MANNER OF MAKING A BOUQUET.

stick of convenient length for the center of the bouquet is cut off. As it is customary to use a rose, camellia or other large flower for the center, that is fastened to the end of the stick by running a wire through the flower cup and fastening its ends to the stick by means of small twine as shown in *figure 3*.

Then the bouquet is gradually built up by adding the other flowers, and securing them in place by turns of small twine. *Figure 3* shows two of the small flowers attached in this way. The shape of the bouquet is governed by desire of the customer, a flat or slightly convex surface in which the flowers are all upon nearly the same level being the commonest form. Any desired shape can be given, and the bouquet will be flat or pyramidal according to the point at which the artificial stems are tied to the central support.

All this artificial work is concealed by an edging of some kind of green—and the extreme of elegance is to have outside of this a white paper cone, bordered on its edge by a rich fringe of white silk. Bouquets made in this way may sell from $5 to $20 or more, according to the season and the flowers used in makin them. Flowers treated in this unnatural manner will keep much longer than one would suppose. Of course it is useless to put bouquets of this kind into water, but an occasional sprinkling will keep them fresh for some days, and if they are put under a glass shade, their beauty can be prolonged for a much greater time. (1864)

Acorns and Oak "Puff-Balls"

These can be used for decorating fancy baskets, brackets, or small tables.

Provide each acorn with a stem of green crewel silk, about two inches long. Remove the cup, and run the silk through it with a large needle, and knot it inside the cup. The acorn can then be firmly glued into its place again.

A bunch of these look very pretty hanging from a ribbon bow, or with a handful of oats or grasses, and can be made useful in many ways. The "puff-balls" are used similarly, by merely running a thread through each of the "balls" and knotting one end. (1883)

Preserving Autumn Leaves

The leaves of forest trees are so beautiful when they take on their varied autumnal tints that many have a desire to preserve them. For those who would like to do so,

here is a method of treating the leaves in order to best preserve their colors.

Gather the leaves as soon as they begin to change color, as they then retain their bright hues longest and best. Medium and small leaves are most suitable for wreaths, pictures, and crosses; a few larger ones are desirable for leaf bouquets, fine sprays of tiny ones for that purpose being highly prized. To dry the leaves, any book of soft paper will do. Begin to place the leaves in at the end of the book, but not too close on a page. When one page is filled, turn over five or six, and continue in this manner through the book; then put it in a cool, dry place with a heavy weight upon it, as it is very essential to make them as smooth as possible.

In one or two days another book will be needed into which to change the leaves. The first can be left open to dry, to be used again. In about a week the moisture will be extracted so that they can be placed in any book to remain until needed. About a month will insure their being thoroughly dry.

For all the leaves *not pasted* on paper, use boiled linseed oil, rubbing it on with a flannel rag, just enough to give a rich gloss. Keep the leaves spread out for a few days after oiling. For mucilage, to paste leaves upon Bristol board, use two parts gum arabic and one of sugar. When the wreaths or groups are pasted on, press them between books until smooth and dry, and then apply carefully, with a small brush, one or two coats of copal or white varnish.

For wreaths, cut a circular piece from stiff paper of the size and width required, sew a piece of steel hoop around the back to keep it from warping, and add a loop

at the top to hang up by. Then begin at the top, arrange and sew on small leaves, increasing the size as you near the bottom. When one half is covered, begin at the top again and make the other side in the same way, and finish with the most brilliant leaves. The oval is another form that might be used. Hanging against a light wall they look very bright through the winter, and retain their beauty until June.

Lampshades, ornamented with leaves, are something new, and very beautiful as well as useful. Cut six pieces like the pattern in the engraving, in perforated Bristol board. They should be 6½ inches long, 5¾ inches wide at the bottom, and 3½ inches at the top. Arrange a group of oiled leaves, flowers, or small ferns, on each piece—tacking them on very slightly. Then line the back with white tissue paper, and cover the leaves with tarlatan or lace. Bind around the edges of the pieces with narrow brown or crimson ribbon, and sew them together. (1868)

STARRY SCABIOUS.—(*Scabiosa stellata.*)

Winter Bouquets.

Winter Bouquets

Bouquets of everlasting flowers, as they are called, are pleasing or the reverse, according to the care that has been given to collecting and preserving the flowers, and the taste displayed in making them up. Most of these unfading flowers bloom late, some, such as the Helichrysums, coming into perfection just at the time of hard frosts. With the majority of these plants it is best to pick the flowers before they fairly open, remove the leaves from the stems, tie them in small bundles, and hang them, flowers down, to dry in the shade. If too many are put together there is danger of mildew, and it is moreover difficult to keep the stems straight.

The Globe Amaranth (*Gomphrena*), should not be picked until the heads are well developed and feel papery. If in making up, the natural stems are not manageable, or if the flowers become broken off, as they are apt to be, artificial stems made of slivers of broom corn may be attached by means of a thread or fine wire. Seed-vessels of various kinds are introduced into these bouquets with good effect. A species of Scabious (*Scabiosa stellata*), is sometimes cultivated for this use, under the name of Starry Scabious. This old but not very common plant is so pleasing in its appearance in fruit that an engraving is here shown. Each seed-vessel is surmounted by an expanded and prettily marked calyx, and which holds its shape and beauty when dry. It is an annual and may be readily raised from the seed. (1868)

Grasses for Winter

Most beautiful are the grasses, whether made into bouquets by themselves, or used with the dried or everlasting flowers. The grain fields, the meadows and roadsides, as well as the swamps and marshy places, afford a great variety. These should be cut when they seem to be in perfection, and dried rapidly in the shade. Those of a stiff appearance, such as have their flowers in an erect spike, may be tied in small clusters, and hung to dry with their heads downwards.

Other grasses, with their flowers in graceful panicles, would be spoiled by this treatment. For these, provide a box of convenient size, filled with dry sand; the stems of the grasses can be stuck in the sand, and the flower clusters will dry in a natural position. A garret or any unused room will answer for drying the grasses, and they may be left in the boxes of sand until wanted for making up into bouquets.

A well arranged bouquet of dried grasses will make a welcome Christmas present. Select a damp time for making up the dried grasses into bunches or bouquets, as otherwise they may be so brittle that many of the smaller stems will be broken off. Some give directions for coloring, bronzing, and otherwise giving grasses an unnatural appearance. All of these are in bad taste. Colored grasses are quite disgusting; those that are dried in the shade will keep their beautiful natural colors. (1883)

A BOUQUET OF DRIED GRASSES AND FERNS.

Grass Bouquets

The introduction of a number of annual flowers, which, when dry, retain their form and color, has made winter bouquets very popular. These everlasting flowers, as they are called, when carefully dried and made up with skill, form pleasing ornaments for the household; but at their best they are not, to our taste, so desirable as bouquets of dried grasses. Many of the grass bouquets that we see are failures, for the reason that the maker of them tried to crowd too much into them. A collection of the rarest and most elegant grasses, if tied into a bunch and crowded into a heavy vase, will fail to be pleasing. The beauty of grasses depends upon their ease and freedom from restraint. Some color the grasses or incrust them with alum crystals, processes which do not add to their beauty, however much it may to their showiness.

Seeds of several kinds of "ornamental" grasses are to be had of the seedsmen, but few of these produce anything more beautiful than may be found growing in the wild state. There are numerous wild grasses which are suitable to use in bouquets, but as they have no common names as a rule, it is not worthwhile to enumerate them by their botanical ones. The best way is to collect whatever grasses seem suitable that we meet with in our rambles, tie them in small parcels, and dry them in the shade in a place free from dust. Some berries of the Wax-work (*Celastrus*), and ferns dried between paper, or in a large book, will be useful to combine with the grasses. For a grass bouquet the great trouble is to find a suitable vase or receptacle. Those sold as flower vases are altogether too heavy in style to correspond with the airiness of the grasses they are to hold.

Here is a suggestion for a container that is most suitable for an ornament of dry grasses. As no water is needed, some such stand could be very easily contrived. A glass tube or solid rod of glass, ½-inch or a little more in diameter, and about 2 feet long, is to be fitted into a round block of wood, heavy enough to answer for a firm base, and at its top furnished with a funnel or trumpet-shaped receptacle to hold the stems of the grasses. This receptacle may be covered with some paper of some neutral tint, or may have mosses and lichens gummed upon it.

For the pleasing arrangement of the grasses in such a stand as this no directions can be given; each individual can display her taste in the matter. The aim should be to avoid all appearance of crowding, and allow each kind of grass to show its natural habit. The wooden base of the stand can be concealed by the dried fern leaves, and cones, berries, and nuts may be introduced. Those who are fortunate enough to find the delicate climbing fern can add much to the beauty of such an ornament by twining one of its stems around the glass rod. Here is an illustration of an ornament of grasses arranged in the manner suggested. (1870)

A Moss Vase

The cut above represents a vase for holding flowers which is of novel construction and so simple that any one can make it. The frame is made of two pieces of board, the lower one 10 inches or a foot square, the other an inch smaller, with an upright square or round stick fastened to the middle. It will be firmer if let into a hole in the base.

For the top, take a common straw hat with rather a low crown, and sew a piece of wire around the rim to stiffen it. Another piece may also be sewed around the top of the crown on the inside. Cover the wire and edge of the rim with green ribbon, which may be put on with glue. Set the hat, crown downward, on the upright stick, so that it will be supported by its center. Lay a small piece of leather in the crown over the stick, and fasten the hat down with small nails driven through the leather. This completes the frame.

The whole is then to be covered with lichens, the flat moss that grows on trees, rocks, etc. These are fastened on with glue. Mosses cannot be fastened as well as lichens, but a trimming of them fastened around the edges of the rim would look tasteful. The lichens are of different colors, green, red, and yellow, and may be arranged to look very neat. We have seen several specimens like the above. The idea came originally, we believe, from a valuable little work on "Leaf and Flower Pictures," recently published. (1859)

Miniature Rustic Plant Stand

Here is an engraving of a beautiful miniature rustic plant stand. It consists of a simple oval-shaped box, with slips of wood tacked around the sides, the bark still adhering, and an arched frame of vine-work raised above it, the whole being nicely varnished. A shell containing a trailing plant rests upon the top. Underneath this is suspended a miniature globe filled with water in which swims a small goldfish. Ferns and other plants are grown in soil covered with moss in the box at the base, and delicate vines are trained to the side frames. The whole forms a unique and tasteful ornament for the sitting room, costing but little to make or to purchase. (1863)

Miniature Rustic Plant Stand

A Rustic Jardinet

The French word *jardinet* (pronounced jar-de-nay) means a small garden, and is usually applied to small enclosures or beds margined with ornamental pottery work. The name is also given to large terra-cotta vases intended for growing plants. Some very beautiful ones of this description are now imported, some of them made in imitation of the trunk of a tree.

138

RUSTIC JARDINET.

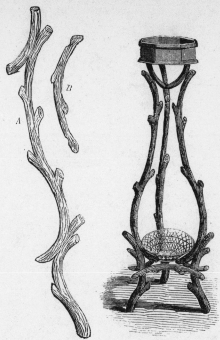

Fig. 2.   Fig. 1.—FLOWER STAND.

One of our friends, not wishing to pay the high price asked for the imported article, has invented a home-made one, which is more "rustic" in appearance, and answers every purpose of the more costly affair. The lower part of a keg furnishes the receptacle, and split staves, nailed to this, support it at the desired height. The whole is then covered with bark neatly tacked on. Lichens—those ashen-colored and brownish plants found on the trunks of trees and often incorrectly called mosses—are used here and there with good effect. Such plants as are suitable for hanging baskets are appropriate for a *jardinet* of this kind. (1869)

A Handsome Flower Stand

Rustic stands for the tasteful arrangement of flowers are often coarse in material and in construction. This example, while it has much the effect of rustic-work, is neat and more in keeping with the furniture with which it would be surrounded in the parlor. *Figure 1* shows the stand as it appears when empty. Above is an octagonal box which contains a zinc pan that may be filled with earth, and used for growing plants, or may serve to hold cut flowers. When used for the last named purpose, a convex zinc cover is placed over the pan; this is perforated with numerous holes through which the stems of the flowers are thrust. The pan in this case, of course, contains water. Below is a wire basket which can be lined with moss, and hold a pot of ivy, the stems of which may be entwined around the legs of the stand.

The legs are of the shape given in *figure 2, A;* they are first sawed out of a black walnut plant, and then worked

into a rounded shape by use of the drawing knife, spokeshave, or even a jackknife. The shape of the curved cross pieces near the bottom of the stand is shown at *B, figure 2*. After the pieces are rounded, a "rustic" appearance is given to the work by lining it with shallow grooves by means of a small gouge, such as is used by woodcarvers.

The whole is finished by oiling it with linseed oil. When the stand is not occupied by flowers, it may be converted into a useful article of furniture by means of

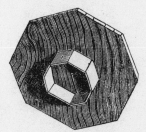

Fig. 3.—TOP OF STAND.

the circular top, *figure 3*. This has a projection to fit into the upper part of the stand in place of the zinc pan. Any one who is at all handy with tools can readily make this really pretty article of furniture from the engravings given. (1868)

A Neat and Tasteful Ornament

During the Fall season of the year there will be little difficulty in finding plenty of the cones of evergreen trees scattered about the woods and lawns, which have partly opened and perhaps shed their seeds. Gather a few of these, sprinkle grass seed among the openings, and set the cone in a wineglass or other small vessel which will support it well. Partially fill the vessel with water.

In a few days the burrs will close upon the seed, and they will germinate, sending out their shoots to the light, and forming a beautiful little pyramid of green, looking all the brighter by contrast with the brown color of the cone. (1859)

Beautiful Floral Ornaments

Hyacinths, as ordinarily grown in glasses and pots, are deservedly favorites. Few flowers give better reward for the little pains required to raise them successfully. A very tasteful arrangement of these with other bulbs is common in Germany. Single hyacinths, together with snowdrops, crocuses and other small bulbs, are placed in shallow dishes and arranged in any form to suit the fancy. The roots spread out and intertwine until the flowers rest on a network that keeps them in place.

Having selected the bulbs, place a foundation of charcoal, and on this a layer of damp white sand. Set the bulbs a little distance apart and remove the dish to a dark room where they may remain for about three weeks. This treatment encourages the roots to form plentifully before the buds appear. At the end of that time a little water may be given (being poured down the sides of the dish), and if the roots are pushing the bulbs up out of place, pour dry sand over them, so as to surround them at least half way to their crowns. When the blossom buds and leaves have made a little growth, they should be brought to the full light of a window, and in all respects treated like those in glasses.

Dwarf hyacinths are best for this use. They are raised from well-ripened bulbs of the same kind as the large ones, but not much exceeding a large walnut in size. (1862)

Paper Flowers

General Instructions

Flowers made of fine tissue paper are most elegant, and the art of forming them is capable of being carried to a high state of perfection. Unlike the art of forming wax flowers, this may be made to give satisfaction in the hands of a mere amateur. When executed by a skillful and practiced artist, however, it is so charming in its various combinations that it will amply repay a patient and persevering study of its many technicalities and a continued series of attempts at forming any and every flower and bud that comes within the reach.

Materials: These consist of the finest tissue and glazed papers, which come in sheets of different sizes and of every shade and color, and many pleasing combinations of color, suited for carnations, mottled roses, and other variegated flowers. Wire of different sizes to be used for making stems; bristles and thread; also wild grasses (best is manilla grass) for stamens and pistils. Glue, colors of various kinds (in watercolor powder form), and some absorbent cotton.

Tools: The tools used are a molding pin; scissors of small size with sharp points, a pair of tweezers, and if convenient, it is well to have a pair of wooden goffers, which will form several sizes; also a brick to be used as a rest for crimping. These materials and tools (with the exception of the brick) may all be obtained at the arts and crafts stores, where the various articles for fancy-work are always kept.

Petals: The petals of various flowers are cut from paper patterns, taken, if possible from the natural flower, or procured from the stores. [The flowers discussed in the pages following may be made from the patterns illustrated therein.—Ed.] In dissecting a flower, mark every petal with numerals or letters, and write down the number of stamens, form of pistils, calyx, etc. Never cut more than three thicknesses of paper together, as the edges will be rough and uneven, and the scissors injured. The petals are sometimes required to be rolled on the ball of a molding tool, or pressed between the goffering tools; others will be merely notched on the edges; others finely cut into a fringe, while some will need crimping. These points will be best seen in the natural flower.

Crimping: Crimping is done by laying a petal on the brick and laying it in plaits by taking hold of a piece with the tweezers or pliers, and drawing them down, pinching the paper between them, so as to form regualr, crisp-looking creases, noticed in the petals at the heart of a rose and other flowers. Some persons make these folds or crimps with the fingers, but the tweezers do it more effectually.

Calyx: The calyx is made of stiff green paper or tissue paper, painted with glue, and cut into the proper form. Many prefer to purchase these already formed from the art shops.

Hearts: Stamens and pistils connected and covered by a calyx are called *hearts;* and these are also sold ready-made for various flowers. But a neat and skillful person with deft fingers may readily form them, and this is far less expensive. The method is as follows: For fine threadlike *stamens,* use glazed cotton thread, waxed, and the ends dipped in glue, and then dipped in yellow, brown, green, white or other colored watercolor powder, suited to the natural flower. Some are more natural formed of bristles or horsehair, cut into suitable lengths, while others require paper shred fine. Others are made of zephyr, formed into moss by clipping. Feathers and manilla grass are best suited to some kinds.

Pistils: The pistils should be made of fine threadlike wire, covered with green silk. Upon the end twist a little pellet of wax, or a bit of cotton; dip into glue, and then into colored powder—emerald green, rich brown, yellow or orange, according to the flower.

"Cement" for forming flowers: [The modern craftsman is advised to purchase Celluclay or Craft Dough or any other commercial product readily available for this purpose. But for those "purists" who wish to learn how the craft was practiced in the late-nineteenth century, a "recipe" for "cement" follows.—Ed.]

A ball of cement is required for the foundation of the petals and heart of the flower, which is made of the following: Take two ounces of gum tragacanth and as much powdered alum as will rest upon the point of a tea-knife. Put into a cup or wide-mouthed bottle. Add cold water, in which plaster of Paris has been rubbed to a paste. Mix this well with a slender stick, and add a little sugar of lead [lead acetate—Ed.]. This will answer for a large number of flowers and should be kept closely stopped in little bottles, cutting out as much as is required from time to time.

[In the directions for individual flowers that follow, the "cement" or Celluclay or Craft Dough will be referred to, consistently, as "dough."—Ed.]

Leaves: Leaves are rarely natural in appearance when made of paper unless done by machinery or professional hands. It is better, therefore, to procure store-bought ones or make them of wax. If however, a person desires to try paper ones, take stiff green paper and, making it a little damp, press it carefully into the leaf molds used for wax flowers, making both a light and a dark-green side. Place a wire upon the inner part of the

HYDRANGEA PANICULATA GRANDIFLORA.

141

dark part, and paint it over entirely with glue. Then place on it the light outer side and press the edges together carefully. This will form a fair leaf, but not so perfect as the bought one. (1876)

Lilies

The common white is a beautiful and conspicuous flower, with a heart formed like *E, figure 5*. The stem is made of stiff wire, the top extended and tipped with a knob of green wax dotted with brown spots. The stamens are of fine wire, with large filaments made of yellow wax. These are placed round the pistil, as shown in the illustration, and are six in number. A ball of dough at the base holds the petals cut by *Nos. 28 and 27 (figure 8)*, from thick glossy white paper, three of each. Vein them with five straight marks down the center, and small ones converging each way. Place the three smaller ones round the stamens, at regular distances, and the three larger ones outside between the spaces.

Of *No. 31 (figure 8)* cut three smaller petals, crimp them at the points so that they will close together as a closed bud. Cut six of *No. 22* in pale-green, opaque paper and put three round the bud first; and afterwards the other three. Roll the paper stem with cotton or paper until as thick as the little finger, making it into an elongated ball, with dough, just below the petals, and painting green or covering with the paper.

The *Pink Japan Lily (rosea)* and *White (alba)* are cut from *24 and 25 figure 6*, with hearts of the same form as the common white lily; but the white paper in *rosea* is covered on one side with pink tissue, which is dotted or marked with oblong spots raised upon the surface by repeated coats of opaque white and afterwards colored with dark red. Vein them very deeply and curl them and then fasten to the heart with each one reflexed. *No. 25* is the calyx. *Alba* is white with spots of crimson. Make little balls of dough or cotton, just at the base of each flower and bud and color green. Twist the stems with green paper, then bend the wires into drooping form, and arrange in clusters with buds of two or three sizes and leaves. (1876)

Narcissus

The different varieties of narcissus look well in paper. The single has its petals of light yellow, with the cup of bright orange. The double of a light cream-color with clusters of small petals in place of the cup, and the polyanthus narcissus, which is perhaps the most charm-ing of all, its delicate and beautiful little flowers clustered on a long, graceful stem.

The *Pheasant Eye* is very beautiful, and made thus: Cut for the center two rounds of double yellow tissue, or single thick paper, *No. 33 (Figure 8)*. Tinge with a little yellowish green at the base, and, clipping the edge into a narrow fringe, color it an intense scarlet.

On a rather thick stem (made of wire covered with cotton and then wound with green paper) fasten a ball of dough, and on it fasten five little short stamens, ⅛-inch in length, formed of little pieces of wire, dipped in glue, then in dark brown powder, with a little yellow speck in the center of each. Press these into the cement, and slipping the bowl on the stem press it up to them. The petals, *Nos. 34* and *32 (figure 8)*, are a pure white. Cut from stiff white paper and vein each one, carefully curling the edges towards each other. With moist fingers pinch the center into a little twisted point. Put on the smallest set first, then the larger between them. Finish with a sheathed calyx of light-green tissue paper.

The old-fashioned "daffodil" is made of bright yellow paper, with large, full cups in the center, and may be easily made from the natural flower, and the martagon, tiger and California lilies are of various shades of orange, yellow, scarlet, etc., and all very effective in paper. (1876)

Sweet Peas

The *Sweet Pea* is of an entirely distinct form from any flower thus mentioned, and its description will enable a person to form the rose acacia, wistaria, laburnum, dolichos, and all pea-shaped flowers. Cut *No. 32 (figure 6)* of double white tissue paper, and *No. 31* of thick pale pink paper, and *No. 33* of thick deep pink paper. Or the colors may be shades of purple, the *No. 32* of white, merely tinted with lavender; *No. 31* light lavender; and *No. 33* is pretty and rich looking when formed of velvet, stiffened with glue on the wrong side, and creased down the center.

Take a stem of green-covered wire, and turning the end over, fasten a little oblong ball of dough on it, around which press the pieces *No. 32*. After rolling them into hollow cylinders, *No. 31* is placed over the white piece, the double part covered by the open part of the white. *No. 33* is then curled a little on the edge and rolled back towards the stem. The calyx *No. 35* is then slipped on the stem and a little white powder rubbed on the sepals of light-green paper, which are curled over from the base of the flower. (1876)

Fig. 6. Diagrams.

Fig. 5. Diagrams.

Fig. 8. Diagrams.

Asters and Daisies

The *China aster*, daisy, and other flowers with what are called "button-centers" or "hearts" are made as follows: Take a cloth-covered button and glue over it some fine net or lace. The form should be rounded on the top. Coat this thickly with dough, and, when almost dry, cover it with yellow mustard seed or seed-beads, set thickly together. When these are dry and firm, paint it over with glue and dust with yellow powder. *No. 8, figure 4,* shows this heart.

Around this is placed the corolla made by drawing three circles, *No. 35, figure 8,* divided into quarters by horizontal and perpendicular lines. In each of these regular divisions draw a line dividing them in half and making three petals. Fill each small division, increasing in size towards the outer edge, where each one is separated into two points. *Nos. 29, 24,* and *21* give the three other sizes, and, if a full double flower is desired, continue to decrease them until a mere tuft of cut paper finishes the center.

Daisies, if the wild-field variety, are made with a similar center, and two circles of white petals cut from *24* and *21.* The double daisy is made like the double aster without any button center, and the petals are streaked and spotted with carmine. (1876)

Verbenas and Hibiscuses

The *Verbena* has five petals cut from thick white paper like *No. 4, figure 8,* with calyx from *No. 3* and the corolla cut in an entire circle, to save trouble. A heart is formed of a little tip of dough on the point of a short stem, colored with brown, yellow, black, red, etc., and surrounded by a number of threadlike stamens. A number of these are made and colored, then clustered into a head containing from twelve to thirty. They may be of any color desired, plain or with centers and edges of different colors. A change is also made by cutting each petal with a division in the center, thus forming two little scallops, and in others the ends of the petals are not so much pointed.

The scarlet *Hibiscus* is a large and imposing-looking flower. The petals cut of scarlet paper from *No. 8* are shaded into black at the center. The pistil, *No. 7,* is made of wire covered with wax and has a number of stamens made of thread and tipped with glue and powder closely covering it. The anthers on the end of the style (the slender part of the pistil) is of triangular form, made of wax colored yellow and dipped in a very little yellow powder. Finish with a calyx from *No. 11* and stem wound with light-green paper. (1876)

Passionflowers

Passionflowers are always beautiful and appear to possess a peculiar attraction, probably on account of the legend connected with the vine. On the night of Good Friday, according to ancient tradition, after Jesus's body was taken from the cross, where His blood was shed a vine sprang up and blossomed, which, upon being examined, proved to contain in its leaves and flowers all the principal features of the crucifixion. The pistil in the center with outstretched arms was a miniature of the cross itself; the five stamens represented the nails, spear and hammer; the ten petals, the ten faithful disciples who stood around the cross; the little upright fringe round the bottom of the pistil, sometimes red or purple in color, the crown of thorns with blood upon it; the fringe or rays, the halo of glory; the three-lobed leaf, the three Marys, united in heart in their love for their Savior; the tendril, those faithful of the multitude who clung to the vine to the last; and the calyx, with its three sepals supporting the flower, the Trinity. This beautiful idea, though only legendary, is nevertheless so full of sacred meaning that it has always accompanied this beautiful and curious flower and given it a certain importance which renders it valuable. A collection of wax or paper flowers is, therefore, never considered

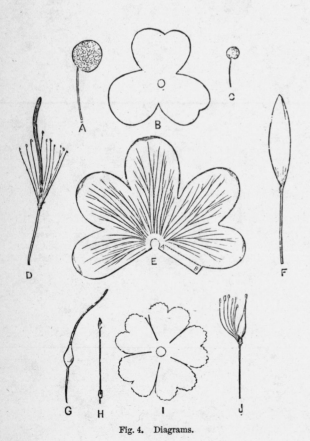

Fig. 4. Diagrams.

The Passion-Flower.

into a fine fringe almost to the center. The small green one curl up with a small knife into a tiny ruff and slip it on the stem and curl up over the yellow ovary. Then take the large circle and color it with bright purple paint ¼-inch on the edge, and a stripe rather broader midway between this and the center of the circle. Curl it slightly, and having cut a circular piece of thin cardboard a trifle smaller than it is, cover it with purple paper. Make a hole in the center sufficiently large to fit round the yellow ovary below the green fringe, and place the purple and white rays on it in such a manner that they curl gracefully over the edge

Then cut a tiny circle as large as the outer edge of *No. 21*, and ⅛-inch wide. Snip it into a tiny fringe and touch with purple paint. Glue the underside and fasten round the upper edge of the rays, where they rest on the cards.

Then cut the ten petals—or rather the five petals and five sepals of the calyx; for the calyx, or what is called the calyx in this flower, is rightly an involucrum. Cut five from *No. 14*, and also five of *No. 13*. They must be as large again as in the diagram and of thick white paper. Tint *No. 14* with very light lilac and *No. 13* with very light purple in which a little pink is rubbed, lining with green. Goffer and roll the center and edges of each one, and place them round the circle beneath the fringe, the smaller ones above and the large purple ones behind, and alternating with them. The calyx, or involucrum, is in three divisions, like *B, figure 4*; those for the buds are smaller and pointed. There are two of these calyxes cut from thick green paper and placed so that the sepals alternate.

The buds, *No. 12*, should be of three or four sizes, made like a rosebud, with foundation of cotton, covering with petals the size given in the diagram. The tendrils, like *No. 16*, are made of fine green silk-covered wire, wound round a knitting needle until it curls. (1876)

quite perfect without its being added. Here, then, it is described as plainly as possible.

Make a ball of dough as large as a filbert and place it on the end of a wire stem, the end turned over. On this fasten a short pistil, made round and thicker at the top than below. On this place anthers, made of three pieces of wire 1 inch in length with spade-shaped ends; color these purple and dot with yellow paint. After covering them with wax or tissue paper, have them arranged so that they stand equidistant about ½-inch apart and gracefully curled. Just beneath the base of these, and on the narrow part of the style of the pistil, the five stamens of white silk-covered wire with filaments of yellow wax or dough, covered with yellow powder, are fastened by pressing them into dough or wax, of which the pistil is formed.

Next color the ball on which the pistil and stem are fastened a deep yellow color, and cutting two circular pieces of the thick white and green paper, one from *No. 15, figure 8*, the other from *No. 21*, proceed to cut them

Camellias

The *Camellia* is perhaps the most perfect of paper flowers. It may be made in various shades of crimson, scarlet, and these combined with white. But the pure white are the most beautiful. Cut them from thick paper, like *No. 13, figure 6*, and goffer or roll them until well curled. Arrange these round a ball of dough, made flat on the top, using the smallest around the top and folding them one over the other. Over these arrange a set cut like *No. 14* and in the same manner as just described and with the rolled or goffered edges folded around the center.

Then cut and goffer all the rest, five of *No. 15*, ten of *No. 16*, and twelve of *No. 17*. Place these around the preceding, reversing the order and placing the hollow part downward, with the edges towards the stem.

Cut of thick light-green paper twelve each of *No. 3*. Put three around the base of the flower and the other three over and between them. (The patterns figured in all the diagrams are but one-half the real size to be cut.) (1876)

Fig. 9.

the natural color of the wild poppy. Laying them on the cushion, crimp each one around the edge a very little, rolling and pressing with the head of a molding pin. Then, having a natural center, color it green, with brown dots on the top. Putting a little stiff dough round the base, fasten it to a stem. Cut a number of stamens from black ducks' feathers and tie them in close little bunches and arrange around the base, fastening the petals around regularly. Wild grasses, barley, and wheat should accompany these poppies, and form, alone, an elegant winter ornament. (1876)

ESCHSCHOLTZIA MANDARIN.

Poppies

The *Poppy, 5, figure 8*, is handsome in paper, and requires but little skill. Make five petals from *figure 9*, of scarlet paper, unless other colors are desired, as this is

Campanulas and Other Bell-Shaped Flowers

As lilac-color flowers are always a pretty addition, here is described the method of making one or more of the campanulas. The *Canterbury Bell* of the garden is cut from lilac tissue paper, using *No. 1, figure 8*. (This diagram will answer for all bell-shaped flowers, such as hyacinths, lilies of the valley, harebell, abutilon, etc., by altering the size and shape of the margin of the bell.) *No. 1, figure 8*, is the size for the single hyacinths, with smaller sizes in the center, around two white-tipped stamens. Three times the size illustrated forms canterbury bells. Form the bell by joining the side piece, and the swelling portion of the lower part by neatly joining the edges of the five points. The points at the top are curled over, and the corolla is slipped on the wire stem which also forms a pistil, around which five stamens are clustered. A calyx with broad appendages finishes the lower part. These may be made of white or deep purple if desired.

The *Lily of the Valley* is cut one-fourth the size of diagram *No. 1, figure 8* from white paper. Each bell is fastened on one of the slender white stamens, and a

146

number is clustered on one stem, curled into a drooping form, with the larger ones below.

The dotted lines on the diagram show how to form larger or smaller bells, by ruling four horizontal parallel lines, and dividing these perpendicularly into five equal portions. Then make the points above and below, and a perfect pattern is formed. (1876)

Sprays of Flowers of Natural Woodland Materials

Nearly similar to the subject of paper flowers is that of making flowers of natural woodland materials. The two sprays here illustrated may be made of paper—or in a much more beautiful manner by the use of cones, nuts, etc., in addition.

The materials used are the cones of pine and larch trees, beechnuts and their hulls, acorns, etc., moss, fine and coarse flower wire, cardboard, tissue paper of a wood-brown color, amber varnish, a fine brush for painting, a small brush, and glue.

These flowers are not only suitable for trimming coarse straw hats, but also for decorating brackets, bookstands, mirrors, and picture frames, etc. For gathering the materials which the forest yields in greatest abundance, autumn is the most favorable season. The materials must be first cleansed from dust with a brush, then soaked in river water in order to make the hard crust soft enough for a needle or wire to be passed through. At times it is necessary to cut some of the scales into the proper shape for leaves. The various leaves, petals, etc., when completed, are varnished with amber varnish by means of a small paintbrush.

Spray of Roses. The inner heart of the rose consists of a dwarfed pine cone. This is surrounded by flat scales, cut from a large cone, turned outward, till the desired

size is attained. The two last rows of petals must be bent over towards the outside. Beechnuts pasted over with moss and dyed brown serve as rosebuds.

The little pansy is made thus: The two upper petals of larch-cone scales and the three lower of pine-cone scales. They are twisted together by means of their wire stems and finished off in the center by a little knot of fruit from a linden tree. The veins on the pansy petals are done with pen and ink.

The pretty bellflowers are made of acorns, cut in half, hollowed out, and cut into four round petals. Pretty branches may be made of beechnuts, three of which always pasted together and held fast by wire produce pretty buds. Leaves interspersed here and there complete the spray. The stems are wound about with brown tissue paper.

Spray of Dahlias. The flower petals for the dahlia are made of the scales of large pine cones. Five of the smallest scales, provided with wire stems and placed close around the capsule or cup of an acorn, constitute the center of the flower. This is surrounded by rows of scales, growing gradually larger in size, each folded together in cornucopia-like manner. The wire stems which are visible at the bottom are best covered by little branches of moss, dyed brown. The dahlia buds are made of cones of the dwarf pine, provided with wire stems and pasted over with moss.

The starflowers are made of large pine-cone scales cut in a pointed shape, sewed around a circle of cardboard, and finished off in the center by the lighter-colored head of an acorn. Pretty bellflowers can be made of the hulls of beechnuts, with stamens such as are yielded by the stork's bill (geranium). The leaves are made of scales, either plain or scalloped at the edges. The large, broad leaves, made from dried foliage of the beech, give an elegant appearance to the spray. Although not very durable, they are employed for the sake of the pretty effect they produce. The coat of amber varnish which is applied to the whole, makes them durable for some little time. (1876)

Hyacinths of Tissue Paper

The materials used are colored tissue paper, bond paper painted green, and florist's wire. Involuntarily the head bends down over the pretty hyacinths to inhale their fragrance, yet though this expectation meets with disappointment, the agreeable discovery that they are unfading flowers which will ornament a room all the year round affords ample recompense. The blue, pink,

Fig. 12. Hyacinths of Tissue-Paper.

yellow, purple and white tissue paper requisite for their construction may be procured in any good stationery store. In order to make speckled hyacinths, pencil and brush must be resorted to.

Figure 13 very clearly shows the simple manner in which each blossom is constructed. Cut strips of tissue paper 7⅕ inches long, some 1½ inches wide and some 2 inches wide. Then cut fringes to a depth of about ¾-inch along one side, after which curl them with scissors or knife. Then lightly roll the strip together, and pressing together at the bottom, give the calyx a shape as nearly that of the natural hyacinths as possible. The number of such blossoms for each flower varies from twelve to fifteen.

These blossoms are tied with stout cotton thread to a stem of florist's wire 8½ inches long, beginning with the smallest blossoms at the top and continuing downwards in transposed rows. The best model for doing this is a natural hyacinth. Care must be taken not to place the blossoms too close to each other, so that each one remains distinct from the other. When the last blossom has been affixed, fasten the thread and cover the stem

148

Fig. 13.

Fig. 14.

Fig. 15. Full Pink.

Full Pink. If tissue paper is chosen, the pink requires four circles of petals; but if, as in the illustration, the paper is a little thicker, then three circles will suffice. *Figure 17* represents such a circle spread out. *Figure 16* represents one folded eight times and is the size required for a natural-looking pink. Cut this folded part into small scallops and make a short incision at every second scallop, just as the illustration indicates. When spread apart, curl all the edges with the aid of scissors, taking care to curl them all one way.

with a strip of brown tissue paper. The leaves, made from the bond paper and six or seven of which enclose each flower, are cut in strips ⅘-inch wide and from 5½ to 7½ inches long. They are pinched along the middle and rounded off at the top. Three or four of the smaller ones are first affixed to the bottom of the flower, reaching to its top; then several of the longer ones which, as may be seen in the engraving, tower over the first. (1876)

Pinks and China Asters

The materials are carmine and pale-green paper without a gloss, bright green paper, figured pink and lilac tissue paper, and plain green tissue paper, and fine flower wire, etc.

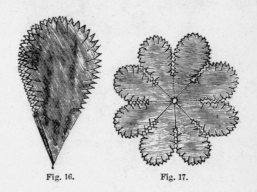

Fig. 16.   Fig. 17.

Fig. 18.   Fig. 19.

Full China Aster. Two circles of petals of figured tissue paper, each 1⅖ inches in diameter and two other circles, each ⅕-inch larger in diameter, serve to make the China aster which may be proportionably increased in size. Two circles of paper are folded double, cut into round scallops at the rounded side, then fringed as represented in *figure 21.* Spreading them open in the palm of the hand, the fringes are curled singly over a knitting needle.

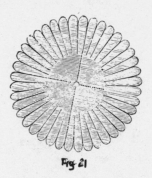

A piece of white tissue paper fringed to a depth of little more than an inch, curled and twisted round a wire stem, constitutes the stamens as illustrated in *figure 18.* Up this wire slip the circles of petals, then pass the flower between the thumb and forefinger of the left hand in order to make the petals fall close to each other. The calyx, whose edges are pasted over each other, is cut of green paper according to *figure 19.* Fill it with a little cotton, and then slip the flower stem through it. The bottom of the calyx is hidden beneath the strip of green tissue paper which is used to wind around the stem. The long pointed leaves of pale-green paper are folded along the center, passed over the scissors, and provided at the bottom with a short and thin wire stem covered with green paper. The buds are shaped of cotton and covered with a mixture of green wax and glue. Buds that have already opened are made of but one circle of petals and a calyx having but three points.

The center of the aster consists of a small ball of yellow worsted combed out and fastened to a wire stem. Around this the two smaller circles of petals are placed, and these are succeeded by the larger ones. The calyx consists of a circle of like petals ⅘-inch in diameter and made of green tissue paper. The bud consists of one circle of petals and a calyx formed of a scalloped strip of green tissue paper ⅕-wide. The leaves are to be bought ready-made, and the stems are all covered with green paper. (1876)

Fig. 20. Full China Aster.

Morning-Glories, Lilies of the Valley, and Starflowers

The materials used are tissue paper, fine white writing paper, wire, glue, yellow worsted, yellow farina or cornmeal, and stiff white thread. What follows are descriptions of some very pretty sprays of flowers suitable for the filling of vases. The manner of their construction is very simple. The requisite tools, scissors, pencil, etc., every lady has in her workbox. The shape of the leaves is soon imitated from the illustrations, and the veins are produced by ribbing them on the roller described in a subsequent page (see Fuchsias). They are each furnished with a fine wire stem pasted at the back. The tissue paper used in the manufacture of the flowers may be bought in any color, and even shaded. The latter is particularly suitable for tea roses,

150

pinks, morning-glories, etc., making them quite true to nature.

Morning-Glory. Cut a strip of lilac tissue paper 5⅕ inches long, 1⅗ inches wide, and paste it neatly together to form a ring. Gather one side around the wire stem provided with stamens made in the usual manner of fringed tissue paper. Arrange the gathers evenly, turning the upper side outward. Affix a calyx consisting of three green tissue-paper petals, each ⅕-inch long. Cover the stems with green paper, and the flower is completed. The tendrils are curled by winding them around a coarse knitting needle. They are of course also covered with green paper.

Lilies of the valley and Starflower. For the lilies, cut out of fine white writing paper various strips ⅕- to ⅖-inch wide and 1 to 1⅕ inches long; these scallop on one

of the long sides, and paste neatly together over round lead pencils of various sizes. When quite dry, slip each circle to the bottom of the pencil, the scalloped edge towards the top; when half slipped off, fold together at the bottom, turn the scallops outwards, then slip off entirely. In each flower insert stamens of stiff white thread, the ends glued and dipped into yellow farina or corn meal. The buds are formed of small balls of cotton, the size of a pinhead, covered with paper. From two to four such buds are affixed to the point of each branch.

The center of the starflower is composed either of short loops of yellow worsted cut open and combed out, or of flat balls of cotton glued and strewn with yellow farina or corn meal. This center is surrounded by circles of petals 1⅕ inches in diameter. These are cut of gold-colored tissue paper, scalloped all around and cut into

A GROUP OF BELL-FLOWERS.—*Drawn and Engraved for the American Agriculturist.*

151

Fig. 22. Morning-Glory.

Fig. 23. Lilies-of-the Valley and Star-Flowers.

fringes to the depth of ⅕-inch. These petals are carefully rubbed with the round point of scissors. One circle
of petals gathered in at the center and provided with a
calyx, consisting of several pointed green leaves, constitutes the bud. (1876)

Fuchsias

The materials used are purple-red and dark-purple
tissue paper, light and dark-green paper for the leaves,
brown tissue paper, fine wire, red thread, farina, small
green calyxes; wooden bodkin and roller, such as *figures 26* and *27* represent.

The construction of this pretty flower will amply
reward the maker for all trouble, as it resembles the
natural fuchsia to the life. The flowers may be made of
various colors, partly scarlet with white or purple
sepals, partly of light and dark pink. The latter are
made of red and white stout writing paper, and painted
on either side with a few strokes of the brush after a
natural model.

The scalloped shape of the outer flower-cover is
ribbed on the so-called "roller." *Figure 27* represents
this instrument, which is indispensable in the making
of flowers for the veining of leaves. It is of wood, 9⅗
inches long and 4⅘ inches in circumference at the

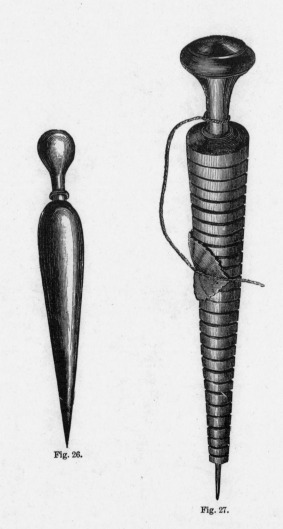

Fig. 26.

Fig. 27.

152

widest part. Deep and shallow incisions are cut close beside each other around the roller, a stout nail is attached to the lower, narrower end and a piece of silken cord tied to the handle. This, as well as the wooden bodkin, *figure 26,* for shaping the blossoms, can be purchased or can be constructed by any woodcarver.

The veins are formed by placing a leaf on one of the incisions and passing the silk thread up and down it, so as to form a deepening in it. The manner in which this is done is represented in *figure 27.* It is requisite to hold the point of the instrument against the edge of the table, and brace oneself against it so that it is held firmly in a horizontal position. The two petals, when rubbed, are placed around the bodkin, the edges glued and pasted together in the shape of a cornucopia, the points falling outward. A small opening must be left at the pointed end, so that a thread may afterwards be passed through it.

For the construction of the inner part of the flower, take a piece of red thread, wind it three or four times around three fingers; pass a thin wire within the loop thus formed and twist it tightly. Cut off all the ends, with the exception of one which must be left 2½ inches long, to a length of 1³/₅ inches. Moisten the ends with glue and dip them into fine farina. These stamens are surrounded by four small petals, rolled in the palm of the hand with the head of the bodkin, and lying partly over each other. They are tied on singly, the wire then cut off, but the thread left hanging. It is drawn by this thread into the cornet-shaped flower, in the manner illustrated in *figure 25.*

A small green-wax calyx is slipped over the bottom of the flower, and close beneath it a piece of fine wire about 5 inches long, fastened to the thread in such a manner that the fuchsia hangs loosely and gracefully. This stem is wound over neatly with brown tissue paper. Half-opened blossoms are constructed in like manner, the only difference being that the longest stamen is wanting, and the points of the petals fall inward and close to each other. The foliage is cut according to *figure 25,* smaller ones toward the ends of the branches. These leaves are all ribbed on the roller, and have fine wire stems attached along the backs. The easiest way to do this is to place each leaf on a board, the wrong side turned upwards, and firmly press the wire stem on it with a cloth. They must be allowed to become perfectly dry before being arranged into sprays. With a little taste and skill, flowers and leaves may be twined into a graceful bouquet. The main requisite is to have good materials to work upon. (1876)

Fig. 24. Fuchsia.

Fig. 25.

Fig. 28. Full Pinks.

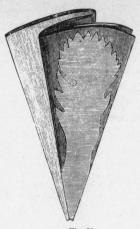

Fig. 31.

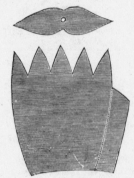

Fig. 32.

Full Pinks

The materials used are dark-red and yellow or white, speckled with red, tissue paper; green paper for the leaves; green stem-paper; flower wire, glue, etc.

Although the Pink is classed among the nobler flowers, and its full, beautiful form outshines many more modest flowers that grow beside it in our gardens, it may be very easily constructed of tissue paper. First cut the shapes of the leaves and petals out of cardboard after a natural model. Then, of the tissue paper selected for the pink, take a double strip 4 inches square, so that two circles of petals may be constructed at one and the same time. Fold them in the middle, then crosswise— which will again produce a square. Of this now cut the fourth part of a circle, and fold into three equal parts as indicated in *figure 31*. Then place on these the shape of cardboard; draw the outlines with a lead pencil. Then cut them out carefully, and snip off a small bit at the bottom, so that a small hole will remain in the center when the circle is spread out. In order to give these twelve-petaled circles the crumpled appearance peculiar to the petals of pinks, take the lower end of the circle before unfolding it in the first three fingers of the left

hand, twist it from the left to the right between a piece of soft muslin, then carefully unfold and smooth out the edges. In this way construct eight circles of petals for a large, four for a small, pink.

Figure 32 shows, full size, the shape in which the cup of the flower is cut of green paper. With the head of a hatpin roll the upper and lower edges in the palm of the hand, taking care, however, not to roll top and bottom on the same side. Then join the strips in such a manner that the points fall outward.

On a piece of not too fine wire, 8 inches long, tie a small piece of the feathers of a goose quill, which, when curled with knife or scissors, serves well as stamens. Cover the wire with a little cotton, and wind about with green tissue paper. On this stem slip on the circles of petals, having previously put a little glue on them so that they will stick to each other slightly. Shove them up closely together, and twist tightly at the bottom. Now slip on the cup or calyx, which is glued inside, and complete by adding a few green petals at the bottom cut of green paper, according to *figure 32*.

The leaves consist of a strip of green paper, ⅕-inch inside and 5 inches long, pointed at the ends, bent along the center, and curled here and there. They are affixed to the stem in bunches of two and three at intervals. In order to imitate the knots peculiar to the stems of these flowers, cover thickly with cotton at the requisite spots and attach the leaves, after which wind about with green tissue paper. However, as these flowers are mostly used for vases, it is unnecessary to waste time and trouble on what will scarcely be noticed. Buds and calyx as represented in *figures 33* and *29* are much more effective when made of wax than of paper, of which it is very difficult to construct them. (1876)

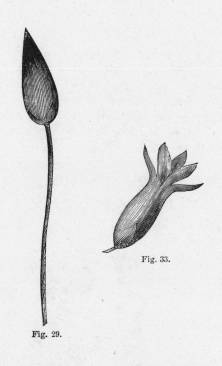

Fig. 33.

Fig. 29.

THE MOUNTAIN CLEMATIS—(*Clematis montana*).

SANVITALIA.

Feather Work

General Directions for Making Flowers

The wild and uneducated inhabitants of the Pacific isles form the most beautiful feather flowers that can be imagined. Roses, lilies, pinks, orange blossoms, and the other lovely and brilliant flowers of tropical countries are made of the most exquisite workmanship and appear as if some accomplished artist must have taught them how to form such wonders of grace, neatness, and exquisite combination of form and color.

But the art of forming flowers and leaves with feathers is also one of the most beautiful and satisfactory employments in which a civilized lady can engage. We

155

Fig. 1. Spray of Feather Leaves and Flowers.

In forming flowers, cut patterns from natural ones from the diagrams given elsewhere in this book for paper flowers. When cutting out the feathers, leave the stem of the feather at least half an inch longer than the petal of the flower. The feathers for this part of the work must be free from down, except a trifle on the shaft. After thus cutting, bend with the thumb and finger to the proper shape. Make the stem from 2 to 6 inches long; bend the end over and fasten on it a piece of cotton by tying thread round it and winding until of proper size. If a single flower is to be made, cover the cotton on the stem with velvet, yellow or green, and arrange round it the stamens. These may be made of various materials, as will be explained, or can be purchased at a crafts shop if preferred, as they are made in all sizes, colors, and varieties.

Having fixed the stamens and pistil, the next step is to arrange the petals. The petals having been arranged, cut the stems of the feathers even and fix on the calyx, which will be made of stiff green feathers cut into points, or green silk may be used. If desired, these also may be purchased by the dozen of all varieties, but better than either are those formed of wax, which may be molded round the flower and touched with umber or sienna according to the kind.

know of some persons who have been collecting feathers for many years, and to examine the beautiful and brilliant collection they have amassed is a most enjoyable occupation for a leisure hour. Many imagine that to form feather flowers they must purchase the ostrich, bird of paradise, and other elegant feathers sold in the stores. But this is not the case, and where a lady desires to form a collection of these airy beauties she should commence hoarding every feather she can lay fingers upon. Our common birds, every one of them, have feathers exactly suited for some parts of a group, and the pheasants, ducks, pigeons, doves, and other birds constantly brought to the cities for sale, or obtainable in the country, are all necessary in this work, so that the inability to purchase feathers should never deter anyone from attempting to learn this beautiful art.

"Fine feathers make fine birds," is a trite old saying, so also "fine feathers make fine flowers," and surely no more brilliant plumage can be desired than we can obtain from many of our barnyard fowls, game and singing birds, and many others scattered here and there wherever we go. Persons in the country are ever occupied in the delightful occupation of gathering flowers, but do you ever hear them speak of gathering feathers? Yet were they to watch closely as they walk through yard and field, many a choice treasure in this line could be obtained. Any one may obtain the best white swan or goose feathers, and if possible they should be plucked fresh from the bird with great care, and these are always required.

[Modern readers are advised to use contemporary "craft dough" in the directions that follow. Purists, however, will relish these 1876 recipes for "paste."— Ed.]

A paste for forming various parts, as hearts, calyx, buds, etc., is made thus: Take white starch and mix with gum arabic mucilage until as thick as syrup, then color as necessary with the dye-colors used for the feathers. The best paste for buds, etc., is made as follows: Mix common ground rice into a stiff paste with dye of proper color; dry it before the fire, and when quite hard reduce it to a fine powder. Into this powder dip the stamens, buds or berries, which are first formed of cotton-wool dipped in thick gum, forming them with the fingers. One or two coats must be given.

There are also necessary for this work stiff and curled feathers; tissue paper; assorted green papers for covering stems; covered and plain wire in three sizes (thin, thick, and extra thick), the first two covered; a little green and white wax or glue; and colors for dyeing the plain feathers.

Leaves are formed of green feathers of various shades, also brown and dun-colored, using the stiff kind from the wings and tail, some of which should be cut into shape and veined by imitating a natural leaf. Thus a cock's tail feather of pretty green is cut off at the end, shaped, notched, and fastened to a wire. The midrib is formed by the hard stiff part of the feather. A few veins and markings are made with a small camel's hair brush, and you have a very pretty leaf with little trouble.

The *colors* used for this work are generally the aniline [commercial coal-tar dyes—Ed.], though in some cases the old colors may be preferred. The old-fashioned colors may be had as follows:

Blue.—Mix equal parts of oil of vitriol and the finest indigo powder. Allow it to stand twenty-four hours, and when required for use shake well and put a tablespoonful into a quart of boiling water. Immerse the feathers and let them boil slowly for ten minutes; shake out gently and dry.

Pink.—Pink saucers [a pink tint used for rouging the cheeks and readily available in nineteenth-century drugstores.—Ed.] are best for feather-dyeing. Put three of them into a quart of boiling water, and add a little cream of tartar upon the point of a knife. If rose color of a deep shade is desired allow four saucers. Allow the feathers to remain in the dye for half a day.

Yellow.—Put a tablespoonful of superfine turmeric into a quart of boiling water, and place the feathers in this for one hour. Use more or less turmeric according to the shade desired.

Orange.—Add a little bicarbonate of soda to the yellow dye.

Scarlet.—Take one teaspoonful prepared cochineal and then add a teaspoonful of cream of tartar and a few drops of muriate of tin. This dye is expensive, and the fine aniline colors are really superior to it.

Purple and Lilac.—Take a quart of boiling water into which stir two teaspoonfuls of cudbear for the lilac. For the purple add another teaspoonful of the powder and a little cream of tartar.

Making Individual Flowers

Roses are formed by making a ball upon the end of a stiff wire stem. Around this fasten four small feather tips of a deep rose color, six around these rather lighter, six still lighter outside of these, winding with fine wire. Outside of this heart arrange loops of curled feathers of a light pink. Below this make a calyx of small pieces of green feathers fastened on with a little ball of green wax, curling the sepals with a knife, etc.

Asters are made of various colored feathers, first forming a heart of small yellow strands of feathers upon a little ball of green wax and arranging fine tiny feathers as petals.

Daisies are made of soft white feathers of very small size. A flat button is placed on a stem and covered with

VIRGIN'S BOWER—(*Clematis Virginiana.*)

glue upon which yellow feathers, chipped fine, are fastened, thus forming the yellow heart. Around this the little white feathers are placed, one row below the other, until three rows are formed, using glue to secure them.

Camellias are formed of stiff snow-white feathers, using the tips and cutting them carefully by the same pattern as used for wax flowers. The leaves here must be of a rich dark green.

Sprays of *orange blossoms* are beautiful made of feathers. Make the buds of fine white starch and thick gum arabic mucilage. Place a leaf at the junction of each flower or bud and stem, larger and deeper colored ones below, and small light-colored ones at the point.

In this work so much depends upon the taste and judgment of the operator that it is almost impossible to give explicit directions for each flower. Everything depends upon the feathers that can be made available and the proper coloring. Certain feathers may be dyed, but many must be formed of white feathers and afterwards tinted with moist colors. Pinks and other striped and blazed flowers are thus colored. (1876)

TROPÆOLUM LOBBIANUM.

FORSYTHIA VIRIDISSIMA.

A Sweet Jar

The following combination of sweet odors will be pronounced the perfection of fragrance and will retain this property for twenty years at least.

When the rose season is at its height, gather from day to day the very finest of rose petals, the common old sweet-scented annual varieties being the most odoriferous of any, especially the hundred-leaf, as it is called. The weather should be dry and sunny, and they should be gathered in the morning as soon as the dew has dried off. Pick the petals from the stalks and calyx, and do not use any that appear decayed. When four quarts have been collected, take a porcelain bowl and over the bottom of it strew a layer of fine table salt. Then add a couple of handfuls of petals. Again, add salt, then petals, continuing this process until the petals are all used. Cover the top with a layer of salt, and press the mass down gently with a plate that fits within the bowl. Allow them to remain thus for one week, stirring, turning, and mixing them each day. They must be separated and exposed to the air during the process. When the entire mass appears moist, and water appears drawn from the petals, add three ounces of allspice grated into coarse powder; this forms the stock. Turn the mass thoroughly for three more days, adding each day a quarter of an ounce of allspice and the same of ground cinnamon.

Then put the mass into an ornamental jar in which it is to be kept, adding the following ingredients: One ounce coarsely-powdered cloves, one ounce cinnamon, one ounce nutmeg, one ounce mace, one ounce allspice, one ounce orange and lemon peel, ¼-ounce black pepper, one ounce anise seed and sliced root, 6 grains musk, ¼-ounce of oil rose geranium, lavender, rosemary, or any essential oil preferred. At any time when the mass appears dry, moisten with rose, orange-flower, Florida or lavender water.

The following flowers can be added as they come into bloom or can be procured: violets (picked from the stems), orange blossoms, myrtle leaves, pinks, jessamine, honeysuckle, mignonette, heliotrope, and lemon verbena. These may be added yearly as the flowers come into bloom, as well as rose petals, prepared as at first, and mixed through annually.

The jar must be frequently stirred and shaken, and various perfumes may be put in as obtained. Add also three ounces of orrisroot [iris roots—Ed.] in thin slices. Keep the mixture tightly closed for a month after the final mixing. Then open whenever the perfume is desired and it will permeate through the apartment or through the entire house in a very short time, filling it with a delicious, fresh, spicy odor like the perfume from a thousand flowers. Never allow the mixture to freeze nor to become very dry, and always moisten with some one of the fragrant waters or extracts as preferred. (1876)

How to Make Geraniums, Sweet Peas & Wild Roses

Large clusters of scarlet geraniums arranged on long, stiff stems like those that support the natural flowers are especially striking when used to adorn a lampshade. No particular color is advised for these blossoms because one person may fancy a very vivid tone, while another may deem a light-scarlet tint most appropriate. Having chosen French tissue paper in the admired hue for the geraniums, cut pieces the shape and size of the diagrams shown at *figure 177*, and with a scissors blade or dull knife cut the petals in the manner depicted at *figure 178*, until the effect displayed at *figure 179* is obtained.

FIGURE No. 177.

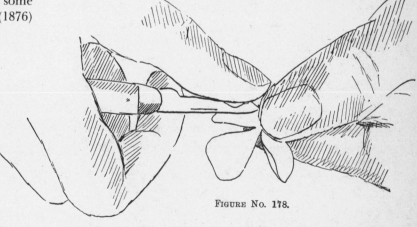

FIGURE No. 178.

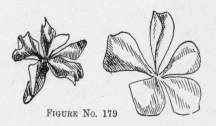

FIGURE No. 179

GERANIUM, LADY PLYMOUTH.

159

Fasten the pieces together with 1½ inches of fine wire, the point of which is covered as shown at *figure 180*. The wire forms the stem and must be wound with a section of dark-green tissue paper cut after *figure 181* and painted with red-brown watercolor below the dotted lines. The tips of the petals may be very delicately tinted with a little India-purple or carmine, or may be left the color of the paper, as preferred. *Figure 179A* depicts the completed flower.

FIGURE No. 182.

FIGURE No. 179 A.

FIGURE No. 182 A.

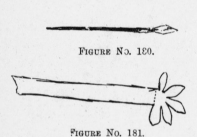

FIGURE No. 180.

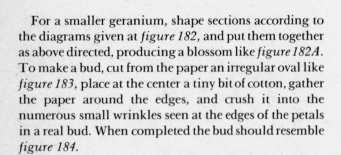

FIGURE No. 181.

FIGURE No. 183.

For a smaller geranium, shape sections according to the diagrams given at *figure 182,* and put them together as above directed, producing a blossom like *figure 182A*. To make a bud, cut from the paper an irregular oval like *figure 183*, place at the center a tiny bit of cotton, gather the paper around the edges, and crush it into the numerous small wrinkles seen at the edges of the petals in a real bud. When completed the bud should resemble *figure 184.*

In putting the flowers and buds together to form a bunch, closely follow nature's own arrangement. Place the larger blossoms at the center and the smaller ones outside, and let the buds, which should be made in two or three sizes, curl gracefully downward about the large stem, as clearly shown at *figure 185*. The large stem should be at least ³⁄₁₆-inch in diameter.

FIGURE No. 184.

FIGURE NO. 185.

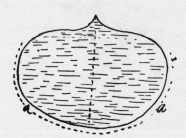

FIGURE NO. 187.

To make sweet peas, which are massed together in stiff bunches, first cut petals like *figure 188B* from French tissue paper, and like *figures 188A* and *188C* from crêpe paper, and shape them with a small knife blade to appear as at *figure 189*. Put them together in the manner illustrated at *figure 190*, and finish with a stem shaped like *figure 191*.

The leaves must be made of crêpe paper. Cut a strip 2½ inches long and 1½ inches wide, and gather one edge and stretch the other, so that, when the gathering string is tightly drawn, the paper can be laid flatly upon the table or workboard. Make a pattern exactly like *figure 186*, place it upon the crêpe paper, and shape the latter by it very carefully. Then with a camel's-hair brush and some chrome green slightly darkened with black or sepia, imitate the shadings and veinings on a natural leaf, as at *figure 187;* and finish the leaf with a stem as directed for the flowers. Vary the leaves slightly in size if many are used and arrange them prettily and naturally.

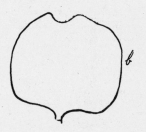

FIGURE NO. 188 A

FIGURE NO. 186.

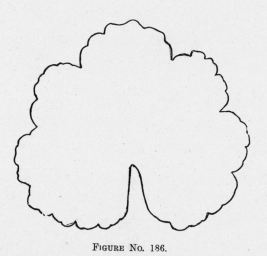

FIGURE NO. 188 B

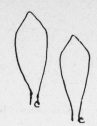

FIGURE No. 188 CC.

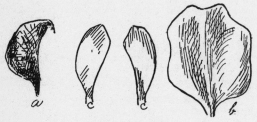

FIGURE No. 189.

FIGURE No. 190.

Sweet peas usually grow in small clusters, and three or four of the artificial blossoms may be easily wound into a single large stem, as displayed at *figure 192*. As the leaves of the sweet peas have not much character, it will be found advisable to use the flowers and stems as a bunch decoration. The large petal is nearly always of a darker shade of pink, red, or purple than the small inner ones, and this effect may be attained by choosing paper in the proper tints or by painting with watercolors. Equally pretty flowers may be made wholly of crêpe paper that has its crinkles smoothed out.

Wild roses are among the most admired flowers for decorative purposes, and can be made of crêpe or French tissue paper, although the former is to be preferred. The most natural effect may be produced by procuring a branch of a rose bush, stripping off its leaves after they have become dry and shrivelled, and then adding paper wild roses made according to the accompanying illustrations. (1895)

FIGURE No. 192.

FIGURE No. 191.

FIGURE No. 193 A.

How to Make Snowballs (Flowers)

To obtain a natural-looking snowball, such as is shown at *figure 241*, proceed as follows: Take a piece of white tissue paper 4 inches square. Fold it four times and cut as shown by *figure 243*. Then unfold the paper as shown by *figure 242* and cut in halfway to the center, as indicated by the dark lines. Next take a fine brush, dip it in gold paint and dot the center of each flower. When dry, twist the flower a little. Use five such sections of

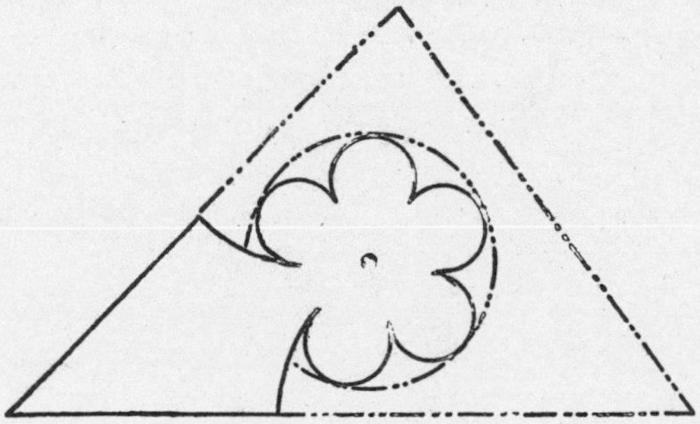

FIGURE No. 243.

FIGURE No. 242.

FIGURE No. 241.

FIGURE NO. 244.

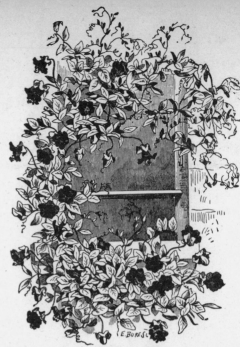

COBÆA SCANDENS.

Nile green and ten of white, placing one over the other, with the five green ones on the bottom. Draw a needle with coarse thread through the center of them, tie the thread tightly and sew on the stem, which is made of coarse cord wrapped with dark-green tissue paper.

The leaves, which are cut as shown by *figure 244*, are of dark-green paper. Fold each over a hatpin to crease the center. After fastening each snowball on the end of a stem, arrange them as you like, tie them together, and fasten the leaves on with a little glue. (1895)

MYOSOTIS DISSITIFLORA.

GERANIUM, "HAPPY THOUGHT."

164

VII. Miscellany

A Jelly Bag

The brilliancy of jellies is secured by careful filtering through a flannel bag. The old chemists, under the name of Hippocrates' sleeve, made use of the same thing that we call a jelly bag. It is a conical bag of stout flannel, shaped as in the figure, stretched upon a hoop. One 14 inches deep, and 7 inches across the mouth, is a convenient size for ordinary use. The seam should be double stitched to make sure that no liquid will pass through it. As the bag requires to be washed, it ought not to be permanently attached to the hoop. A broad hem may be made at the top into which a wire hoop may be inserted, or the mouth of the bag can be finished by sewing a cord to it to make a strong edge. It can then be easily sewed to a hoop each time it is used.

In straining jellies which solidify when cold, the bag should be hung near the fire. The first portion which runs through will be turbid, and should be poured back into the bag. (1870)

A Home-made Toast Holder.

A Homemade Toast Holder

This simple contrivance will be found a very convenient article, particularly for those who use coal wood fires and are often troubled to toast a slice of bread quickly by holding it near the coals. If the bread is laid upon a support on the top of the stove, it dries hard before the surface is browned, impairing the sweetness, and requiring either very good teeth to masticate it, or to be moistened by hot water or milk. Or if a common fork be used, the fingers are burned, and the forks heated and loosened in the handle.

To make the "holder," take two pieces of common wire about the size of coarse knitting needles, each 3 to 3½ feet long. Twist them together within about 5 inches of each end, bend the twisted part double, to bring the ends together, and then form the arms or supports as shown in the engraving. They can easily be sprung apart to receive a slice of bread, which can then be conveniently held in any desired position, without burning the fingers. A ring may be added to the end, by which to hang up the apparatus when not in use. It is an unpatented article and is free to all. (1863)

How to Make Hard Soap

Take 3 lbs. of unslaked lime, and 6 lbs. of soda, and put in 5 gallons of water. When they are dissolved, pour off the water from the top, (throwing the sediment away), and add to it 6 lbs. of fat. Boil till thick, pour in a tub, and when cold, cut in bars and dry. It is injured by freezing before drying. (1863)

How to Make Soft Soap

Take 5 lbs. potash, 5 lbs. grease, and 16 gallons of water. Break the potash in pieces the size of walnuts—if large, it will not dissolve so quickly. Put it in a clean tight barrel, melt the grease, and pour it in. Any grease will answer, as skimmings, old lard, etc. Have the water hot, and pour half of it immediately into the barrel, stirring it until the potash is dissolved, which will require from twenty to thirty minutes. Then add the rest of the water, stir again until thoroughly mixed, and afterward occasionally for three or four days.

This will make about a half barrel of white soap, hard enough to cut with a knife. Should the potash be very strong, it sometimes requires more water, which may be known by small crumbling pieces remaining in the lye at the end of four or five days. In breaking the potash, be careful to prevent it from adhering to the clothing, as it would soon spoil the texture. (1863)

A Fruit Drying Frame

The extreme simplicity and ingenuity of this drying frame puts it within the reach of every housekeeper. Secure from the carpenter (or build it yourself) a

DRYING FRAME.

wooden frame, made light, but strong, and about 5 feet square. Also a small ball of white, but strong twine. Cut a quantity into lengths of 7 feet, and to one end of each fasten a tack, which is hammered firmly on one side of the frame. About an inch and a half from this another string is secured in the same way, and exactly opposite to each tack a shingle-nail is driven firmly into the frame.

When stringing apples or peaches for the purpose of drying, use a darning-needle, threading the loose end of the string, and when a sufficient quantity is threaded, take off the needle and wind the string around the shingle-nail opposite. As the fruit dries it may be slipped along the thread and more added until the frame is full of dried fruit. This is a very convenient frame as it may be taken in at night or during a rain storm without disturbing the fruit, and may also be adjusted over the kitchen stove and used for drying apples during the winter months. (1868)

A Chimney Sweeper

Here is a sketch of a device for removing soot from a chimney. It consists of a bundle of flax straw large enough to fill the flue, to which a rope is attached in its middle, each half being long enough to reach through the chimney. If the rope cannot be dropped readily from the top, attach a weight of some kind to it to carry one end of the rope through the chimney.

The sweeper is operated by two persons, one at the top and the other at the bottom, one pulling up and the other down. The illustration herewith given shows the arrangement of the flax, weight, and the rope. (1882)

Mending Broken China, Etc.

In the first place, take excellent care of the pieces of any broken dish or vase. Do not handle the broken edges, or allow them to become dusty or greasy, but lay them carefully away, and do the mending as soon as possible after the breaking. The best cements often fail because the parts united by them are not clean.

Another general rule for all kinds of cement or glue is this: Make the layer of cement between the parts as thin as it can possibly be, and yet entirely cover the edges. A very thin layer is much stronger than a thick one. Where the shape of the pieces will allow, rub the edges together after each has been smeared with the cement, so as to even and work it well together. Press very closely, and keep up this pressure (usually by tying the parts together) until the cement is dry.

An old and well-tried way of mending broken glass and crockery still remains in excellent favor, and is well worth trying by housekeepers who can get plenty of skimmed milk. Dishes badly cracked should be set away until they can be boiled in skimmed milk. Those broken apart should be tied firmly together, and boiled gently in carefully skimmed milk for an hour or so. Leave them tied together for several days before using, and they will be found almost as good as new. The milk should be cold when the dishes are put in to boil.

Broken crockery is sometimes mended with white paint. Dishes so mended should be left to dry for several months before being brought into service.

A better cement is made of white lead and copal varnish mixed to the consistency of cream. Apply this carefully to each edge of the broken dish, work it together and press closely, tie it strongly together, and lay it away to dry for several weeks. This cement is said to bear hot water better than any other. It is cheap and very strong.

A great deal may be saved by attention to these little matters. And yet your own time may be worth so much that you really can better afford to buy new things than to tinker up old ones. Each of us ought to be on such a pleasant human-family footing with our neighbors that all the odds and ends may go to the right place and be *saved by somebody*. Common beggars would not care for your broken things, but some careful grandpa or half-invalid might delight to mend them up for use in another home than yours.

In addition to the hints above given, one should add that cements formed largely of isinglass or other forms of gelatine often fail upon common crockery on account of the porosity of the material, while they cement glass and true chinaware well enough. When these cements are used upon the ordinary whiteware or stoneware, the surfaces should have a thin coat of cement, which is to be allowed to dry; then warm the pieces, and give each another thin coat, and put them together. Vessels cemented by means of white paint or white lead should be kept to contain dry and inedible articles exclusively. Preserves and other foodstuffs ought not to stand in them. (1873)

Husk Mattresses—Cheap, Comfortable, and Healthful

Rural friends are very hospitable. When visited they treat city folk during the day with the greatest kindness, but they are often cruel at night, and most always consign them to a feather bed in the smothering depressions of which a sleepless night is passed. That a feather bed is a fit thing to sleep upon is an idea rapidly disappearing; yet in many communities feathers still prevail, and they are looked upon as silk dresses are, in some measure an index of the wealth, or competence of the owner. It is quite time that all this was changed, and comfort and health consulted, rather than show. Yes, comfort—no one after having slept for a few weeks on a hard bed would willingly return to feathers.

Curled hair makes the very best mattress, but it is expensive. The next best thing is corn husks, a cheap material, and accessible to all. The inner husks, or shucks, as they are called in some places, allowed to curl up a little, are often used without any preparation. A softer bed is made by slitting the husks in strips, half an inch or so·in width. A fork may be used to facilitate stripping. The best husk beds are made from the husks of green corn that has been shredded by drawing through a flax hatchel.

Husk beds should be opened about once in six months, the husks shaken free from fine particles and dust. The husks are then sprinkled with water and allowed to lay in the sun for awhile. Treated in this way the husks will be almost as good as new. This timely hint is given in order that, at husking time, those who would enjoy the luxury of a husk bed may take measures to secure the necessary material. (1866)

Straw Beds

Most people who use feather beds in winter put them away in the summer and sleep on straw beds. These should be very full, and they will not be found hard or

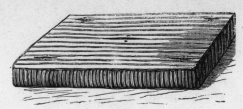

Fig. 1.—STRAW BED.

uncomfortable by any except the sick or aged, and usually not even by them. Our grandmothers, who wove their own linen-ticking, used to call nine yards of three-fourths-yard-wide linen a bed tick pattern, but the modern bed requires cloth a little wider. Good striped ticking is best.

The best form is box-shaped (*figure 1*), with four small holes near the corners, in the upper side, and one longer one in the middle. This admits of adjusting the straw all over the bed more easily than in case of a single slit. Each one may be fastened by a single strap under one side and a button, or by narrow tapes.

For a comfortable bed oat straw is the best. It is more soft than wheat or rye straw. To make it lie evenly, do not be contented to pull the straw up light and simple, but pull it from the higher parts into the lower ones, until the bed is of even thickness in different parts. It is aggravating to find the same hollows in the same spots night after night. Never fill them up by stuffing pillows or other articles under the mattress or under the lower spots in the bed, as some bedmakers do. There is no trouble in making an even bed, if care is taken in stirring it. A mattress, or a comforter, or at least a bedquilt, should lie between the straw bed and the sheet.

Husks are preferred to straw by many; they are cleaner and more durable. But nervous people are sometimes much annoyed by the rustling of the husks. (1872)

A Homemade Tent

It is easy to make a tent which, if not as pleasing in outline as those for sale in the stores, casts quite as graceful a shadow, and is fully as comfortable.

The first thing needed is a light but firm frame put up in a substantial manner. The cover is made of canvas awning cloth, and is just large enough to fit easily over the frame. The top is in one piece, and to it are sewed the

A CHEAP LAWN TENT.

Foot Scrapers or Boot Cleaners

Some people (men in particular) do not pay due attention to the removal of dirt from their boots and shoes and often walk into a kitchen or sitting room, upon a clean floor or carpet, with much mud and dirt adhering to their footgear. This may be prevented by placing a foot scraper or cleaner near the door, and in laying walks between the house and the barn, and other outbuildings.

To aid those who desire to make boot cleaners, here are several, and of sufficient variety, so that there need be no excuse for an absence of this necessary article near the door. Any of the forms shown may be attached to the step at the door, or secured to a piece of board 1 inch thick, 1 foot wide, and about 2 feet in length.

side pieces and those for the ends, cut in scallops around the lower edge and bound with woolen braid of a color to correspond with that of the stripe in the cloth. The pieces must all be sewed together very firmly, and the seams bound on the wrong side. Cords are attached to each corner of the cover, by which it is tied to the frame.

If the tent is to stand in a very exposed situation where there is an entire absence of shade, an extra curtain will be desirable. This should be supplied with rings and hung on the side needing the protection from the sun. It should be as wide as the tent and long enought to reach the ground. Two frames may be put up—one on that part of the lawn which is most pleasant in the morning and the other in a favorite after-dinner gathering place. If the frames are of the same size, one cover will do for both. In this way, two tents can be made with but little more trouble and expense than one. (1883)

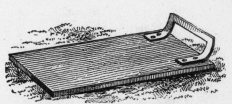

Fig. 1.—A FOOT SCRAPER.

Fig. 2.   Fig. 3.

The scrapers shown in *figures 1*, and *2*, are of iron, and attached by screws to the bottom piece. An ironworker can bend an old piece of iron into the form desired.

Figure 3 shows a piece of hardwood, 1 foot in length, 4 inches wide, and nearly 1 inch thick, with one edge made quite sharp, the whole being nailed firmly to the end of a piece of board.

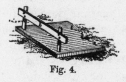

Fig. 4.

How a Footscraper Is Made

Improvise a scraper in this manner: Hunt up an old broken spade and the head of a worn-out broom. By picking out a little of the mortar between the bricks of the house-wall, fix the cutting end of the spade firmly in. Then drive a short piece of timber a foot into the ground, and fasten the broken handle into the top of it with a nail. Then with two strong nails the old broom head is fixed to the wall, just above the spade, and now you have a better farmer's scraper at your door than any costly apparatus you have ever seen.

As all do not live in brick houses, two strips of wood, nailed perpendicularly to the house, and just far enough apart to hold the edge of the spade, will answer the same good purpose. (1882)

The plan shown in *figure 4* consists of two wooden pins 1 inch in diameter firmly secured in holes made in the bottom board near one end, 3 inches from which is a bar, *b*, either of hardwood or of iron, fastened upon the pins. This form has some advantages, as the tops of the pins, if made flat and sharp, will aid in cleaning the sides of boots.

A mat should be provided, and in absence of anything better, a piece of old carpet will serve a most excellent purpose. The housekeeper may need occasionally to refer the careless members of the family to the foot scraper and mat. (1882)

A Shoe-Blacking Stand

Well-blacked shoes are a necessity, but the operation of blacking them is irksome, and the apparatus used is a nuisance in the eyes of the housekeeper. Hence the blacking and brushes are banished to some out-of-the-way place, to which the one who would use them must follow them. Stores sell neat blacking stands made like the one shown in the engraving. They are made of

SHOE-BLACKING STAND.

black walnut, and when closed no one would suspect their use. Upon lifting the lid a place is found for the brushes, one for the blacking, and a stand upon which to rest the foot while performing the polishing. Probably the majority of people do not find it necessary to black the boots in the house, but a stand of this kind, even roughly made, would be found a great convenience in the shed or other place devoted to this part of the toilet. It would keep the brushes and blacking together, and free from dust, and prove a comfort in affording a footrest of the proper height. A person trying to black his boots with his foot in an inconveniently elevated position, shows himself in an attitude, the awkwardness of which is as amusing to others as it is uncomfortable to himself. (1870)

TIGHTENING THE STEMS.

How to Make Your Own Brooms

Every man or boy with a little skill and a few simple tools can make a broom. The apparatus here shown consists of a rope, long enough to reach from a rafter, *figure 1*, to a stout board, about 6 feet long, near the floor. This rope should be strong enough to bear the weight of a heavy man. A half or ¾ inch rope will be sufficient, and a coating of hard soap will make it work easier.

CLAMP FOR BRUSH.

A clamp, *figure 2*, consists of two pieces of hardwood (white oak is best), each 2½ feet long, 2 inches thick, and 4 inches wide, with a ¾-inch bolt, 8 inches long, *a*, through the center of the wooden pieces. Two hardwood pegs, 8 inches long, fit ⅜-inch holes at *b, b*, these holes being from 6 to 8 inches from the bolt to regulate the width of the brooms while in the clamp. A wrench turns the nut at *a*.

The needle is 8 inches long, with a flattened point, and an eye large enough to admit large twine. These, with a strong knife, a mallet, a few small nails, broom handles and the necessary twine, complete the outfit.

A sufficient quantity of the broom corn for a broom, about one pound and a quarter, should be tied into a bundle—the small and crooked in the middle, the fine and straight outside make the brush ends as even as possible. If kept in a cellar or other damp place over night, it will work more readily.

Make a turn in the rope as in *figure 3*, and in this place the bundle of broom corn. Be sure the rope passes around at the point you wish to tie with the twine. Several inches of stem may be between this and the brush, particularly in short corn, as so much may thus be gained in the length of the broom. By putting the person's weight upon the board, the rope will compress the bundle. Rapidly rotate the bundle, repeating the pressure, and compress the mass into the size required. Have the twine ready.

The wooden pegs can be adjusted to the size of the broom—wider, of course, for the seam nearest the brush end. By turning the burr, *a*, sufficient pressure will be given to produce the desired flattening. A loop of twine is passed around the brush at *c*, and the free end, a yard or more long, by means of the needle, is used for sewing. The manner of passing the twine back and forth is shown in *figure 5*, *a* to *b*. The twine is taken once around the loop at *b*, and then passed, by means of the needle, from *b* to *c*, where it is cut close, this being sufficient to secure the end. The bundle may be put into the clamp and sewed before it is broken with the rope, as in *figure 1*, or tied with twine, as in *figure 4*.

After being tied and sewed, the broom is ready for a handle which should have an evenly tapering point about 4 inches long. If the handle is pointed straight and inserted into the center of the cut ends of the stems, there will be no trouble in driving it in properly. Keep the broom off the ground, and use a mallet or hatchet to strike the end of the handle. The point of the handle should extend past the upper sewing. Drive a nail through the twine into the handle at *g*, *figure 4*. One at the opposite side may be necessary. Trim the stems neatly within half an inch of the twine that binds them securely. Cut the brush end evenly and a cheap and durable broom is ready for use. (1883)

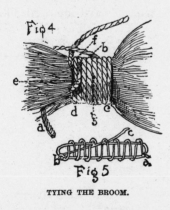

TYING THE BROOM.

Brooms

A cleanly horse or cow stable is very desirable, and will be appreciated, especially by the women folks, who often are troubled to find a clean spot whereon to place their milking stool, to say nothing of their spreading robes. If cleanliness is next to godliness, in the house or person, very surely it is equally so in the stable or barnyard. Many highly improper feelings and expres-

Make a small loop at one end, and a large one about 4 feet from the end, to be held by the feet. Place the small loop around a stem, *a*, *figure 4*, and pass it between the ends of the stems to the opposite side of the bundle, *b*. With the thumb, hold the twine at *b*, pass around to *c*, and over the first twine, *b*, at every turn, until you have completed eight or ten turns. Cut the twine, leaving 6 or 8 inches which you pass around the last turn of twine, as at *e*. The twine may be cut here; but if it is carried by means of the needle through the bundle, passing between the last two turns of twine, as at *f*, and out at *a*, on the other side, it will be more secure. Two bundles thus tied can be placed in the clamp, *figure 2*, to be sewed.

Fig. 1.—STABLE BROOM.

173

sions arise through contact with dirt or filth in places where it ought not to be. The want of brooms, or scrapers, is made an excuse for dirt lying about where it is not wanted, and this excuse is valid to a great extent, as a stable-broom, fit to use, is rarely seen.

Fig. 2.—BOX FOR MAKING BROOMS.

The broom represented in *figure 1*, is made of twigs, birch being the best, as it is long and straight. Any stiff woodland brush, however, will answer. Cut the twigs of a proper length—30 inches will make a good broom. Lay them in a box, made like that shown in *figure 2*. Draw them tightly together with the binders (*figure 3*), which are stout sticks placed through eyes at the end of a short rope, wound once around the bundle. When pressed apart, they draw the twigs together with great force. Tie two pieces of cord (which should have been already laid across the box in the slots) around the broom. Then it may be taken out and well bound with several rounds of strong twine.

For a handle take a stick long and stout enough, sharpen the point, and drive it into the center of the broom, until it has a good hold. The broom is then ready for use. It is hardly necessary to say that this is not a lady's broom; and yet we have seen a lady handle one with vigor, rather than not have a clean place to milk in. (1871)

Holder for Brooms

Every housekeeper knows that it is ruin to a good broom to stand it on the floor, brush-end down, and that it is equally hard on the wall to stand the broom so that the brush, fresh from contact with the dusty floor, is leaned against it. But even if the broom is provided with a string at the top of the handle, the servant is usually in too great a hurry, or too careless to hang it up, and prefers to stand it up against the wall in such a way that it is ready to tumble down at the least jar. A holder like the one illustrated in *figures 1* and *2*, will therefore be found a very useful little contrivance.

To make one, cut a small piece of board into the shape given in *figure 2*, and fasten it to the wall by two screws through the back. It is quite as easy to place the broom in the holder as to stand it on the floor, and a few

Fig. 1

Fig. 2

A BROOM HOLDER.

such holders, placed in the kitchen, on the back porch, and in other places through the house where brooms are kept, will be found very convenient. If space will admit, it is desirable to have a small closet opening out of the hall, where all the brooms, dust brushes, pans and suters used in sweeping and cleaning the front rooms of the house can be kept, and a similar closet opening from the upper hall, where everything needed for the upper floor has its place. It is much more convenient than to carry the broom, pan, and brush from a kitchen closet every time they are needed. (1883)

A Straw-Mosaic Box

Figure 2 represents the manner of covering a box with a mosaic of colored straw. The straws are first dyed of various bright hues, then carefully split and pressed flat. A plain wooden box may be marked with any patterns to please the fancy; the straws are then cut of suitable lengths and gummed on. This is very neat work for young people on winter evenings. (1867)

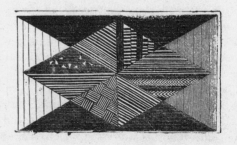

An Aquarium

A properly managed aquarium is not only a pleasing household ornament, but it is capable of affording no small amount of instruction. The aquarium is a vessel of water containing plants and animals, and is in fact a miniature lake. A globe or other vessel containing fish, the water in which is daily changed, is not an aquarium proper. In the aquarium there is plant life as well as animal life, and the main condition of success consists in keeping the plants and animals properly balanced. The plants as they grow in the water give off oxygen, a proper amount of which is necessary to the life of the fish or other animals that may be there. Reciprocally the fish, etc., give off carbon dioxide, which is needed for the growth of plants. Too many plants are objectionable, as they diminish the room needed by the fish; but an overstocking with fish will soon prove fatal.

The first thing to be considered is the vessel, or tank, as it is generally called. A pleasing aquarium may be made by using a large glass jar, holding a gallon or more. Such jars as confectionary is kept in (*figure 1*) answer well, and they are to be preferred without bands or hoops. Large glass covers, such as are used by confectioners to cover up cake, make a good tank. They have to be supported in an inverted position by means of a base, which has a hole for the reception of the knob upon the glass as in *figure 2*. Vessels with curved surfaces have the objection that they distort the objects within when viewed through the sides. Regular tanks

INTERIOR OF A SALT WATER AQUARIUM

175

Fig. 1.—JAR.

Fig. 2.—GLASS COVER.

Fig. 3.—SQUARE TANK.

The plants, being washed clean, are made into convenient bunches, to the lower end of each of which a small stone is tied to sink it, and as many plants as are desirable are anchored in the tank. It is best to allow the aquarium to remain thus for several days before any animals are added, exposed to the light at a window that has the sun for a part of the day. For animals, very small fish, water newts, snails, mussels and tadpoles are the principal ones. If the vessel is quite small, care must be taken in introducing fish, as they consume oxygen much more rapidly than newts, snails, and less active animals. (1870)

(*figure 3*) are made with metallic bottom and frame with the sides formed of glass; these are sold by the manufacturers at prices varying according to size and finish. The flat, glass sides allow the interior to be distinctly seen.

An aquarium may be made with a wooden frame, black walnut being the wood usually preferred. The glass is fastened in with a cement of rosin and beeswax applied hot. The bottom of the tank and all the parts of the woodwork that come in contact with the water should be covered with the same cement, spread on while hot. Four parts of rosin and one of beeswax, with a small proportion of tallow, are used for the cement. Enough tallow is used to give toughness to the cement, so that it will not break readily when cold. The quantity is best found by experiment, probably a fourth as much as there is of wax will answer. Those who do not care to procure a tank of the regular style can find sufficient to interest and amuse in an aquarium made in a large jar.

An inch or so of clean gravel from which all fine particles have been washed is to be put into the bottom of the jar or tank, and then the vessel is nearly filled with river or rainwater. The plants are next in order, and it is a little difficult to indicate which are most desirable, as there are few that are known by common names. Almost any plant which naturally grows quite under water in ponds or slow streams will answer. One of the best is tape grass, or eelgrass, and those who will take the trouble to search the ponds will find a number of others well suited to the purpose.

An Aquarium

Fig. 3.—AQUARIUM.

A small aquarium, made in a jar or vase is shown in *figure 3*. Clean white pebbles are put in the bottom of the jar. Next are placed some of the plants that live entirely under water and which may be found in almost every pond or slow stream. *Anacharis* and *Valisneria* are very good, but any with fine foliage will do. A few small goldfish may be put in after the plants have been established for a few days. This will make a handsome ornament for the center or dining table, and may also be used to hold a bouquet. (1867)

An Aquarium Tank

The frame of this is sometimes of wood, but this is often troublesome, and an iron one, though more expensive at first, is much better. But it is advised not to get a square or regular tank, at least not at first, but to use a glass jar. Much about managing an aquarium can only be learned by practice, and the jar answers for this, while the animals will be quite as well off as in a more elegant home.

What is an Aquarium?

A vessel of water holding fish, tadpoles, etc., in which water must be changed every day or two, is not a proper aquarium. Fishes and other creatures live for years in a pond, or deep pool, but in such an artificial pond, the water must be changed or they will die. To imitate nature we need plants, as well as animals in our artificial pond. In real ponds, slow running streams, and ditches, there is an abundance of plant life. You do not want the large plants growing on the margins with their roots only in the water. If you look closely you will find a great number of smaller plants, some of which grow entirely under the water, and others with their greater portion below the surface with a few leaves floating above. If we place such plants in our artificial pond, all will go well and we need not change the water to keep our fish, etc., alive.

Procure a Glass Jar

The larger the better, though a two-quart one will afford much amusement. Place in the bottom an inch or so of clean pebbles, or coarse washed sand—that from the riverside is best—and fill up with river or brook water, or if neither of these is at hand, use rain water. Now get some of the plants that grow wholly under water, wash them, tie small stones to the lower ends to sink them, and place them in the jar. Let all stand for a few days, or until the water is perfectly clear.

Add Animal Life Slowly

Begin with snails from ponds and ditches, and a few tadpoles—funny fellows they are—and when all has gone well for some days, you may add a very small fish or two. Frogs and turtles breathe the air, and you must so arrange that they can leave the water. The engraving of a Frenchman's aquarium for frogs shows how he provided a ladder and branch of a tree—willow will answer—to give them exercise. All is covered with a net to prevent escape.

Plants and Animals

Fishes, tadpoles, and some snails can live entirely underwater. They breathe the water, or more properly the air dissolved in the water. When these are confined in a jar of water, after they have taken out all the air it contained—breathed it out—they will become uneasy, go to the surface and try to breathe the air. If not given fresh water, they will soon die. Of the air dissolved in the water only a small part of it is life-supporting. This is *oxygen,* that part of the air which sustains the lives of all animals. In breathing air we use up the oxygen, and we return to the air a deadly poisonous gas, *carbon dioxide.* A man or other animal shut up in a close, tight box, or small room, would soon die; the oxygen would be used up and the gas breathed out would soon cause death. Animals that live in the water breathe more slowly, but in time, they take all the free oxygen out, giving back this very poisonous gas.

What About the Plants?

Plants growing in the water give out to it oxygen, just what the fishes, etc., need, so if we have enough plants and not too much animal life in the water, our artificial pond, or aquarium, will keep on for years, without need of changing the water. Where do plants get their oxygen?—a very proper question. The carbon dioxide the fishes, etc., give out in breathing is just what the plants need. This is in part oxygen, so united with something else as to make a deadly poison to animals, while it is just the life of the plants. These take it in through their leaves, split it up, or take it apart, so to speak, and send the good oxygen back into the water to keep the fishes, and all other animals, alive.

Just Look at the Arrangement

We have plants and animals, fishes, etc., in our jar, both in water. The animals are all the time taking oxygen out of the water, and giving back to it a deadly-poison (carbon dioxide). The plants take up this poison, which would otherwise kill the animals, and in return give out the life-sustaining oxygen to support them. Can anything be more beautiful? Your little jar, which should now be all the more interesting to you, shows in a small way the round of life in the ponds and other bodies of water.

A Practical Point Here

In managing your jar, do not have too many animals, fishes, snails, etc., for your plants. This can only be learned by experience, but if the plant life and animal life are in the right proportions, the plants and animals will give to each other what they need year after year. (1883)

A Wire Holder for a Flower Pot

The engravings show a wire holder for a flower pot. A brass wire, about an eighth of an inch in diameter, is stout enough for ordinary use. A ring is made by

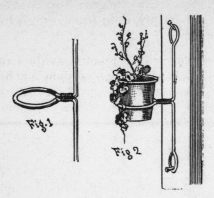

Fig. 1.—COVER FOR FLOWER POT.

bending the wire as shown in *figure 1*. This may be done around an empty pot to get the loop of the desired size. The arm of the loop is bound securely with fine wire. The upper end is continued into a loop by which the holder is hung to the side of the window (*figure 2*). The lower end is bent into another loop that may pass over a nail to securely hold the wire and pot. (1883)

Supports for Potted Plants

A stick or rod, even a very light one, appears clumsy when used to support very slender plants, such as the stems of carnations, etc. Not long ago was seen in an English journal a device which since has been used with much satisfaction.

The support is made of small galvanized iron wire. This is formed into a spiral with its turns wide apart, by winding it around a rod, leaving that portion straight which goes into the soil of the pot. The stem of the plant can be passed into the turns of the wire, which when nicely adjusted will be so concealed by the leaves as not to be unpleasantly conspicuous. Galvanized wire will answer admirably to make other supports, such as balloon-frames, for which rattan and similar material is generally employed. The effect of all plants needing a frame or other support is much detracted from if these are made at all conspicuous. (1873)

Fan Cover for Flowerpot

A green, thrifty, growing plant, even in a common pot, is in itself an ornament to any room, but some kind of a cover to put over a plain pot is often an addition that does much to increase its beauty. Very pretty covers can be made out of the Japanese fans which can be so cheaply bought.

Remove the fastening which holds the sticks together at the bottom, and cut them off close to the lower edge of the fan. Make two holes in the sticks at each side of the fan, one an inch from the upper edge, and the other the same distance from the lower. Run a fine thread through each fold of the fan at the top and bottom, and fasten at each end after drawing it up to the right size to fit around the pot it is to cover. If very fine thread is used, and small stitches taken, they will show but little. Put a coarser thread through the holes in the sticks, and fasten the cover on the pot by putting the thread through the opposite holes and tying it.

Fig. 2.—POT WITH COVER.

It is well to select the fan with some regard to the color of the flowers of the plants it is to be near. For the cover of a pot holding a geranium with bright scarlet flowers, a fan with a gray ground, covered with figures in which black, blue and gilt predominate, would look best, but for a rose geranium or an ivy, a bright colored fan could be used with good effect. (1883)

A Rustic Calling Card

The engraving represents a very neat and tasteful frame for holding a *carte de visite* (calling card) or other small picture. It is made of slender twigs of some evergreen: larch is best, but pine may be used. The parts are

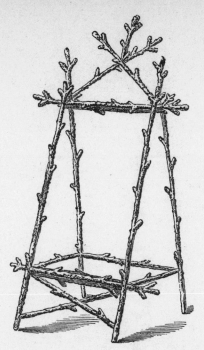

A Rustic Carte de Visite Frame.

fastened together by common pins, and the whole is varnished over.

It makes a pretty ornament for the mantelpiece or table, very easily constructed by every one. Any variation suggested by the fancy can readily be introduced. (1864)

STRAW FRAME.

Straw Frames

How do you like these new picture frames? They are perfectly simple, and, like simple things generally, are pretty. It takes but a little ingenuity to learn how to make them. Those who are fortunate enough to live in the country, and more fortunate still to have a wheat stack in the yard, can readily obtain the straws.

Select any quantity of white or dark straws, as preferred, being careful to use none but perfect and unbruised ones, and choose those as uniform in size as possible. Some narrow ribbon will be required for trimming, or you may use instead, colored worsted,

chenille, or silk, as convenient and to your taste. A straw carefully split and flattened out, first wetting it, makes a very neat fastening.

When ready to make a frame, take three or four straws, lay them in a horizontal position, and holding between the thumb and finger, pierce with a needle and thread, securing firmly. Do both ends alike, and make the four sides in the same manner. Adjust according to the size of the picture to be framed, fastening the corners together with the needle and thread. Some cut the ends even with a pair of scissors, but it gives a prettier effect to allow the central straw to remain a little the longest, as shown in the engraving. Trim the corners, paste the pictures on the back, and it is done. If it is desired to hang the picture on the wall, a cord and tassel of worsted may be made, or a simple band of the ribbon may be used. Two straws with a third across may be fastened to the back to form a support, which will allow the frame to stand upon the table or mantlepiece. (1868)

FRAME OF PINE TWIGS.

Frame of Pine Twigs

It is often a convenience to be able to hang a photograph or small picture by the writing desk or dresser to be always in sight. The illustration shows a rustic frame of suitable size. It is made of the smallest twigs of the Norway spruce about ⅛-inch in diameter. The twigs may be cut at any time when it is convenient, and after lying a few days, the leaves will drop off. The natural color is pleasing to the eye, and nothing needs to be done to prepare them for the frame.

Cut the side pieces of suitable length, with cross pieces for top and bottom. These are to be fastened at the joints with pins. The additional pieces above and below

179

are fastened at the crossing with needle and thread, and the picture is kept in its place by a stitch at each corner. These can be made very readily by boys and girls with a little help, and a great variety of tasteful patterns may be wrought with the small twigs.

If stouter limbs, a half inch or more in diameter are taken, the frames can be made much larger and of a more substantial character. If stout enough they can be fastened with glue and they will last many years. Skillfully made, they are nice presents for friends, especially when they enclose the donor's likeness. (1868)

Painted Fans and Panels

Now that art in every form is attracting so much attention and is spreading its refining influence over all classes of society, it may be of use to girls who live at a distance from the great cities if a few hints are given in regard to painting in watercolors and oil.

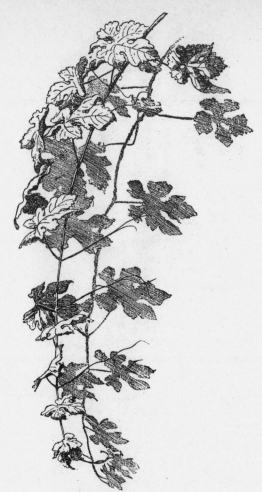

DESIGN FOR PAINTING ON SILK OR SATIN.

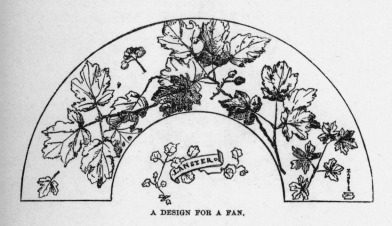

A DESIGN FOR A FAN.

A pretty design for a fan is a spray of vine leaves to be painted in watercolors. The best quality of silk or satin should be used or it will be very likely to crack in the folding. To prepare a mounted fan for painting, it must be stretched upon a board, and thumbtacks placed at short distances just beyond the edge so as to hold it firmly in place without piercing the material.

If the design is to be transferred to the silk or satin, black carbon paper must be used upon light colors; red or blue transfer paper is used to mark upon dark fabric. Care, however, should be taken to remove the superfluous color from these papers by rubbing them for some time with a cloth, else the fabric will very likely be spoiled. If you can draw the pattern with a brush dipped in white, or neutral tint, it is much the neatest way. Silk is easier to paint upon that satin, but both require a

sizing; and for this, the white of an egg will be found to answer the purpose.

All the colors used for silk or satin must be mixed with Chinese white, and it is a good plan, first, to go over the whole design with white. If the colors do not run readily, add a little soap. In painting this vine design, use only flat colors—green or gray—that is colors without shades. Put in the veining and outlines in dark brown. Clusters of daisies are extremely pretty upon white, and garlands of tea roses upon black satin, when the stems may be carried down upon the sticks.

Wooden picture, and looking-glass frames are very effective painted in oil with some bold design. They are about an inch thick, and may be of walnut, showing the natural grain of the wood, or else of common pine, well rubbed with gilt or bronze powder. It is considered more artistic to have sprays only across the corners, as in the illustration.

The picture here given shows a vase of chrysanthemums, the light tints of which would be well thrown out by a dark brown frame. (1883)

French Pastilles Aromatiques

These are little cone-shaped lozenges which, when ignited, send forth a fragrant odor, more or less spicy, according to the particular substances used in their composition. There are various kinds of these pastilles, the odor of some, perhaps, suiting one person's olfactory organs while a different combination will better please another.

Vanilla. Galbanum, 24 parts; cloves, 16 parts; vanilla extract (or bean pulverized), 35 parts; essence of cloves, 1 part; essence of vanilla, 16 parts. Powder all the spices and rub up with the liquids, mixing in mucilage of gum arabic as thick as jelly. Dry and form into cones. If too moist, add powdered cinnamon sufficient to stiffen into a mass.

Pastilles à la d'Orange. Galbanum, 24 parts; dried orange peel, 32 parts; oil of orange, 5 drops; oil neroli, 2 drops; powdered charcoal, 124 parts; potash, 16 parts. Dissolve the potash in a few drops of rose water, pour over the charcoal, and thoroughly dry. Then powder all the materials and mix into a paste with thick gum arabic.

Pastilles à la Rose. Use the same body as the previous, and instead of the orange, etc., use powdered rose petals, 40 parts; oil of rose, 5 drops. Use gum arabic to form a paste.

Pastilles à la Fleur d'Orange. Again, use the same body and add oil of orange flowers, two drops, or extract of orange flower, twenty drops; oil of neroli, 5 drops. Use gum arabic to form a paste.

Pastilles à la Millefleur. Use the same body mixture along with powdered millefleur, 12 parts; olibanum, 24 parts; storax, 24 parts; extract millefleur, 1 teaspoonful. Make into a paste with gum.

Pastilles à la Nuit. Benzoin, 4 ounces; charcoal, 7 ounces; niter [saltpeter—Ed.], three drams; cascarilla bark, ½ ounce; myrrh, 1 drop. Powder all the materials separately and mix them together. Mix into a stiff paste with gum arabic. Make into cones with the fingers or put into molds to harden.

Pastilles à la West End. Gum benzoin, 16 parts; charcoal, 48 parts; niter, 2 parts; balsam of tolu, 5 parts; cloves, 1 part; cinnamon, 1 part. Make into a paste with gum arabic.

Pastilles à la Violette. Charcoal, 50 parts; orris root, 25 parts; oil of rose geranium, 5 drops; olibanum, 16 parts; storax, 16 parts; niter, 2 parts. Use gum arabic to form a paste.

Pastilles à la Lavender. Charcoal, 45 parts; lavender flowers, 16 parts; oil of lavender, 15 drops; niter, 2 parts; gum tolu, 5 parts; bark of cascarilla, 5 parts; benzoin, 2 parts. Mix with thick gum arabic and mold.

These pastilles above are all delightfully fragrant. Place your favorite on a plate and ignite. For a liquid version, however, see the following:

Liquid Pastille Aromatique. Gum benzoin, 40 parts; gum galbanum, 24 parts; cloves, bruised, 17 parts. Bruise to a coarse powder and put into a glass bottle with sufficient deodorized alcohol to dissolve the gums. Place the bottle in a warm place until this takes place. Then decant the clear liquid and bottle for use, stopping closely with wax around the cork. Add to this liquid any perfume preferred—rose, rose geranium, violet, etc. When desired for use, pour upon a little tin or porcelain plate and ignite. (1876)

RAIN-GAUGE.

How to Make a Rain Gauge

A rain gauge is used to mark the amount of rainfall. It is, therefore, only necessary to procure a proper receptacle to receive the rain, and another in which the rain gathered may be measured and preserved from loss by evaporation. The annexed engraving shows how one of a very simple character may be made.

It consists of a glass jar with parallel sides and of a regular cylindrical form. A cork is glued closely into the neck, and the side of the jar is marked with a file, so as to show inches, halves, quarters, or, preferably, inches and tenths of inches when possible to do so. A porcelain or metal funnel, the inner edge of which is exactly the same circumference as the inside of the jar, is fitted into the cork, and the joint sealed with glue so as to be airtight. Although this gauge will not be exactly accurate, it will be so nearly correct that it will serve the purposes of an ordinary observer, and its construction and use will be found of interest to many, especially to young ones of an inquiring disposition who may learn by its use a habit of observing closely those things which are occurring hourly around them, but which are now often passed unnoticed.

Nothing is more interesting than the study of the natural sciences, and the means and appliances for much of this study are, like this simple contrivance, readily procured and easily used. One thing, for instance, learned in a very short time by the use of such a rain gauge and by observing the rainfall, will be that the idea that drops of rain falling directly downwards are nearer together than when they fall in a sloping direction, forced into such direction by a strong breeze, is incorrect. On the contrary, it will be found that exactly as many drops will fall into the funnel when the rain falls in a slanting direction as when it falls directly

downwards. The explanation of this fact, which to some seems improbable, we leave to others to study out.

The position of the rain gauge should be such that the rainfall is not interfered with by sheltering trees or eddies or irregular currents of wind. A clear, open space should be chosen, and the jar should be enclosed in a wooden box, leaving the funnel projecting above the cover. (1873)

Design for a Weather Vane.

Design for a Weather Vane

People are often at a loss to find a pretty pattern for this useful as well as ornamental article. Here is an engraving of a very tasteful one.

The "fly" is of tin, shaped and painted like a flag fluttering in the wind, and of any colors usual to little flags. It is fastened upon an iron rod (or wooden staff if the size be great). This is attached to a cylinder of brass which moves loosely upon the pole, and is supported by a ring that is fast to the pole. At its lower end the rod to which the fly is attached is stayed to the pole by means of a loose ring and wire.

The top of the pole may be protected by a ferrule or cap of any kind. A star and crescent may be constructed of sheet tin. (1864)

Binding of Periodicals, Pamphlets, etc.

(A) The first method is to open two consecutive numbers, as January and February, in the middle, and place them back to back, that is, outside against outside

Fig. 1.

Fig. 2.

(C) A third method is to begin with two pieces of strong cloth tape (as for Venetian blinds) ½ to ¾-inch wide and about 3½ inches long. Draw them through paste and dry them in the form of *figure 3*. Place the periodicals evenly together, press them well awhile, and then place them on the tapes as in *figure 4*. Mark down each side of the tapes as a guide. Then sew the periodicals upon the tapes, letting the strong sewing thread to pass along on the *inside* of each issue and over the *outside* of the tapes just as books are sewn on to cords. Round the back a little, and coat with thick glue.

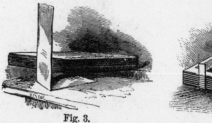

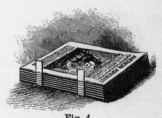

Fig. 3.

Fig. 4.

(*figure 1*). Run a needle with a strong thread in at *a*, up on the other side to *b*, bring it through to you, put in again at *a*, bring it through at *c*, and up to *a*, and tie the two ends in a fast knot. Close the magazines, and bring them round to their proper position, one upon the other. They may then be cut and read as desired.

When the numbers of a volume are all thus stitched in pairs, lay them together in order (as in *figure 2*), and with a straight awl punch six holes as near the edge as you can and be sure to catch inside the running thread previously sewed in. Put the needle in at the upper *a*, bringing it back at *b*, in at *a*, back at *c*, and tie at *a*, as above. Repeat the same at the lower three letters. This is all quickly done, and will leave the whole a strong book, with a back entirely elastic. The thread first sewed into the pairs will be caught by the through threads, and hold the whole firmly.

Let the thread be strong and doubled. It is better still to put strips of pasteboard along the edges and sew through them in the final binding. Or full sized pasteboard covers may be fastened on in the same way. A leather back may be added, and colored or fancy paper be pasted upon the pasteboard, and over its edges. Single issues may be sewed as described for two, though this leaves the thread exposed at the backs.

(B) Another method of binding starts with the cutting of two pieces of stiff card or box-board a little larger than the magazines to be bound. Cover the edges and outside of the boards with any fancy colored paper. Make four holes about ½-inch from one edge of each, and fasten into each hole firmly a common eyelet. Take four short pieces of red tape, tie a knot in the end of each, and put the other ends through the front cover. As each new issue is received and read, make holes in it, then take off the back cover, put the issue in and the strings through, and tie them in two pairs. The knots will hold the other ends. This method has served the purpose very well.

For covers cut two pieces of stout paste- or cardboard, ⅛-inch larger on all sides than the trimmed periodicals. Glue the projecting tapes to the inside of the covers in book form, and glue over each tape-end a bit of canvas to hold it firmly to the cover. Glue a piece of coarse canvas over the back of the book. When all is dry, the whole may be covered with paper, cloth, or leather, according to fancy.

Fig. 5.

(D) Yet another method of binding is to cut two pieces of pasteboard large enough to cover the periodicals, and pass twice through them thus (*figure 5*), leaving ample space between for at least six months' worth of issues. As the issues are received and read they are stitched in in bookbinder's style. (The thread is run along the inside of each paper, but put through the back and around each cross string at the back, as above described.—Ed.) At the end of six months or a year the ends of the cord are drawn down and tied firmly, making a strong volume. This is not very elegant, but it is substantial and cheap and is far better than to have the issues scattered around in loose form.

Fig. 6.

(E) A final method of binding is to make a cover to two pieces of pasteboard, and a piece of calf- or sheepskin long enough and wide enough to cover the back and lap about ¾-inch upon each side cover. Stitch it on firmly, as in *figure 6*, using strong, well-waxed thread. If desired, hide the stitches by pasting on a piece of cloth or paper (which may extend over the whole cover.— Ed.). Put in the papers, and run a strong waxed twine or shoemaker's "wax-end" (shoelace—Ed.) through the whole, four times. (1866)

Christmas Presents

1. Lampshade

The common round lampshades when used, leave the whole family in the dark. You will want something to shield the eyes, and yet allow the rest of the room to be flooded with light.

Procure a heavy wire frame *(A, figure 1)*. Moisten a little plaster of Paris and fill an old tin box with the creamy substance, and place the lower end of the standard in the center, where it is held firmly with your left hand until the mixture hardens. Meanwhile, with your right hand, expeditiously arrange a row of coffee berries around the edge of the box; which, as well as the standard, will soon be securely held in place by the hardened plaster.

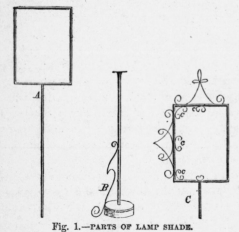

Fig. 1.—PARTS OF LAMP SHADE.

Next take four pieces of wire, which must be bent and fastened to the standard and box as at *B (figure 1)*. This can be accomplished by means of very fine wire and small bits of putty. The edge of the upper part, or screen, should be ornamented with fancifully coiled wire, making the figures *c, c, c,* (at *C, figure 1*), double. Upon the edge of a round board, two inches larger in diameter than the tin box, putty a row of coffee berries; fasten wire feet to the bottom, and glue this second and broader base to the first one, already at the bottom of the standard. (In fact, if you screw the box and wood together before using the plaster of Paris, it will be much better.)

Then give to the whole three coats of dark brown paint, and as many of varnish, letting each one dry *thoroughly* before applying the other.

Fig. 2.—LAMP SHADE.

Cut a transparency from Bristol board and give to each side a coat of white glue and, afterward, two of varnish. Insert it between the double wires at *figure 1 (C)*. When complete, it presents the appearance of *figure 2*, and will be pronounced by all, beautiful. (1870)

2. A Footrest

An old wooden box, 14½ by 17 by 17 inches, furnishes the foundation for a foot rest. Remove the top and cut the sides and one end down to 8½ inches, as in *figure 3*. Point the other end as at *a, b, a*, around which nail two small boards, *c, c, (figure 4)*, so as to form a box in which to keep the slippers. (A cover to this part would be an improvement, if you are carpenter enough for that.)

184

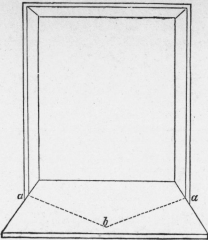

Fig. 3.—DIAGRAM OF FOOT REST.

Fig. 5.—FRONT OF FOOT REST.

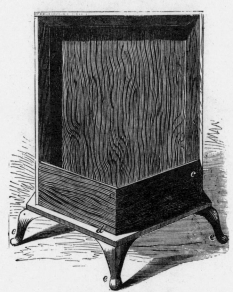

Fig. 4.—BACK OF FOOT REST.

Next nail a second bottom or baseboard, 1½ inch projecting, to the rest when thus prepared. Then screw to the corners feet 2½ inches in height, *e, e, e*. These feet or legs can be purchased of a carpenter. They should be stained to imitate black walnut.

Then carefully cover the whole with walnut-grained paper, fastening the edges and corners securely, and being sure that no air bubbles are left under the paper. When dry, give it one thin coat of glue and three coats of varnish, after which it would take a skillful eye at a little distance to detect that it is not really walnut.

Cut a piece of rep 16½ by 14 inches. In the center of this embroider a medallion with initials, and tack it over the front, as shown in the engraving (*figure* 5), with upholsterer's gimp and white headed nails. The finished footrest will look "just as boughten as can be,"

which is, of course, a high term of praise. American men are noted for wanting their feet, while sitting, nearly as high as their head. This rest enables any man to indulge in his favorite attitude without occupying an extra chair. He will declare it a splendid affair for warming the feet. When not in use, keep it in the chimney corner, the pointed back fitting in so as to occupy but little room, and the front being very ornamental. (1870)

3. Paper Holder

For the paper holder procure two butternut boards the size of *H*, and *J*, *figure 6*. *H* is 17 inches from *i* to *k*, 16 inches from *i* to *l*, 28 inches from *m* to *n*. *J* is 13 by 14 inches. *O* is red kid, 13 inches long, and 4 inches wide at the top, where it is bound with narrow ribbon. There are two such pieces for the ends, and also a strip 13 inches long by 2 inches wide.

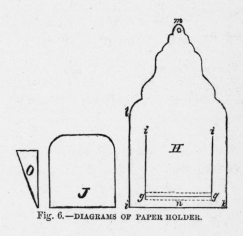

Fig. 6.—DIAGRAMS OF PAPER HOLDER.

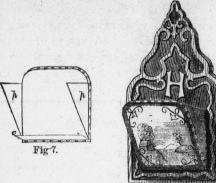

Fig. 7.

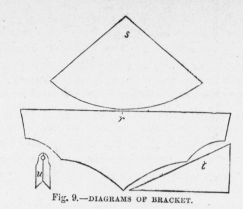

Fig. 8.—PAPER HOLDER.

Fig. 9.—DIAGRAMS OF BRACKET.

After smoothing the boards with sandpaper, draw upon them the design (*figure 8*). Stain the body of *H* a rich brown, leaving the ornamental work of the original color; while on *J*, the corner figures and a wavy margin around the edge is stained and the remainder of the board left in its natural state.

To heighten the effect of the designs, paint a narrow band of black around their inner edges. Then varnish *J*, and immediately press upon the center, face downward, an engraving previously soaked in water, from which the white back should be carefully rubbed off. When it becomes thin enough to show the picture through, allow it to dry, after which it again should be wetted and still more of the paper back rubbed off. Do this until only a very thin film of paper remains, which becomes so transparent by varnishing as to allow the grain of the wood to show through and seems to have been engraved upon the board.

Both *H* and *J* receive four coats of varnish, which give them a very high polish. The three pieces of kid are then tacked upon the sides and bottom of *J*, with gimp and white headed nails, the gimp and nails being carried around the top. Held with the back toward you, it now presents the appearance of *figure 7*. With carpet tacks fastened *o, o,* upon the line *q, q* (*figure 6*), in the manner shown by dots. When the pieces *p, p* (*figure 7*) are brought up to *r, r* (*H, figure 6*), this seam is left inside the holder. Gimp and white headed nails are used in fastening the kid to the lines *q, r*. This article is hung upon the wall by a large picture nail, and is for holding newspapers. (1870)

4. A Bracket

Figure 9 shows the parts of a bracket shelf, 13 x 17 inches, which is papered and varnished the same as the footrest. Each of the side pieces, *t*, is 7 by 13 inches. A bit

Fig. 10.—BRACKET.

of tin, *u*, is cut from an old tomato can and is papered, varnished, and nailed over the junction of the side pieces to act as a ring by which to hang the bracket (*figure 10*). An embroidery canvas, *r* (*figure 9*), is 19 inches long and 8 inches at the deepest point. There are also two other pieces of canvas, the same shape, but an inch larger each way than the side boards, *t*.

In the center of each canvas embroider a group of bright autumn leaves, filling in the body with crystal beads, a bead in each stitch. Then tack the canvases over the side pieces, and around the foot of the bracket, as in the engraving, hiding the tacks under a bead hading, and finishing off the lower edge of the curtain with a heavy fringe of the same.

When finished this will be far prettier than any of the brackets sold in the stores. There is great satisfaction in providing so many acceptable presents with so small an outlay of money. Perhaps these hints will help others to prepare gifts for friends at Christmas time. (1870)

Rustic Pictures of Natural Materials

Rustic work has, within the past few years, obtained a popularity exceeding that of any other branch of fancy-work, and yet there are those that condemn all work of this class as among the things that are "common and unclean" inasmuch as its materials are found "in the woods and on the shore" and are not costly articles sold only in large cities—or else, perhaps, because those who thus condemn it have never examined any fine specimens of the work. Those they have seen were in all likelihood the clumsy attempts of some novice, devoid of taste or judgment.

The following section on rustic pictures endeavors to give such particular explanations and minute directions for forming baskets, anchors, grottoes, and both summer and winter landscapes, that a person with even a mediocre amount of taste and skill will be enabled to accomplish the task successfully. One point in regard to these pictures is to be particularly observed; that is, that the arrangement must be such that what is termed the perspective by artists is kept perfect. This is accomplished by the proper arrangement of the background and by the disposal of objects in the mid-distance and on the foreground so that when viewed from a short distance the view will appear like a miniature view of natural scenery.

These pictures may be of any size—from one of a few inches in a small recess, to one 24 by 36 inches, or even larger if desired. They may vary in style from a basket or bouquet to an elaborate landscape or scene. But the correct idea of their beauty will best be given by describing minutely each kind in detail. Let us now endeavor by explanation, description, and diagram to make each separate design distinct and clear as possible, advancing from the simplest to more complicated forms.

The implements and materials for this work are as follows: A sharp knife with large and small blade, coping saws, small gimlet, tack hammer, bradawl, small brads, small brush for glue, one or two small-sized chisels, and several small mesh sieves or kitchen strainers.

Also required are all kinds of natural products, such as ferns, mosses, green and autumn leaves, dried grasses, tendrils, lichens, fungi, twigs and small branches of any pretty trees (such as birch, or those with mossy bark, gnarled roots, and knots), stones, pebbles, shells, a-corns, berries, sand of various colors, flowers (dried or pressed), seaweed (or any treasures from the ocean), nuts, and various colored wood.

Useful, as well, are glue, powdered paints of various shades, and putty.

Many may wish to purchase as forms for rustic work the various-shaped pieces sold by florists [now available in styrofoam—Ed.]. Many, however, prefer to use only natural materials, forming faces of figures of tiny nuts, building castles and ruins of small stones, dressing figures with colored leaves or the outer and inner husk of corn, etc. This, however, is entirely a point of taste or opinion, and is optional with the artist. (1876)

Starch Paste Models

Unless this material has been tried for making models for rustic pictures, its beauty and the ease of forming it cannot be well conceived. It is made by soaking gum tragacanth in water, and when soft, mixing it with powdered starch and a little double-refined powdered sugar until it is of the consistency that can be rolled like paste for pastry on a board or marble slab.

This material is infinitely superior to any other for modeling all fine work such as modern houses, porticoes, temples, pagodas, etc., and will form all delicate molding, fine tracery, small figures, etc., better than any we have described. (1876)

Transparent Rustic Picture

There is another style of rustic picture which is beautiful beyond description, but inasmuch as it requires the aid of light to bring out its exquisite loveliness, it must be placed against a window. Sometimes there is a window which is entirely, or almost, useless; and here such a scene as is about to be described will be found a happy thought, not only utilizing that which before was but an aggravation, but changing it into one of the most charming features of the house. These pictures may be of any size desired, but must be night scenes, such as an illuminated city, scattered hamlets, and a conspicuous building in the foreground, with abundance of windows. The making of these pictures can be explained so that any person may not fear to undertake one.

Fig. 14. Transparent Rustic Picture.

Take, for instance, such a scene as shown in *figure 14*. You will need a strong cardboard box, of any size desired, but from 3 to 4 inches deep. First make the sky, which, as it is a night scene, must be a deep dark blue, excepting around the moon, where it should be lighter. Then fasten a background against the sky by gluing tiny fern fronds in groups, as distant forests, along the line of the horizon. Also add pieces of white card cut into points as distant mountains, shading certain parts with a soft lead pencil. Spaces of green, as far-distant fields, may be made by gluing pieces of green and brown moss, of the soft cushion-like kind, between and in front of this line of forest and mountain, making tiny fences of thin cardboard around a portion. Next take a sharp knife and remove a section, of greater or less extent according to the size of the picture, from the back of the recess, and from thin white Bristol board cut any number of small buildings, houses, spires, domes, towers, etc., as shown in the illustration. Color these in various shades of stone and white, and cut tiny gashes where windows should be, merely pressing the point of the knife through so as to admit the light. As the foreground of the distant parts is approached, make the holes larger, and in those directly in front cut out the windows and fasten two or three shades of yellow gelatine-paper [modern readers should use cellophane —Ed.] behind them, the lighter farthest back. Any spaces upon the outer edge should be covered with moss, little trees and bushes, tiny fences, etc., making the roads and open spaces of sand and powdered moss, sprinkled on glue, with which the ground should be painted.

Make the railroad depot and train barn of wood or heavy cardboard, sanded, forming these parts carefully like perfect miniature houses, always recollecting to cut out the spaces where light is to appear. On the left side fasten two pieces of mirror, one beneath each bridge, placing each one so that it will dip downward slightly, covering the edges with moss, ferns, etc. Make the bridges of cardboard, sanded, and cut or marked to imitate stone. All coloring must be dark, as the time is night, it should be remembered.

Next make the remaining mid-distances, the two churches, houses, etc., which will require care, as they should be an imposing part of the scene. Soak cigar-box lids, and while the wood is pliable cut out the various parts, removing window spaces; then cover with thick glue and sand heavily, marking off rough stones with black crayon. The colors should be varied in the different buildings. Let a vine of pressed ferns and moss cover the parts of the sides and towers. The cluster of houses on the right should be made as described above; but the windows must have crimson paper instead of yellow.

The large church in the foreground, being the most important feature of the whole, will require unusual care. Cut all the parts out carefully and put together so that the front, or projecting side, is perfect; but cut away the back so that the parts rest flatly against the recess, which must be cut out to admit the light. Cover the windows, on the inside, with colored paper, or colored glass, if preferred.

The vines, shrubbery, etc., overhanging and clustering about the buildings, and over the stone wall in front, add great beauty to this mimic night scene, and are made by fastening delicate sprays, fern fronds, and moss on slender wire. The old house, to the left, should be literally covered, with only the light gleaming through the ivy-covered windows. Trees, etc., may be added, but are omitted in the illustration lest they should prevent the clearness of the description, as regards the buildings, etc.

As in other rustic pictures, moss, bark, lichens, and other natural materials enter in largely to make the effect one of wonderful picturesque beauty. All lovers of the beautiful should appreciate these really artistic creations which are more like miniature scenes in nature, liliputian realities, as it were, then mere pictures. (1876)

Basket of Woodland Treasures

This basket may be of any desired size and shape, from 6 to 15 inches in diameter of the round style, and 3 by 4 to 7 by 11 inches of the oval Swiss basket.

Form a recess of stiff cardboard, of suitable depth and width, and line it with white cardboard. Cut the basket in half, lengthwise. Touching the cut edge of body and handle with glue, fasten it in the center of the back of the recess. Below it place a pretty mossy branch imitating a log, selecting one with little branches at one end. If this should not be sufficiently mossy, fasten pieces of moss upon it with glue. Place a few stones below the log upon a foundation of card covered with moss, and group a few grasses and ferns among the stones.

Fill the basket with grasses, small ferns, berries, sprigs of evergreen, a few small cones and acorns; also clusters of bright-colored flowers and leaves which have been preserved in sand or carefully dried. Secure each piece by touching the stems, etc., with glue. Begin at the back part and place flat pieces, such as pressed leaves, grasses, etc., against the back. Then fill in towards the front, finishing at the front with fine delicate sprays placed in such a manner that they may fall gracefully over the edge with a long tendril twined around the

handle. Enclose the basket in a rustic frame of russet-colored oak leaves and acorns, fastening the nuts into the cups with glue, and suspend by cords made of strung acorn cups with cone tassels.

The other half of this basket may be made into a suitable companion piece by placing it in a similar recess and filling with shells, pebbles, seaweed, etc., and by placing it upon a single large shell of great beauty and resting it upon a strip of mirror. Finish upon the outer edge with a narrow margin of sand, moss and tiny shells. Touch all parts of the contents of the basket with clear mucilage and dust with sparkle powder. An appropriate frame for this is made of coral. (1876)

as deep as this part of the anchor, although in placing it it may be rested in such a way that the bar will stand at an angle of about 22½ degrees. The recess should be lined with azure-blue velveteen. Cover the anchor with silver or tin foil and encrust with tiny pearl shells.

Make a chain or cable with fine rice shells strung upon thread and either looped into links or twisted into a cable rope. Form the ring of the smallest-sized shells strung on fine pliable wire.

Make a foundation shelf to imitate an area of sea beach, with sand, shells, seaweed, curious specimens of barnacles, starfish, claws, etc., of lobsters and other marine treasures that have been carefully preserved. Upon this build a little piece of rockwork of pretty

Anchor and Shells

Cut an anchor of graceful shape about 8 or 10 inches long, as shown in the engraving. The recess must be deep enough to admit the bar of the anchor as it is placed at a right angle with the arms and horizontal with the flukes. And of course the recess must be at least

fragments of rock built in with moss and cemented together to form a thing of beauty.

Against this rest the anchor; or, if preferred, a large shell of unusual beauty may be used as the rest. Cover the bottom of the recess with mirror and fasten long graceful sprays of seaweeds, grasses and moss with the tiniest of shells clinging to them, along the edge of the shelf, so that they will be reflected in the mirror below. Twine the chain around the bar and beam of the anchor, and let it trail upon the ground. Frame in a shell or sea-foam [meerschaum—Ed.] frame, and for suspension cords string long narrow shells on strong twine, using a bunch of small shells for tassels. (1876)

Ruins of Melrose Abbey

Obtain a strong recess of any desired size, from 12 by 18 inches to 36 by 42 inches, and line the sides and bottom with brown or bronzed paper; the top with light blue.

Commence with the sky, which we will suppose to be a sunset. We would observe here that in making a landscape it is of great importance to have a good picture, either in oil or watercolors, a chromolithograph or even an engraving, as a guide. As was observed, some may prefer to use only natural materials for these pictures; and in this case, even the sky may be made with colored paper, cotton, etc., as entire pictures were thus formed centuries ago, and finished so artistically as to appear as fine as an oil painting. In the present case the sky may be painted in oil, watercolors, or pastels, or, as we are about to describe, by using natural materials.

The natural method follows: Procure tinted tissue paper and lead-colored and white cotton. Then, commencing at the top, take a strip of deep sky-blue paper, and touching only the edges with glue, fasten it along the bottom line, leaving the paper loose in the center. Proceed to cover the lower edge with another strip of lighter shade, making the two deep enough, combined, to reach two-thirds the way down. Cut another strip of light straw-color, and fasten it against the light blue. Then add another shade, and perhaps two or three more, making each one of a deeper shade, until at the horizon it is of a bright golden hue.

This neatly accomplished, proceed to form clouds, the long flat ones, of white and bluish-white tissue paper, crumpling it first in the hands, and arranging in such a manner that the lower part of each division is hidden by the top of the one below. For light fleecy clouds use in the dark parts stone-colored cotton, pulled into loose feathery pieces. Make the white soft clouds of white cotton which may be pulled so thin as to appear like veritable clouds. Arrange the banks and clusters of clouds to hide as much as possible the lines of connection on the foundation of blue and gold. Such a sky may be made to appear very beautiful and far more natural than any one would suppose from merely reading the description.

The sky finished in whatever style desired, proceed to form the background. Directly against the sky, upon the left side, make a distant forest by fastening the pointed divisions of fern fronds in irregular clusters, using various light shades, and grouping them properly, with deep vistas made of the darkest pieces. Along the center make a different forest of autumn leaves, with a few distant hills of light bark. Upon the right side form distant mountains by cutting cardboard into pointed pieces and shading with small thin pieces of bark. Below this line of background, finish down for a little distance in the same way, only increasing the depth and brightness of color in the forests, hills, and mountains.

Next, upon the left side, make a distant village by cutting small houses, spires, turrets, domes, etc., of card, and coloring of different shades of stone and white. Make the windows of black paper, or mere lines of black paint or ink. Small sprigs of evergreen or leaves or tiny branches will answer for trees.

In the middle, between this village or city and the mountains, make an open field of green tufts of moss. Form sheep, cows, figures, etc., of putty, and dress the figures in bright-colored silk, cotton, or paper.

The mountains, upon the right side, should be made more distinct as the front is approached. This result is produced, first with light-colored bark upon a foundation of putty, or what is better still, with the German preparations or papier-mâché used for dolls' heads and toys of various kinds. It is made by boiling brown paper to a pulp, straining off all superfluous water, and adding to each quart of soft pulp half a pint of thick-boiled flour-paste, and one pound of glue, adding burnt umber or potter's clay if the color is not suitable; but this addition is not necessary. This rude papier-mâché is most valuable as a foundation for various things, and also for molding into figures, animals, and other objects.

Then upon the front build up with stones or fragments of rocks. The foundation of prepared paper prevents undue weight which would be produced by using a number of heavy stones or rock.

The conspicuous parts of the picture may now be commenced. The mid-distance is made upon the right by a deep and bright green forest, using small branches trimmed into shape as trees, and covered with various-colored leaves of ferns or tiny pieces of moss, etc. This forest will reach about two-thirds the distance from the top of the case.

Fig. 6. Ruins of Melrose Abbey.

Below it let a strip of ruined stone wall extend, made of putty and marked off into irregular and broken stones. Paint with thick glue and cover with coarse sand. Form a gateway, partially ruined, about midway, with rough stone steps leading down a mossy declivity to a strip of sandy shore. Upon the shore place an old post with a little iron ring. Cover the bottom of the recess—partially at least—with mirror, in which, near the post, have a hole cut in which to place a miniature boat. The hole can be cut with a glazier's diamond, which is a useful instrument in this work.

The little grassy ascent from the water to the wall may have bushes, flowers, wild entangled vines, stones, etc., scattered upon it; and the wall and gateway may be covered with moss and ivy, made of grapevine tendrils and little leaves cut from ferns, with little purple berries made of wax. Cluster this vine thickly upon the top of the wall and on the posts, and make it appear to run in wild, uncared-for luxuriance upon the ground and over the bushes.

Next to this wall, in the center of the recess, the castle is placed. This is carefully cut and sawed out of wood. A cigar box will answer well, as cetain parts of it may be allowed to remain almost uncovered, and the red color of the wood gives the effect of the sunset glow. The large arched window must be cut with such exactness that each piece of tracery, every slender pointed part of the

broken frame must be distinctly seen. The cluster of turrets may be made from thin cardboard or skillful carpenters may use wood.

The central tower, immortalized by the poet Scott, must be cut in sections; the high end with its three Gothic windows, partially ruined, requires unusual care in cutting, as the pointed arches, brackets, etc., must be very delicate and frail. Various ornamental parts require to be cut in tiny pieces and glued together; and various little decorations which will enhance the beauty of the work will suggest themselves to the artist.

When all the parts are finished, they must be coated with thick glue and covered with colored sand. A little brown sand will give the sides towards the sunset a warm glow, while the dark parts in shadow may have a little burnt umber touch on them. Lighter parts can be brightened with raw sienna. The taste and judgment of the artist must be exercised in regard to coloring, as it is impossible to explain this in writing.

Colored sand should be used for the various parts of the ruin, either natural or with paint-powders mixed through them. Care must be used in drying both wood and cardboard parts to prevent them from warping, which is best accomplished by placing them, while damp, under a heavy weight. When these are dry, commencing at the far back parts, proceed to put the pieces together, using care to place them so as to produce the proper effect. This is done by letting the parts next to the back be perfectly flat, but allowing all the projections of corners, roofs, etc. to project towards the front, showing every angle distinctly.

When entirely finished, the large window in front will appear as if standing out at a distance from the back parts, and through its open frame may be seen the wild growth of vines, etc., growing in the grounds around and even in the main building itself. The large arched doorway to the left should have a rich molding in fretwork and carving, and appear deep. This effect is produced by placing two pieces of colored card within the frame and placing behind them a piece of wood covered with black. The roof of the nave is quite dilapidated, and a thick growth of ivy covers it partially; on the front place a stone cross above the large mullioned window, and a bell gable on the wing to the left, with a little tower above.

When done, arrange a clump of bushes, ivy, vines, etc., at various points, and cover all parts, here and there with a luxuriant mass of creepers, ivy, etc., in various shades of green, dark in the shadows and bright in the sunshine. Let ivy also climb up and over the windows of the high central tower and then fall in festoons and garlands from various points. Creepers should fill the open, ruined roof with its deep green and also the space within the towers. Cover the roofs, mullions, gallery, arches, and ornamental brackets, supporters, etc., with moss, and let tufts of ferns and grasses cluster in every nook and corner. The ruins finished, proceed to arrange the ground in front.

Here let there be considerable wild, entangled growth of grasses, low bushes, flowers and vines near the building, with fragments of broken turrets, windows, pillars with carved capitals and heavy stone bases, etc. Farther out place broken gravestones made of white marble or of wood dipped in liquid plaster of Paris, and the usual crosses of wood, marble or stone to each one, some partially covered with graceful vines and blossoms. Here a road sweeps round in front of the abbey, and is lost in the woodland, beyond the stone wall; upon the right, it is carried on over an old, partially-ruined bridge, with two or three broken arches and stone supports upon which a rude moss-covered handrail rests. By the bank, down on the water edge, two or three deer stand, one bending to drink. Crossing the bridge are two horsemen.

Beyond the bridge, high up in the far distant mountains, a thread of bright, white and blue water is placed, made of a strip of tissue paper, crushed and crinkled, on which sparkle dust is sprinkled. This stream widens and becomes more and more distinct as it approaches the bridge and sometimes appears to flow over the rocks in sparkling cascades, made by painting the course with glue and covering with large pieces of white and blue frosting. [Commercial frosting is made from coarse flakes of powdered glass.—Ed.] Where ripples or foam are formed by the stream rushing over rocks, a little plaster sprinkled upon it gives the white foamy appearance and forms the natural ripples. As it is the most difficult task of the whole to make this water look well, it will be found a good plan to hide and veil it in various places—here by an overhanging rock, there by a clump of shrubs or tangled wild vines upon the margin; a rustic bridge or a fallen tree in this place, and a low overhanging tree in another. By these means the stream, although still sufficiently visible to be seen, will not be so conspicuous as to be offensive.

Figures may be introduced if desired and tend to give life to the scene. They may be made of a stiff paste, made of wheat flour and water, and molded upon a tiny china doll, or with wax or putty, with faces made of small nuts. But perhaps, after all, it will be found advisable to procure the beautiful and suitable little figures readily sold in the toy shops.

In forming or purchasing the figures of whatever kind for these pictures, great care and discrimination must be used with regard to the size. Figures at a distance must be rather imperfect, often mere straight pieces of wood, cut in shape and colored. Those figures used towards the front must increase in size and distinctness of form and color. But even in the foreground the figures, trees, etc., must be apportioned to the size of the buildings.

The stream of water should be finished up with care. Along the bank, let the moss be green, and rise in swelling curves to the mountain range. Bright flowers, creeping vines, tufts of pretty grasses, green feathery ferns, tangled brushwood and groups of low growing bushes should be scattered along the margin, and the whole will be more or less obscured from clear view by the objects in the foreground, viz., by the bridge, horsemen, etc.

Many and varied may be the views and scenes produced by this style of work, which will create and enshrine within a case a collection of mementoes or beautiful treasures and portray each incident and feature of the scene with such perfection and precision as to vie with nature itself. With care and patience you can create, in miniature size, a very liliputian scene of mimic beauty and rare delicacy. (1876)

Fig. 11. Swiss Hamlet.

Fall Bouquet of Oak Leaves

Line a shallow recess with tinted paper—lavender or rose color. In the center place a group of the large, thin, curled oak leaves of various colors—brown, dun, etc.—upon pretty twigs, with clusters of acorn cups and whole acorns. Make the nuts, if you wish, of putty, colored with umber, and fasten them into the cups with glue. Form a wreath of frostbitten fern fronds around the edge of the recess, and clusters in the corners of autumn leaves and scarlet berries. Or make the wreath round in form, and crossing the stems at the bottom, fasten with a cluster of autumn leaves and a knot of tendrils. A motto formed of tiny leaves is a pretty addition. (1876)

Swiss Hamlet

A winter scene under a glass shade for use on a wall bracket is easily made. The shade and stand for this can be homemade or obtained from a fancy store. Those made by hand consist of a square piece of board set on four feet, ornamented around the edge with a wooden beading obtained of a carpenter, and with leather leaves, or rustic work of cones, acorns, and little branches of oak or grapevine. Pretty feet can be made of spools, with a long screw passed through them and into the stand, and then ornamented with acorns or any other article corresponding with the edging of the stand. Or the common curved clothes hooks make really beautiful feet for these and various other articles, as they look precisely like the feet upon sofas, bureaus, etc., in miniature.

Having finished the stand with a coat of copal varnish, the shade is made of a sash of desired size, filled with four panes of glass for sides, and a square one for the top. Pass a piece of chenille around the base after the shade is placed over the picture. (1876)

Sea Landscape

In strong contrast with the previous scene, will be a sea piece—the ocean near the shore, opening out between high pieces of rock. A perfect model of a lighthouse tower stands out upon a prominent point, with the keeper's lodge down among the rocks. Out upon the waves, made of frosting and alumina [aluminum oxide—Ed.], rides a full-rigged schooner or several of them. Or perhaps one of the Arctic expeditions is delineated, when the ocean will appear frozen, and the vessels fast among the icebergs which float like giant crystal castles upon the icy waters.

The various accompaniments of lifeboats, anchors, etc., may be perfectly fashioned with a sharp knife from pine wood and subsequently painted. The curious fur caps and cunning little rough coats and boots of the officers and crew, and the odd dresses, and appearance of the natives, with their curious huts upon the icy shore, add great interest to the scene. The ice, snow, and general appearance of a rugged Arctic region may be so perfectly copied as to make one's very teeth chatter. (1876)

The Old Mill

A winter scene, as a companion to the foregoing is, perhaps, even more admired than the greenness and luxuriance of a summer landscape. There are numerous views appropriate for winter scenes, of which the following—an Alpine scene—is copied from a chromolithograph called The Old Mill.

Fig. 10. The Old Mill.

Fig. 7. Swiss Chalet.

Fig. 8. Beam, Pulley and High Door.

Fig. 9. Mill Door.

Instead of a bright golden sky, let it present the dull leaden hues, black heavy clouds, and cold colors of winter, accompanying a snowstorm. The background of this scene must be high peaks of far distant mountains, made first of white and stone-colored tissue paper shaded with soft crayons and also dull, russet-colored fern and autumn leaves. In front of and below these, place mountains cut from cardboard, and leaves of rather deeper shades in thicker clusters, standing out more prominently. By placing quite light ones in one cluster, and against these very dark colors, an appearance of prominence upon the one side and of a deep recess within will be given, even when the leaves do not project more than a quarter of an inch. This same effect may be produced in other parts among the rocks and mountains, and upon a field, or on any flat surface.

The ranges of mountains and forests being finished for a short distance down, the mid-distance is made thus: Upon the left side is an Alpine village, made of a number of perfect little chalets, each one of those in front being cut from very thin wood, laying glass upon it for windows, and marking out the panes with thin slips of white paper. In some upper windows place bright green paper, as curtains, and let the tiny balconies and tiers of outside steps and stairways, with the low flat roofs, be cut with the most careful precision. The most satisfactory mode is really to procure the cunning little houses, churches, etc., of all sizes, from the toy shops.

Upon the higher points, and appearing as if at a distance, cut the houses of cardboard, painting them to look natural. Also position long pointed pieces of evergreen cut in imitation of trees; little yards, with miniature fences around them; etc. This village, scattered over the mountainsides, and dotted among the ravines and in the little valleys, will occupy the space between the left side of the recess and the center. Here a frozen stream glistens among the rugged mountain crags, and hangs in long glittering icicles from every projecting rock.

Soft white cotton, covered with crystallized alum, forms perfect snow for the mountain. And thread, subjected to the same process, affords icicles and frozen drops for various parts. The mosses, grasses, evergreens, twigs and leafless branches should also be crystallized. The stream here may be partially screened with overhanging rocks, covered with snow and bare, almost leafless trees, etc., but it is not as necessary as in the former scene.

Upon the right wide, a church or homestead should be made to appear as if only a short distance beyond the foreground. It may be constructed of cardboard sanded, or of dark sandpaper. The windows, doors, balconies, porches, window hoods, etc., should be made quite distinct, and after a pattern of the peculiar style of building used in Switzerland. A rude fence or low wall should surround it, with a rustic stile and gateway. In the graveyard within, crosses, tombstones, and one or two more imposing monuments, designate the purpose for which the ground is allotted. Upon the spire or bell gable of the church, a cross should be placed and the whole thickly covered with ivy made of vine tendrils, fern fronds, sprigs of brown and green moss, all crystallized.

The mill, etc., in the foreground, and now to be described, will partially cover this middle work along the entire line. The mill should occupy the position almost in the center of the recess. It must be formed of thin wood, two stories high, with high pointed roof, covered with cone-scales. There should be a main building with a wing projecting from one end, and a blacksmith's shed at one side. The gable end of the principal building should stand facing rather towards the left. From the top of a long door, in the upper part, a narrow beam covered with two boards are laid together like a roof. From this a ring is fastened, through which a rope and pulley are affixed. A tiny barrel, fastened to the rope, may hang a short distance from the ground.

The window and door facings must be made to appear heavy and quaint, with rough hoods and the general dilapidated appearance of an old building. The wing should stand with the gable towards the right, but turned to face almost directly front, and must be only one story. Let a rough shed run along the entire length beneath the upper square window. Beneath it make a mill-door; that is, a door in two sections, the lower one closed, the upper one swinging open. Behind the lower one, within the mill, may be placed a small doll dressed to resemble the miller.

The mill must be so cut as to fit up against the back recess, and yet each part can be so arranged as to retain the perspective view, showing the various parts of the building in their proper position. The lower part of the main building will jut out over the water, made upon the bottom of the recess with a strip of mirror. The water wheel, one of the chief and perhaps prettiest features of the scene, should revolve upon a round beam, supported in the water by a post or pile of stones, all thickly covered with alum crystals.

Boys skating upon the lake, and a tiny bridge across the rocks in the distance, will add to the beauty of the scene. Very much depends upon the taste and designing qualifications of the artist. Ice upon the sides of the lake is made by touching with glue and placing large pieces of frosting upon it. After all is finished, touch various parts with mucilage, and dust with arrowroot mixed with fine frosting.

197

Fig. 13. The Old Church.

Various additions may be added to improve this old mill and its surroundings; leafless vines and trees, smoke from the chimneys, fastenings for the loose roofs, usual upon all buildings in Switzerland, with ladders, poles, spades, etc., placed in proper positions against the smith's shed. Use your imaginations or a good picture of an Alpine scene as your model.

The recesses for large pictures should not be less than four inches deep. The companion pieces, of which the previous scenes are descriptions, are in cases of this depth, enclosed in frames 36 by 42 inches. (1876)

The Old Church

A companion piece to *figure 11*, "Swiss Hamlet," displayed under a glass shade and mounted on a T-bracket, is "The Old Church." Form a groundwork of dried green moss. Cut out the church of wood or card; make the tower of light cardboard, cutting out windows and door. Over the latter place a quaint-looking porch, and over the windows hoods, made by simply bending a piece of card into an angle. Cover the church with fragments of ferns and moss, and upon the top of the chimneys and on the roof of the tower pile it up to look like luxuriant ivy, letting long, trailing pieces fall down from the edges of roof, porch, and windows. Dust the roof with green and brown watercolor powder, or, even better, crumble dry moss, very fine, and sprinkle upon all parts, having them previously touched with liquid glue or mucilage.

Around the church place a wall made of cardboard, with edge bent over to form a deep ledge. Moisten the wall with glue and cover with sand, etching the sand to resemble irregular stones. Cover the top with moss and ferns. Make a gate, and within this enclosure put a number of white gravestones, a few broken monuments, etc.; also some evergreens and trees.

In the foreground place a quaint old cottage, surrounded by a green hedge, formed of dried mosses, evergreens, etc. To one side may be a tiny garden with gay flowers, etc., and here is an opportunity of forming pretty designs with everlasting flowers, grasses, etc. An old dilapidated barn may go on the other side, with green trees, vines, and any other pretty floral treasures.

The beautiful mosses and lichens found in the South, and the lovely climbing fern, bright and beautiful colored sand, and odd mosses found in the East are invaluable in forming these pictures. Those living in vicinities where such treasures are not found should endeavor to procure them as best they can, as they add great beauty to the picture and enable you, from their varied shades, to form the perspective. (1876)

Basket on Shell Stand

Obtain a pretty basket, or make one of cardboard. Or a pretty rustic one may be made of little twigs and pieces of bark. Cut the basket in half and fasten to the back of a recess which should not exceed more than 2 inches in depth. Place beneath a projecting piece of card, covered with seaweed, if obtainable, or pretty mosses, ferns, and lichens, interspersed with fragments of coral, pretty shells and stones, etc.

Fill the basket with marine plants, if possible, or otherwise with grasses and flowers, such as acroclinium, graphalium, ammobium, waitzia, rhodanthe, polycolymna, zeranthemum, glove amaranthus, helipterum and helichrysum.

Of the grasses suitable for drying for rustic work and for use in this basket, the following are the most recommended: Agrostis laxiflora, stevern, andropogon bombycinus, eragrostis, elegares, coixlacheymae, avena sterilis, arundo versicolor, isolapsis gracilis, briza, maxima, gracilis, and compacta, chloropsis, chrysurus aureus, panicum colonum, capilacum and frumentarcum, setaria machho, stipa pinnata and elegantissima, tricholum rosea and trypsacum dactyloides.

These grasses should be gathered while in fine color and dried in a dark closet in an upright position in order to fall gracefully. Those who prefer brighter colors can dye and then dry them; but with gay flowers, the natural color is in better taste.

Frost the basket with white frosting. Make a stand of cardboard and glue it beneath the basket. Wet with glue, and fasten on various pretty shells, stones, fragments of coral. If you prefer, the various ores and ossified or petrified curiosities are pretty and will form a curious and beautiful stand. (1876)

Easter Cross of Flowers.

Easter Cross

To form this, first make a wooden cross, not less than 18 inches in height, and place it on a wooden base of three steps. Paint this a light stone color, or if preferred, an imitation of granite. Give successive coats, until a smooth, uniform surface is obtained. Procure some colored sand, as near the shade of the paint as possible. Then, having applied a coat of varnish over the paint, dust the entire surface with the sand, and simulate irregular stones with a crayon of lighter shade.

Flowers suggested for this cross are roses with buds and leaves, sweet peas, and ivy geraniums. Pansies, lily of the valley, calla lilies, passionflowers, forget-me-not, wisteria, honeysuckle, camellias, abutilon, convolvulus, ivy, dicentra, and orange blossoms, etc. are also recommended, but others may be substituted if preferred. (1876)

Fig. 1. Shrine Closed.

Making Photo-Mirrors

Persons who have been in France within the past few years, and others who visit the emporiums of foreign art, have enjoyed the luxury of examining a rather recent artwork, called Photo-Mirrors or Mirror Photographs. These exquisite productions are photographs upon glass, prepared as for mirrors, and are as costly as beautiful. We are glad, therefore, to be able to explain to those lovers of artistic beauty, without the means of gratifying their fine tastes, of a mode by which they may obtain these elegant Mirror Photographs. No more beautiful object can be imagined, than a Photo-Mirror of the Madonna, the Mater Dolorosa, or Ecce Homo, encased in an elegant shrine.

Fig. 2. Shrine Opened.

First, procure a suitably large illustration of the figure to be honored. Cut carefully away all the margin and background, leaving the figure entire. Obtain a piece of fine mirror (plate glass is superior and produces the best effect), which has been cut considerably larger than the illustration. For the present purpose it is more artistic to have it cut with an arch at the top; for a cabinet-sized picture, the glass should be not less than 10 by 8 inches. Prepare a sizing by dissolving gelatine and adding it to flour paste, and then apply it to the wrong side of the picture. Lay the picture exactly on the center of the mirror. Press it down firmly with a napkin, smoothing out every wrinkle and patting it gently to remove any air that may blister its surface.

The shrine for this picture must be strong and carefully constructed, as the mirror is heavy and would otherwise break away from its case. Any wood may be used, but a beautiful case is made as follows: Cut the back several inches higher and wider than the mirror. This may be of ¼-inch pine wood. Cut of white ash or satinwood the several pieces for the doors, sides, etc. A framework for the doors, of an inch in depth, should also be cut, and the doors fitted to it, opening down the center. These and a bottom of ¼-inch wood must be lined with crimson satin or velvet.

The woodwork is then ornamented with a design of inlaid wood, pearl, etc., in imitation of Japanese lacquered work. For the sides, and running up over the top, form a vine, cutting the design in paper, and then marking it off upon the wood. Let the leaves and flowers be small; convolvuli are pretty, or an ivy vine may be used. On the doors, ornamental crosses with garlands of flowers are very handsome.

Having marked out the design upon each piece, proceed to cut out the various parts from the colored wood, thin veneers of dyed holly or bird's-eye maple being best for this purpose, using care to cut each part perfectly true, according to the pattern. This done, fasten each piece in its proper position, touching the wrong side with glue and laying a weight upon the pieces until dry. Small pieces of pearl and gold and silver are a beautiful addition.

When perfectly dry, the various parts must be put together with glue and small brad nails. The doors are fastened to the frame with very small brass hinges, and an ornamental lock miniature size is placed upon one of them. At some of the fancy stores, tiny locks with keys may be obtained, which are very beautiful for this purpose. A bracket should be made to correspond with this shrine, upon which it should stand supported upon four ornamental feet. The picture, framed in velvet and gold, is placed against the back, supported by a gilded ledge placed upon the bottom of the case, and a hook fastened in the top of the back, which throws the picture a little forward.

The inlaid work must all be varnished with outside or finishing varnish. The velvet and gilt frame and ledge are made by covering cardboard with velvet and decorating the corners with the gilt ornaments. (1876)

Engraving of Glass

Cleanse the glass to be engraved perfectly and put it aside. Then melt paraffin or beeswax with bitumen in an open vessel. When this is entirely melted, but not boiling, take a flat brush with soft hair and give the plate of glass one or more coats, according to the heat of the wax, the thickness and warmth of the glass, and the temperature of the room. A narrow rim or edge should be formed of the wax immediately around the edge of the glass so as to form a well in which the acid to be used will be contained.

In case of vessels such as tumblers, wine glasses, etc., dip them once or twice into the melted wax in such a way that the part to be engraved may be entirely covered. The article being thus entirely coated over with wax, sketch upon it the design, name, initials, or monogram

with the point of a needle or sharp-pointed instrument. Always make the lines and tracery upon the wax of the precise thickness or delicacy desired to be engraved on the glass, and with care remove all the wax from the lines and grooves.

The design being entirely drawn out and cut upon the waxen surface, proceed to cover the surface with hydrofluoric acid, and expose the acid bath to the action of the sun's rays, taking care, however, not to melt the wax, or the whole effect will be ruined. [Take care as well in handling this corrosive and poisonous acid.—Ed.]. Let the glass remain in this bath for about five hours, when a whitish powder will be seen rising to the surface of the floating acid. If the glass upon examination is engraved satisfactorily, it may be removed and washed free from wax and acid. It will be found beautifully engraved in the precise manner in which the wax was marked. (1876)

Etching Upon Glass

Etching of the most elegant style is done by the following method which is equally beautiful on flat or circular surfaces. The heavier and better quality of the glass, however, the handsomer will be the work. Therefore, heavy French crystal will, of course, produce the most perfect engraving.

Proceed to cover the glass evenly with wax and bitumen in equal parts. Put on one or two coats very evenly. Then, with a very sharp-pointed instrument and a small-bladed knife, commence tracing the design on the surface of the wax, having first marked it off by a pattern pricked in paper and lightly dusted with a colored powder which will bear the tracery upon the surface in tiny dots. First, mark these all out by cutting very uniformly and slightly through the surface of the wax. Then proceed to cut out the heavier parts with the knife and the fine lines with the point of the instrument. Then, dipping up a little wax in a spoon, provided the surface is a level plane, pour it around the extreme edge, continuing this until the entire center is enclosed in a little wall of wax. In this pour a quantity of pure hydrofluoric acid. When the whole has been subjected to the acid under the sun's rays for a couple of hours, stop out the acid from those fine lines intended to be only as if scratched by filling them with blacking. Let the work remain for another hour, and then stop out those parts to be of moderate depth. Then let the acid act for another hour, and stop in the same manner the third class of marks. Finally allow the acid to act on the deepest parts for another hour. After this, wash the glass off perfectly clean, and it will be found that the tracery is as fine as if engraved with an instrument; and the remaining parts of the engraving as rich and beautiful as the most perfect machine-engraved glass. (1876)

Embossing on Glass

Embossing on glass is the reverse of engraving and etching, for by this method the groundwork is made dull like ground glass while the pattern is bright and clear. This is an excellent mode of embellishing window glass as by it those who are within can see without, while the outside individuals find it impossible to pierce the misty veil that envelops those behind it. It is produced by the following operation:

Paint the entire surface with varnish, and draw upon it a suitable design which should be of a rather uniform and decided character and without very much small, fine tracery. Cut a paper diagram, as before directed for etching on glass, by which to trace the pattern. Do not destroy this pattern as it will again be required. Make a wall of wax around the edge of the design, and fill with hydrofluoric acid. Allow the acid to remain until the design is etched only sufficiently to leave the ground raised slightly. Wash off the acid and also the varnish. Then commence grinding off the ground by means of a flat piece of glass and pulverized emery. Use but a small portion of emery at a time, and first cover the design with the paper pattern to avoid its filling up. Thus executed, the etching, having remained untouched by the grinding process, will be bright and clear. The ground, if well done, will have the dull white opaque appearance peculiar to fine ground glass. (1876)

Glass Crystallized and Ornamented in Figures

Glass may be made extremely ornamental by the following process:

From cloth cut out a number of ornamental designs—diamonds, circles, stars, rings, leaves, flowers, etc.—and paste them in regular patterns upon the glass. Next make a hot saturated solution of Epsom salts with which to wash the glass. When dry, very fine crystallizations will be formed.

A saturated solution is one in which the water is allowed to take up all the salt it will possibly dissolve. Keep this liquid constantly hot, and apply with a brush. Sal ammoniac [ammonium chloride—Ed.] will also produce the same effect and form a different crystal. Glass in windows thus ornamented is beautiful. (1876)

An Aeolian Harp

The Aeolian harp is a musical instrument of very ancient origin and carries with it certain poetical associations which render it a pleasant addition to a household composed of cultivated minds. Its rather romantic and weird music is produced not by educated fingers, but through the agency of nature alone. The "breath of the zephyr," "the voice of the wind" sweeping over the chords, simply fastened to the window casement, sends forth sounds which are at first as low and sweet and soothing as the voices of the spirits and which are said to sing an infant's lullaby. This changes, anon, to deeper and fuller notes that swell and rise and, with trembling reverberations, sweep over and over the chords like the wail of some sad, mourning soul chanting a requiem or the *Deus misereatur*. Then, suddenly, the sound changes to a loud, joyous peal that seems to resound with as great exultation as the jubilate of King David.

There are many persons who never allow their window to be without the Aeolian harp, so greatly do they enjoy its strange and frequently wonderful music. These harps may be of very simple construction, and, as with all other elegancies, they may be most elaborately ornamented. Given here are directions for constructing the case, etc., and it will be understood that it may be made as simple or elegant as desired. As regards the formation and adornment of these harps, they should be made as quaint and ancient looking as possible.

The case is made as follows: Measure the breadth of the window, and make a box of pine, walnut, or other wood ¼-inch thick, 4 inches deep, 5 wide, and sufficiently long to fit the width of the window. At the top of each of the ends glue two pieces of oak about ½-inch high and ¼-inch thick. These are for bridges to which the strings are to be fixed. Within the box, at each end, glue two pieces of beechwood, one inch wide, and the width of the box in length. Into one of the bridges fix seven pegs, such as are used for piano strings; into the other bridge fasten seven brass pins of medium size, and to these pins one end of the strings is to be affixed.

Many persons in making these instruments use only one or two sizes of strings, but the notes are much more musical, and capable of producing far greater range of sound if several sizes of string are used, such as those of the harp, guitar, or violin. Fasten one end of the string, whether of various sizes or of fine cat-gut only, to the brass pins in the one bridge, and the other end twist around the pegs in the other bridge. This done, tune them to perfect unison.

Place over these strings a piece of board ⅛-inch thick, supported by four pegs 3 inches from the sounding-board. This will procure a free passage of air directly over the strings. This instrument should be placed in a window with the lower sash drawn down so that the bottom rests on the frame of the case. If a door or window on the opposite side of the room is kept open, the depth and power of the sounds is increased to a great degree.

Where an instrument is intended to be placed out of doors, it should be of much larger size and of heavier materials. It should also be thoroughly painted and dried previous to setting the strings and tuning into harmony. (1876)

Application of Decorated Cork to Articles

Among the many things a woman's hand may fashion outside the realm of needlework is the application of cork. It is very suitable for decorating all sorts of articles made of wood such as boxes used for postage-stamps (*figure 106*), étagères, brackets, etc., or a paper cutter (*figure 105*). The articles to be decorated are of fine wood and generally stained gray, this color contrasting particularly well with the cork applications. The cork must be as little porous as possible and cut in slices as thin as wafers. According to the size of the slices or the application, the latter may be cut either of one piece or in separate pieces.

Transfer any design to the cork with a soft lead pencil; this may be easily done by holding against a windowpane, the design thus showing plainly through. Then with small sharp scissors, cut out the figures and every little stem and tendril if a floral vine design is employed, as in the morning glory design shown in the illustrations. This undoubtedly requires a very sure, steady hand. The wrong side of the cork is the flatter and harder; cover this with glue. Carefully place it on the part to be decorated and press it down evenly.

Fig. 106. Postage-Stamp Box.

Fig. 105. Paper-Cutter.

Take heed that the application is not lopsided and that it retains its graceful curves.

The whole is then completed by making veins and the like with a fine brush and India ink. A little shading with sepia-brown and white will not detract from the delicate appearance of the application. Several coats of varnish finish the work. The large brush with which the varnish is applied must be rinsed in spirits after each application in order that it always remains quite soft. (1876)

204

Bronzing

Statuettes, medallions, vases and other objects in plaster of Paris may be bronzed in perfect imitation of the genuine material by first rendering the plaster non-absorbent with coats of linseed oil. Then the objects are painted with a varnish made by grinding gold leaf with honey.

Another method is by first painting the article, after it has been rendered non-absorbent, with a dark mixture made of powdered tints of Prussian blue, ochre, and green ground in oil. Before this becomes quite dry, bronze powder, of any desired color, must be dusted on the prominent parts to simulate age. (1876)

The manner of forming these boards is to have a pine frame made that will fit closely into the opening. Cover this frame tightly with black cotton cloth. Then procure a number of colorful pictures, the greater the variety the better. Cut these all apart and glue them randomly upon the black ground. Then cover the surface with a thin varnish, laying the screen flat. When the first coat is dry, give a second, being careful to keep off dust during the entire operation. A screen so decorated with floral pictures is shown in *figure 24*. (1876)

Fire or Stove Boards

The old method of filling wide fireplaces and open stoves with huge vases of flowers or bunches of asparagus ferns during the summer months is still a good one. There are, however, other expedients for rendering this portion of the home tasteful. The methods by which a fireplace may be made ornamental are numerous, but the one we shall describe is by means of fire or stove boards or screens.

Fig. 24.

VIII. Projects by and for Children

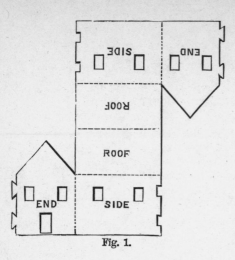

Fig. 1.

A Paper House

Children can get a great deal of fun out of making paper houses. It will teach them how to use the shears and to exercise their minds in calculating length, etc. *Figure 1* shows the form that the paper should be cut into, and also the places for the windows and doors for the house seen in *figure 2*. If heavy paper is used, the house is a substantial structure and may be put up and taken down at pleasure. The size of the "dwelling" may vary according to that of the sheet of paper from which it is cut. The relations of the various lines must, of course, remain the same. (1883)

Fig. 2.

Cutting Paper Toys

Children find wonderful pleasure in the use of scissors. Give them something that it is lawful to cut, or they will probably cut off their eyelashes or front locks of hair, or scallop their own little frocks. At first they cut for the pure pleasure of cutting, but soon they want to "make something." Paper-cutting is one of the occupations of the kindergarten. Good Froebel! No observant mother needs to be assured that he was acquainted with live children. Before we knew what the occupations of the

kindergarten were, paper-cutting had become a favorite employment at many houses.

"I am going to cut something pretty for you," said a young auntie in one household to a three-year-old boy who was whining over some disappointment. She folded a square piece of paper, and after cutting it for a few minutes, unfolded a form of beauty that seemed quite marvelous to the child. "There, sir! That is a toy for you," said she, giving it to him. Now the boy cuts prettier "toys" than she ever showed him. Until very lately he expected someone to mark them for him, but now he does the whole alone. One is delighted to see the little fingers learning care and precision in following the marks exactly with the scissors. Habits of industry will come from such employment, as well as from any other, better than from work that is hated. Are not children sometimes made indolent by parents who think that "good children" are those that "keep still" most of the time, and scold children for getting into mischief, but provide no pleasant occupation for the natural activities of childhood?

In the kindergarten, paper-cutting is scientifically taught, step by step, until the results are very beautiful. The children are helped to mount their cuttings on Bristol board, and give them as presents to others.

Fig. 1.—CUT-PAPER TOY.

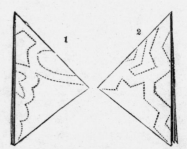

Fig. 3.—FIGS. 1 AND 2 FOLDED AND MARKED.

Half a dozen "toys," doubled and marked, will keep a child busy and happy a good while. For the benefit of those who have had no experience in this line, and who do not get the meaning clearly, here are a few examples. Better ones can be found in Weiber's "Paradise of Childhood." The first ones should be very simple. The fortunate "kinder" who cut paper in their "garten" have soft, colored paper to work with. (1872)

Costumes of Crêpe and Tissue Paper for Fancy Dress Goods

Dresses, caps, hats, sunbonnets, parasols, fans, etc., may be made up of crêpe and tissue paper for fancy-dress parties or balls, or for children's parties. Favors for a party may include all of the articles mentioned above as well as baskets and fancy boxes.

The illustration herewith given represents a child in a pretty fancy costume made entirely of these papers. The latter come in the most brilliant and also the daintiest colors, and costumes may be constructed from them that will match the tints of the rainbow or the soft grays of the dove.

Naturally a little care will have to be exercised in wearing a paper costume, though crêpe paper is fairly strong and can be either sewed or fastened together with mucilage or any paste conveniently at hand. A thin muslin lining could be used in making the waists to crêpe paper gowns. (1895)

FANCY-DRESS COSTUME OF CRÊPE AND TISSUE PAPER.

Window Transparency

A piece of thick Bristol board, 6 inches by 8, will make a transparency to hang in the window. If the design is drawn lightly with a pencil, it can be cut upon a board with a penknife, wherever it is marked, bending all the points out, and pasting a narrow ribbon around the edge, as in *figure 6*. The cross among the leaves will form an agreeable variety with the grotesque figures in the window curtains, shadowed by the moonlight, over the bed and wall. (1867)

Fig. 6.—TRANSPARENCY.

A Doll's House

Departing from the accepted doll's house of the day, here is the description of one that can be pulled down and rebuilt at pleasure.

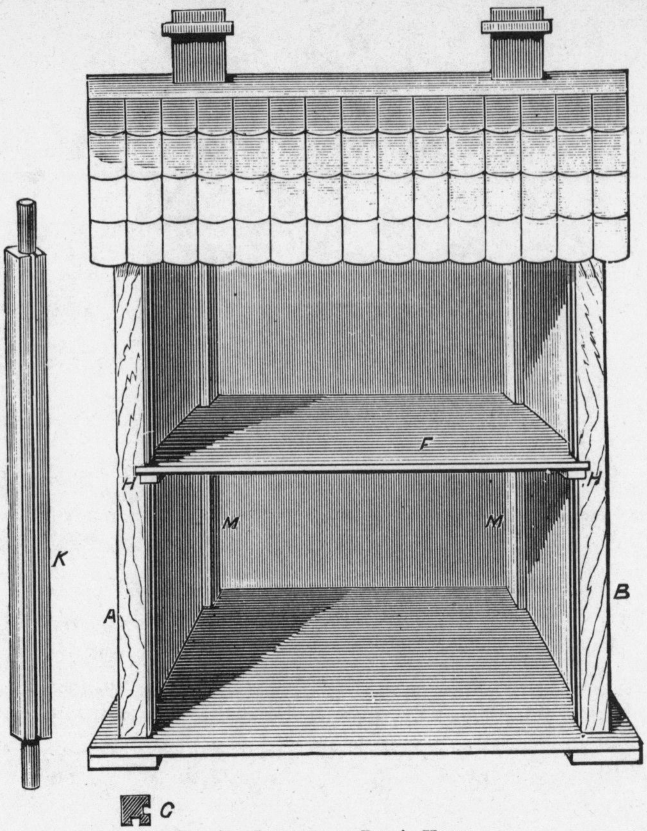

FIG. 42.—FRONT VIEW OF DOLL'S HOUSE.

FIG. 43.—INTERIOR OF DOLL'S HOUSE.

In *figure 42* is shown an elevation of the house complete. The whole front is one board or panel, sliding in grooves like the panels of the windmill just described. The door may be made to open if desired. The bottom of the house is a deal board, about 18 inches long by 9 inches wide and a ½-inch thick. To prevent warping, the strips (*B, B*) of beech or ash, are glued across it at each end, or they may be of deal, a ½-inch wide and ¾-inch thick, attached by screws, or glue, or both. Great care must be taken to make this bottom truly square, and also to plane it nicely on both sides. The piece seen at *D*, forming a door step, may also be a strip so glued on, but made to project a ½-inch, or it may be merely a short piece.

The sole object is to get a good firm foundation that will keep its shape, and not warp and twist; but the two strips (*B, B*) also give more efficient support to the corner pillars by allowing a deeper hole for the lower pins to rest in. Let these pillars be of ½-inch stuff, and 15 inches long, exclusive of the pins. This will allow of an upper room or bedroom, which, like the lower, will be 7 inches high, the floor of the bedroom being but ¼-inch or ⅜-inch thick. This floor must slide into cross notches in the front pillars, and rest on two strips glued on inside the boards forming the ends of the house.

In *figure 43, F,* is the floor, *H, H* the strips, of which, of course, the end only is seen. This figure represents the doll's house open, the front being supposed to have been slid up out of its grooves, as will generally be the case while the toy is in use. *A, B* are the front pillars, which are shown in section at *G,* and *K* is one of them shown in perspective. *M, M* are those at the back, the others crossing them, and concealed by the roof, being (as in the mill) the top frame, half lapped at the corners to make it level on the top. The bottom board should project a little all around, say, a ½-inch, which will give 17 inches as the length of the rooms inside.

This doll's house will take furniture large enough to be strong and durable, but size is, of course, of no importance if the proportion of the different parts be attended to sufficiently to give it a nice appearance. But if it be made very small the rooms will not admit the insertion of even children's hands with the freedom necessary to allow them to move about the dolls and their furniture.

The directions given in the description of the wind-mill ought to suffice to make quite clear the method of framing and fitting the doll's house. The four side posts are capped with others forming a top frame, and the front and sides slide in like panels.

The roof is made with two gable ends (*see figure 44*), the width of span allowing it to project and overhang the front and back of the house to form eaves, which prevent it also from falling off, but this may be further checked by cutting the triangular pieces which form the ends, as at *B,* with a pin or pins projecting below to fit into holes in the cross or tie beam below it. When in use the roof is first removed, then the top front tie beam. The front panel is then slid out, the cross beam and roof

replaced, holding the now open house firmly together. It is stiffened also to some extent by the floor or horizontal partition, which, observe, must be narrow enough to slide in so far as to allow the front to slip in before it. Its chief support will, of course, be the side strips on which it rests, as it can only occupy a very small part of the horizontal groove in the front upright.

It will be seen from *figure 42* that the front of the house is marked out in panels. The framing is a sham, consisting of thin strips glued on and neatly fitted at the junctions. These can be made gay with bright colors like Swiss cottages, or the panels made of deal, and the framing of mahogany. They should project above the general level, but not quite so far as the corner posts. Strips should be placed round the door, and others, rather thicker, to represent window sills.

As it will add to the amusement of the little children, it will be well not to be content with a mere painted roof, but to hang on some representative tiles. For this purpose, after having made the penthouse and gable-ended roof, glue on strips like *1, 2, 3, 4,* of *figure 44* at equal distances. Each board of the sloping roof will be about 10 inches wide, so that if the tiles are made 2 inches in length, rounded off like *C* at the bottom, there will be just room to hang on five rows. The lower ones should be a little longer, so as to overhang the eaves. Each row must just overlap the one below it.

Every single tile, made of the thinnest wood procurable (veneering material by preference), is to have glued across it a little strip of wood, as shown at *C,* which will rest upon the strips glued upon the roof. Thus, beginning at the lowest row forming the eaves, they will be hung on one by one till all have been placed. The top strip, however, it will be noticed, is not at the extreme edge of the roof, so that above the last row of tiles a narrow space will be unoccupied on both sides of the roof. To complete matters, glue together two narrow strips about a ½-inch wide, and as long as the house, to form an angular ridge piece (*D*). This will form a cap, covering the upper edge of the last row of tiles, and put a neat workmanlike finish to the whole. Paint this and also the tiles a bright vermilion. The latter should not exceed an inch in width. If of veneer, they can be easily cut out with a penknife, especially if the wood be first soaked in water and shaped while wet. The tiles so cut out should be bound or put in a press to compel them to dry quite flat.

The windows are to be of glass, fixed on at the back by gluing strips of stout paper round the edges, or a wooden frame to keep it in place. It can then be divided by narrow strips of paper into panes, or, as is often done, a piece of coarse net can be affixed at the back. There should also be pieces of bright colored silk arranged inside to look like curtains, and in one or two there

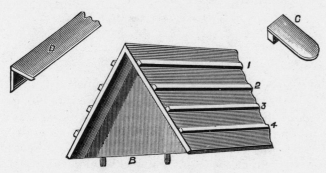

FIG. 44.—ROOF OF DOLL'S HOUSE.

should be a bit of thin callico, white or otherwise, to imitate blinds half drawn down. Attention to these apparently trifling details will give an air of reality and a nice finish to the work.

The chimneys are mere solid blocks, either shaped as shown, or with a flat bit of square board, rather larger than a section of the main chimney, glued on at the top. The block is notched out below to fit over the angle of the ridge of the roof, as shown in the drawings. A wire pin should be inserted to enter a hole in the ridge piece and keep the chimneys safe. Nothing will better imitate smoke that a tuft of cotton wool, especially if some black or grey wool be mixed with the white.

If the toymaker be a neat hand with a paint brush, the whole house should be got up in red, and the mortar lines picked out in white. Window sills should be quite white, and a narrow line of black painted round the windows. Steps of the door should also be white; the frame black. In painting toys we must not, as we should in a picture, aim at gradation of tint and delicacy of color, but use such as contrast strongly. The main and cross timbers, however, taking up, as they do, a large portion of the front of the house, will look better if colored a rich brown, especially if lined with jet black at the edges. But this lining with paint is not very easy work, as it needs a small brush and very steady hand to do it well. (1882)

Doll's House Furniture

The instructions for making the furniture will be confined to a few of the principal articles, as the same character of work prevails throughout, and anyone who can construct one or two pieces of furniture can make others with little difficulty. As the size of the furniture to be made must so entirely depend upon that of the house and on the number of articles proposed to be placed in it, no directions on that point can be given. In regard, however, to the framework of these miniature suites, there is this difficulty, that one can hardly cut a mortice and tenon in very thin material, so must manage to connect the parts in some other way. In a good tool shop a chisel as small as ⅛-inch or even 1/16-inch in the edge could be procured, but in ordinary stores it might be difficult to procure one of ¼-inch, and this, of course, will decide the size of the mortice. Nevertheless, with a drill a still smaller mortice may be managed by making two or three holes in a line, and with a penknife throwing them all into one. This, however, is hardly

necessary, and in very small work the better plan is to drill one or two small holes, and use bits of pins for nails to hold the parts together while the glue is drying, for glue must in all cases be used in addition.

Table

To make a table, plane up some strips of wood of, say, ¼-inch square, to form legs, and some for the top frame, ⅛-inch thick or less, and ⅜-inch wide. Cut off from these four broad pieces of equal length, or two short and two a little longer, if the table is to be oblong for the dining room. Take great care to square the ends truly, have glue close at hand, and some fine twine or strong thread (not cotton). Lay the pieces in position to form an oblong frame, and see whether they fit nicely, then give a touch of glue to each, place in position, and tie securely, or slip over them a rubber band. Cut the legs of the requisite length, and when ready, glue each into its corner inside the frame, which will be easy, if the latter is just tied or secured, and is lying on its edge. The legs are to stand up in the air, and not to occupy their usual position till dry. If other tables are needed make these also so far, as it is always better not to complete a thing of this kind out and out, and then to begin another, but to carry two or more to the same degree of completeness, and then afterwards finish all together. The table will appear like *figure 45*.

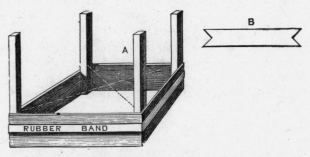

FIG. 45.—FRAME OF TABLE.

The only possible difficulty to be met with at this point is the falling inward of the legs before the glue can dry. These accidents may generally be prevented by simple means. Cut out two little pieces like *B*, notched at the ends, and just long enough to fit from corner to corner inside the legs and frame. Drop them in at the dotted lines, so as to bear against the legs, and they will hold them firmly; but take care not to make them tight enough to force open the frame. Leave all to dry, and then with a penknife clean off any bits of glue, and, turning the table so as to stand upon its legs, see that it bears equally on them all and stands perfectly. If not, correct with a sharp knife where necessary.

All that remains will be to make the top—oval, oblong, or square, as is wished. This must be of thick stuff very nicely faced on one side. It is seldom that it is faced at all on the other. The top of an old cigar box provides famous stuff for a table top, and can be polished or varnished. If plain white wood be used for the table top, the wood stains now so largely used will avail for the imitation of oak, walnut, or mahogany. They should not be used in excess, as a light coat generally looks the best. Then with thin glue give a coat of size, and when dry varnish with hard white spirit or oak varnish; the first is the better of the two for such small articles.

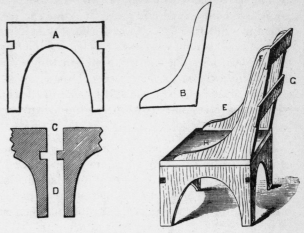

FIG. 46.—DETAILS OF CHAIR.

Chair

To make a chair we have a choice of several plans more or less like the reality. These small and light articles are dependent on glue for their stability, and need no proper joining to unite the parts, so that we can construct them with tolerable ease of any desired form so long as we can tie or pin them together until the glue has time to dry thoroughly. By all means get rid of joints wherever possible, which is to be done by making the article of few parts, and using a little ingenuity in shaping them. In the illustration a chair is shown (*figure 46*) which is made of four pieces, cut like *A*, the back being formed of two more like *B*. For this a cigar box will serve well.

If the pieces are cut like *C, D*, so as to have small tenons and mortices, these will assist more than would be supposed in holding the parts together till dry. *E* shows the chair thus completely fitted. The seat has now to be put on to overlap slightly all round, and upon this are to be glued the two pieces which form the back. A top cross rail fitting in the notch *F*, and a second at *G*, will complete it. The chair thus constructed is shown in the drawing, and if a bit of bright red velvet be glued to the seat *H*, and the different parts are smooth, so as to admit of a coat of varnish, a very neat and effective article of doll's furniture will result.

If, as is probable, three or four are needed, cut out as many pieces of each shape illustrated as are required, pinching them together in a vice and filing all together. The chairs will then match each other as they ought to do. This is a much better and more workmanlike plan than to construct one before commencing the next.

Such is one mode of chair making, and, perhaps, the best, inasmuch as the result is not only very easily attained, but it is a tolerably strong little toy, more so than when framed up out of many small pieces, with each leg separately glued in, for these are always the parts which in doll's furniture are unduly weak, and if we can combine these with the top frame instead of making them as separate pieces, we shall undoubtedly gain in respect of their stability.

Sofa

Precisely the same plan can be followed in making a sofa, but it should be varied slightly by using only a pair of similar pieces forming together four legs and uniting these by longitudinal strips.

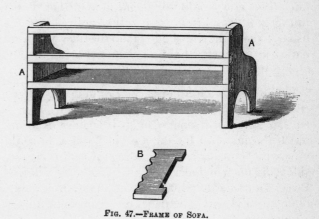

FIG. 47.—FRAME OF SOFA.

Figure 47 represents such a sofa, of which the ends (*A, A*) being shaped as shown, form both arms and legs, and are connected by the seat and the two back rails, which are notched into them and glued. *B* is one end of the seat, and will serve to show how the latter is let into the ends by small tenons, which add much to the stability of the whole article. The seat can, if preferred, slide into a groove in each of the end pieces if these are thick enough; and it can be covered, like that of the chair, with silk or velvet, and still further assimilated to reality by a stuffing of wool.

This, by the bye, is an excellent way of making seats of larger size for household use, and is also adapted for church seats, of which the ends should be thick oak, nicely molded round the edge, and in such case only one broader rail is used at the back. For study use these may be made by the amateur without much difficulty, and the tenons may be carried through, and have wedges driven in on the outside of the standards; thus made they are in a manner portable, as it is easy to drive out the wedges and separate the parts into so many flat pieces. The back should not be so upright as that of the doll's sofa represented here.

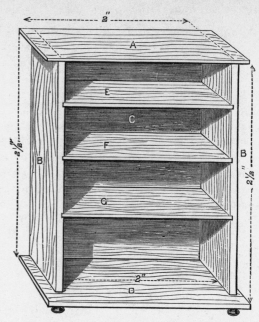

FIG. 48.—SECTIONAL VIEW OF CHEST OF DRAWERS.

Chest of Drawers

A doll's chest of drawers is an article requiring a great amount of care in order to attain anything approaching a satisfactory result. Beyond all question, the chests of drawers sold in the cheaper sets of dolls' furniture are as wretched specimens as can be found anywhere, the front of each drawer by no means representing the length of that of which it is a part, and no attempt at a fit is made.

The material selected must be thin, or the chest will be clumsy, and here again the cigar box will be found to afford the requisite boards. The ends, however, of the cigar box being of thicker stuff, must be rejected. At the same time, one should call attention to the fact of this thicker stuff. In most boxes it will be noticed that it is usual to make the ends stouter than the sides which are nailed to it, a better hold for the nails being thereby obtained.

In the case of a miniature chest of drawers, if large enough—say about 2½ inches square by 1 inch deep—we can follow the same plan, as it enables us to use much thinner stuff for the top and front than could otherwise be managed—say ¹⁄₁₆-inch thick for the two sides, and the remainder ¹⁄₃₂-inch, or half the thickness. Pieces ¹⁄₁₆-inch can be made to hold small sprigs or bits of needles and pins to help the glue, at any rate until the latter is dry.

Figure 48 represents the outer case or carcase of such a chest, 2½ inches high, 2 inches wide, and 1 inch deep,

inside measure. The sides are ¹⁄₁₆-inch, the remainder, including the division between the drawers, ¹⁄₃₂-inch, which is the thinnest stuff that can well be used in this article; but the bottom of each drawer may be still thinner. Veneers can be obtained of all sorts of handsome wood as thin as card, which can be well soaked in water, cut with a knife into little planks while wet, and screwed in a press or put under a heavy weight to dry, when they will be found quite flat and fit to use. Being sawn to uniform thickness, they answer well for work of small size, and will take a fine polish after being sandpapered and brushed with weak glue or patent size, and dried.

Cut out first the ends (*B, B*) of ¹⁄₁₆-inch stuff, and take great care to true them up with a plane or a chisel, square and exact to size; being especially attentive to the edges, which must be at right angles to the sides. Here again it will be the best plan to set a plane bottom up on the bench, and taking the wood in hand, reverse the process by moving the wood over the sole of the tool, which must be keen as a razor and very finely set. Now make up your mind how many drawers you are likely to have patience to make, and prick off with compasses on these side pieces the exact places for the several divisions. It is usual to make the lower drawers rather deeper than the upper, but this is of no importance. It is, however, of the utmost importance to mark the two pieces exactly alike, and then with the help of a square to draw or scribe lines straight across both at the points marked.

At these lines grooves must be made, into which the partitions are to slide, and for this a very fine saw or a file can be used, a key-warding file or knife-edged file being most suitable. Groove both pieces alike, and make all the grooves of equal depth, and exactly wide enough to allow the pieces of wood to be used as partitions to slip in.

Now get ready the top (*A*) and bottom (*D*), cutting these larger than the size of the carcase itself, so as to overlap. Plane and file them true, and then mark on each in precisely the right place where the inner edges of the sides will be. Here draw a decided line with a pencil if deal is used, or a scriber if dark wood is selected, using a square very carefully to ensure exactness. These lines are the inside boundaries, and, therefore, you can drill small holes just outside them for sprigs or needle points, which in this case will help you, even if not driven home, but left partly above the surface, to be subsequently removed by pliers.

Now set on edge one of the sides and the bottom. Hold them in position while you mark with the drill point (or any pointed bits of steel put in the drill hole) where the sprig will come in the side piece, and then make a small hole at that spot. For all such work an archimedean drill stock is the best to use, and the next best is a birdcage maker's awl, which is three-square, like a saw-file, and will not split the thin wood. Mark this, and drill all the necessary holes, and then sprig all together just enough to hold, and see if all is square and true, fit for gluing. Although the top and bottom should overlap in front and at the sides, all may be flush at the back, and this will facilitate putting the parts together in the manner described, because all the four pieces can be stood on edge upon the table or bench, and thus made to fall into place more easily than if the top and bottom were not thus flush.

If all looks right, pull apart, and with glue touch the edges and immediately press together again, tapping the sprigs with a light hammer to drive them home, or, at any rate, to make them take a closer hold. Now, also, set the frame true by a square, so that when dry it will be straight and accurate, as it should be. If this is not done the rest of your work will be most difficult, and the whole affair thoroughly unsatisfactory.

The partitions between the drawers must now occupy attention. It is better to leave these until all the rest is dry, and, while this is taking place, they can be cut out in readiness. If the work hitherto has been well done, these pieces will be exactly alike, but it is not absolutely necessary to work them up together. Care must be taken that the ends are square to the sides, and they must be long enough to fit and slide into the grooves without much pressure, yet still with sufficient tightness to show hardly a crack when in place. They used not to be so wide as the chest is deep, but will be better if nearly of that width, as it will provide more efficient surface for each drawer to rest upon. Three-quarters the depth of the chest will do very well.

These divisions being put in and glued, and the back made of thin stuff, glued on, the carcase should be neatly cleaned off, and sandpapered, and if of veneer or cedar, can now be polished if desired. But the drawers have yet to be made, which in these small chests are merely shallow boxes or trays. They demand, however, very special care, or they will never work as they ought to do. In a real drawer the sides always project below the bottom, so that the drawer may slide on these two narrow edges, while the bottom is clear and does not touch anywhere. You can manage this if preferred, though it is of little importance.

First cut out the fronts, fitting them, each singly, into the place destined to receive them. The better the fit the nicer will the chest look when finished. Therefore take all possible care, and mark a corner of each drawer front, so that you may make no mistake subsequently as to the position it is to occupy. In cutting out the ends of the drawer remember that you must make them short enough to allow the front of the drawer to go in quite flush when in its place. Allow, therefore, for this and for the thickness of the crack.

The precise mode of gluing up the drawers is but a repetition of what has already been done. But remember to glue the sides *inside* the front, as it is sketched at *K* of the drawing (*figure 49*), and either quite flush with it or slightly inside it. The back must be flush in any case. Now with regard to the bottom, we must allow for its thickness in cutting out the two ends of the drawer, and these must not be even in that case with the lower edge of the drawer front, if the drawer is to rest upon the bottom. But if made to rest on the edges of the end pieces as in a real drawer, then in that case let these pieces be truly flush with the front.

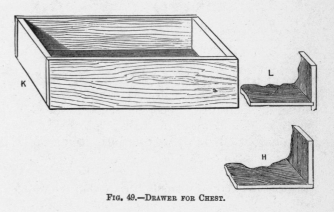

FIG. 49.—DRAWER FOR CHEST.

At *L* is represented the corner of a drawer thus made which can be compared with *H*. Of course, as the drawers are of different sizes, each must be made quite independently, and each must be carefully and separately fitted. For handles to the finished drawers, small brass nails will do driven half in, but if a lathe is at hand, they can be turned of box, ivory, or wood. Four little knobs should also be added for legs, though these can be cut out in one with the sides if preferred, by hollowing out slightly the bottom edge of each, so as to leave projections to serve the same purpose. (1882)

Two Miniature Chairs

For the miniature chair in *figure 1* the quill feathers from the wing of a turkey are the only ones required. The four uprights are made of the thickest portion of the quill and are placed with pointed ends downward to form the legs of the chair. The two in the back are 4 inches in length, those at the front 2½. The lower crosspieces and arms, 2 inches in length, are made of a more slender portion of the quill than the uprights, and are stripped of the plume and smoothed with a sharp knife.

Fig. 1.—FEATHER CHAIR.

The pieces which compose the ornamental back are made from the tips of the feathers and are formed by cutting the filaments into pointed shape, as shown in the illustration. The seat is made of four pieces of a thick portion of the quill, each of which is smoothed on the outer side, and the filaments so cut on the inner side as to form a quarter-section. This must be very neatly done, and the sections cut to slightly overlap in forming the seat. All the parts are held firmly together by medium-sized pins which are driven through the uprights, and lengthwise into the crosspieces.

Much taste can be exercised in the choosing of feathers for this purpose, those with attractive markings being the most desirable.

Anent these miniature chairs, a correspondent writes as follows: "It was my sad pleasure not many weeks since to visit at a home for the insane, a friend I had not seen in thirteen years, and who in the interval had from a series of misfortunes become deranged. Deplorable as her state is, I was glad to find that her hallucinations were pleasant and comfortable ones. In the midst of all these wanderings, she keeps her room, clothing, and person in perfect order, and except when talking to visitors, is very busily engaged.

"As the matron said, 'She made a thousand and one pretty notions.' Her walls were covered with picture frames and brackets, and her tables with really beautiful articles. I examined everything carefully and wondered how a mind so restless and imaginative could fashion so many things, perfect in shape and harmonious in color. I examined so much the novel chair, shown in *figure 2*, that she begged me to take it home. The foundation of the cushion is a portion of the large end of a bottle cork, the upper side is padded with cotton and the whole neatly covered with pearl-colored silk. Embroidery in cross-stitches ornaments the edge and is done in 'single zephyr' worsted of a deep garnet color. The legs are made of strong pins. A small black bead is first slipped close to the head to represent a roller; then the whole is wound closely with the garnet worsted, and a large milk-white cut-glass bead is slipped over the worsted and brought to rest against the black one, and although the pins are closely wound, the worsted will recede from the points and become firm in place.

Fig. 2.—CHAIR FROM A HAIR-PIN.

"The back of the chair is formed of a medium-sized hairpin, with the ends bent outward. Half an inch above the lower end garnet worsted is woven in 'over-and-under-stitch' until three-fourths of an inch of the hairpin is covered; then a white bead is slipped over each prong of the hairpin and placed closely against the worsted. Half an inch more of space is woven of the worsted, then two more beads are added as before, and above them worsted is again woven to the space of one-fourth of an inch. The parts of the hairpin above this point are then wound like the legs, and the white and black beads finish the ends; the black bead should be made secure by wax. The uncovered part of the hairpin is then inserted in a neatly cut incision in the edge of the cushion when it assumes the form of a back. All is made complete by stretching a cord made of the worsted from the points of the hairpin to the lower beads, and from them to the back of the cushion." (1882)

Paper Dolls

As a class paper dolls possess many very desirable qualities. The small space they occupy when carefully packed, the slight charge for postage on them when they are to be sent some distance, and the amount of fun that can be extracted from a paper "Ethel Dorinda" or "Mehitabel," are some of the points that often induce women who make their holiday remembrances with their own nimble fingers to decide upon dainty paper dolls for those juvenile friends whose gifts must be transmitted through the Christmas bag of the post office.

In making a paper doll use cardboard or Bristol board for the foundation, so the arms and feet cannot be bent or broken off. A suitable form for a doll is given at *figure 216*, the outline of which may easily be copied on tracing paper and then transferred to the Bristol board. The face will be most effective if nicely painted with watercolors, but if the worker is not sufficiently skillful, one of the pretty colored heads of a commercially-sold paper doll may be pasted on. Be careful to select a head with the face turned in the same direction as that shown at *figure 216*, as otherwise the hat given further on would not fit it.

On the back of the foundation paste two strips of paper as at *figure 216A* and under them slip the upper end of the standard. The latter is made by securely pasting to a square of heavy pasteboard a section of lighter board cut after *figure 217A*; the tabs marked X are to be bent at right angles with the upright piece, *a*, those at the sides being turned in one direction and the middle one in the opposite direction. After gluing the tabs to the square, cover the entire lower part of the standard with crêpe paper in any desired shade, and outline the square. Cover the entire lower part of the

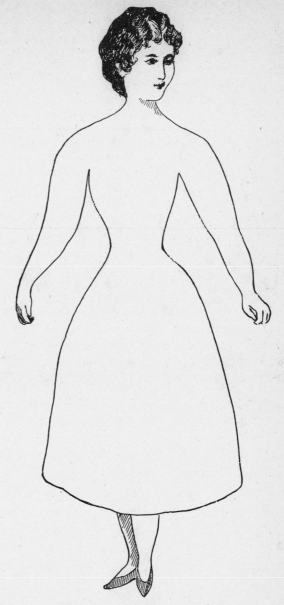

FIGURE NO. 216.

standard with crêpe paper in any desired shade, and outline the square with a cord of twisted paper as shown at *figure 217B*.

If a very strong standard is wanted, purchase at a hardware store a small quantity of iron wire about ⅛-inch in diameter, and bend it with a pair of pincers to resemble *figure 217C*, carrying one end to the center of the square, continuing it straight upward, and cutting it off about ½-inch below the top of the doll's head, so the hat will slip on easily. *Figure 217D* gives another view of the wire stand.

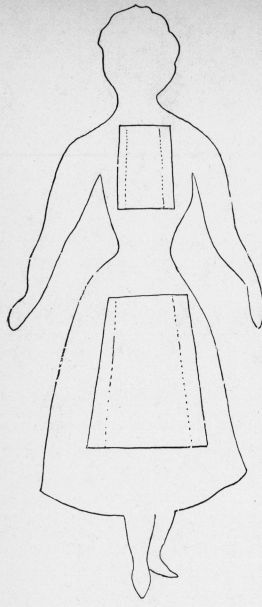

FIGURE NO. 216 A.

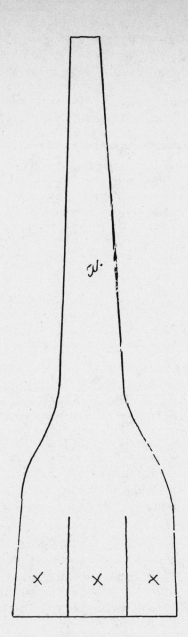

FIGURE NO. 217 A.

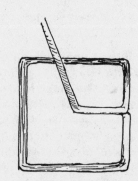

FIGURE NO. 217 B.

FIGURE NO. 217 C.

FIGURE NO. 217 D.

FIGURE NO. 218.

Morning Gown

The question of dress is, of course, a very important one, and the suggestions offered at *figure 218* will be found very helpful. This figure shows a dainty morning gown made of pale-pink crêpe paper over a foundation of heavy white paper, which may easily be shaped by following the outline of the doll at *figure 216*. The foundation should reach only to the neck and should be continued to the ankle, and the lower edge should be properly curved. On this form the dress is to be constructed, and if it is to be sewed, a quality of cardboard or Bristol board must be selected that will not break when sewed. Measure the distance from the waistline to the lower edge of the skirt, cut a piece of crêpe paper ¼-inch longer than the white foundation, and after stretching the lower edge to obtain a fluted effect, gather the paper and attach it with as few stitches as possible. Cut a section as at *figure 219*, ruffle the curved lower edge as in the case of the underskirt, and then gather this overskirt and attach it in its proper place as indicated at *figure 218*. The side edges of both skirts should be passed around the side edges of the foundation to produce the appearance of actual drapery, and the effect pictured at *figure 218* should be carefully imitated.

Form the waist or upper part of the dress of a piece of crêpe paper 2 inches square, gathering it at one side and fastening it around the waist over the upper edges of the skirt and overskirt. Cover the joining with a sash made of a strip of crêpe paper 2 inches wide and about 6 inches long; stretch the paper to its fullest extent to make it soft and pliant, pass it entirely about the doll at the waistline, and tie it in a single knot at the left side in front. Cut the ends pointed, and fold the sash slightly, to produce the soft, drooping appearance noted in a knotted sash-ribbon.

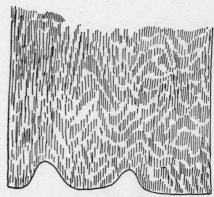

FIGURE NO. 219.

To make the sleeves, cut pieces of paper like *figure 220*. Gather each piece at the top along the dotted lines, and attach it to the foundation at or a little below the shoulder. Before confining the lower edge, stretch the sleeve through the middle so it will puff more softly. Then plait the lower edge as indicated at *figure 221*, secure it about ¾-inch from the lower end of the sleeve foundation, and complete the sleeve by passing a plain piece of crêpe paper about the exposed parts of the foundation and fastening it at the back. The puff of the sleeve must extend about the side edges of the white foundation to present an entirely realistic appearance.

For the broad ruffle around the neck use a strip of crêpe paper 1½ inches wide and 6 inches long. Ruffle the lower edge as directed for the skirt, and gather the other edge to fit the neck. The foundation at the top of the neck should be hollowed out, so that when the dress is on the doll the collar will appear to encircle the neck. Form the collar of a strip of paper folded and applied as at *figure 222*, letting it cover the upper edge of the ruffle. This dress can be varied by adding a second ruffle at the neck, by sewing ruffles to the lower edges of the skirt and overskirt, or by using colored paper for the sash and collar and white for the remainder of the dress.

FIGURE NO. 222.

Afternoon Costume

Figure 223 shows a very stylish afternoon or street costume. The skirt portion is laid in a single box-plait over the left hip, and one side of this plait is a very slight plait, while on the other are arranged a few scanty gathers or folds. The "spring" at the bottom of the skirt is produced by slightly stretching the lower edge.

The body portion of the dress consists of a plain piece of crêpe paper that is not even gathered at the waistline, and the sash is a band of the paper passed about the foundation and pulled in tightly to reveal the curved

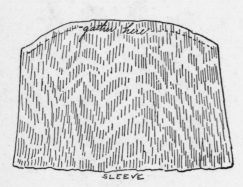

FIGURE NO. 220.

FIGURE NO. 221.

FIGURE NO. 223.

outline of the figure. The ruffles on the sleeves are cut like *figure 224* and are gathered and sewed on exactly as similar adjuncts would be applied on a cloth gown, each ruffle being turned over to conceal the joining seam and fall upon the sleeve. The sleeve is cut the shape of *figure 220*, but is a trifle longer so it will reach to the end of the sleeve foundation; and it is arranged and attached exactly like the sleeve of the dress described above. The collar also, is shaped like that of the other costume, and the bow and band are formed of a strip of paper cut the way of the crinkles, and are entirely arranged before being secured in place as pictured.

The hat is cut the shape of *figure 225*, and the trimming is shown at *figure 226*. A tall loop of paper matching the gown is secured at the back, a bow consisting of two loops of similar paper is secured in front, and a soft fold to correspond is carried over the brim from the back and through the opening for the head, which is cut at the curved line with a sharp knife. The head passes partly through this opening, and the hat is held in place by a strip of paper that is pasted at the ends only, as shown at *figure 227*.

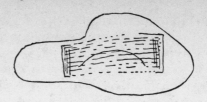

FIGURE No. 227.

Morning Costume

Figure 228 illustrates a morning costume. The skirt is so plain that very little explanation is necessary. The one pictured is ½-inch shorter than the dresses already described, but if a longer gown is desired, the depth may be easily increased. The costume is designed in Empire style and is made over a foundation, which differs from those used above in the length of the waist. The skirt extends ½-inch above the waistline, and the upper edge is properly gathered, while the lower edge is slightly stretched to present the fashionable "sprung" effect. The skirt is finished with a full ruffle that is carried about the side edges of the foundation.

FIGURE No. 224.

FIGURE No. 225.

FIGURE No. 226.

FIGURE No. 228.

221

The yoke-like waist is cut from plain crêpe paper, and the sleeve consists of two ruffles that are slightly curved at the top, one being twice as long as the other. Two rows of coarse, bright-hued embroidery silk are run through the paper at the edge of each ruffle, providing a border that adds greatly to the attractiveness of the gown. A girdle of crêpe paper is passed about the gown and arranged in an upright bow of short loops and ends at the left side, concealing the meeting of the skirt and waist.

Yachting Dress

No feminine wardrobe is counted complete nowadays unless it contains an outing or sailor suit, so we illustrate at *figure 229* a very dainty yachting dress, which is made up in two shades of blue. The skirt is edged with a plain band of dark paper cut across the crinkles. The waist has a pointed yoke cut from light paper and edged with a dark band, and at the center of the yoke is applied a five-pointed star made of the dark paper.

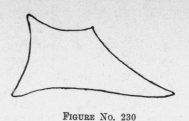

The lower part of the waist or blouse is first stretched, and its upper edge is gathered and attached to the foundation before the dark band completing the yoke is sewed or pasted to position. The lower edge of the blouse is then gathered and turned under, and the sides are made to conform to the outline of the foundation. The sleeve is shaped like *figure 220* and is completed with a dark-blue cuff. The lapels have separate foundations shaped like *figure 230* and covered smoothly with dark paper, as they are attached with paste after the sleeves are in position.

Evening Dress

A very artistic evening dress may be developed according to the design represented at *figure 223*. White crêpe paper may be used, and the skirt may be decorated with tiny festoons of delicately tinted flowers painted in watercolors. The lower edge may be ornamented with a frill of lace an inch or so deep, headed by a plain or loosely twisted band of crêpe paper. The festoons of flowers may be painted above this band, or rosebuds may be scattered over the entire surface of the dress. The ruffles over the shoulders may be covered with lace laid upon the crêpe paper before it is gathered.

"Models"

Almost any of the gowns illustrated in fashion plates may be imitated in paper for the doll's wardrobe, which may thus be easily kept fully in accord with the latest styles. Indeed, there is really no limit to the number of pleasing designs that can be executed in this easily handled material. The woman who possesses manual dexterity and some originality and ingenuity can, if she chooses, make a considerable income by constructing dolls or "models" for dressmakers to show their patrons, who are always eager to know how their gowns will look when made up. For this purpose the pretty china or bisque dolls are even more desirable than the paper ones, their movable arms being of no small advantage. Of course, the mode of dressing them differs considerably from that described above, especially in

FIGURE No. 229.

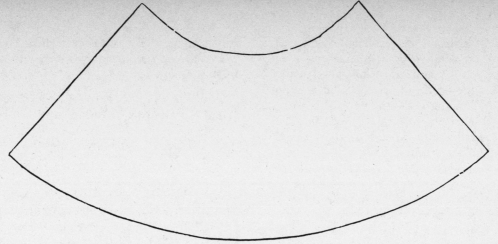

FIGURE No. 233.

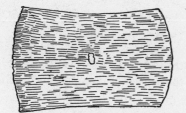

FIGURE No. 231.

the dimensions and shape of the various parts used, but the same style may be chosen.

In making a skirt for one of these dolls, it will be necessary to have a white underskirt and a skirt of the dress material, and both skirts must, of course, be cut to entirely encircle the doll, as the back must be as presentable as the front. The sleeves, also, must be large enough to pass completely about the arms, and the body portion must be so arranged that no joining will be noticeable on the shoulders. It will be best, therefore, to cut the waist after the plan illustrated at *figure 231*, being careful not to stretch the paper in the slightest degree out of its crinkles, that the fit may be correct.

There is a decided liking just now for bands or folds that cross the shoulders. These may be trimmed at the outer edges with ruffles, which will take the place of short sleeves and may be sewed in place before the bands are put on. *Figure 232* shows a dress arranged in

FIGURE No. 232.

FIGURE No. 234.

this way. If the doll is to simulate a grown person, it will be well to make the white skirt of plain notepaper, cutting it after *figure 233*, and increasing or decreasing the length to suit the height of the doll. The general proportions should be observed, and the paper, when arranged, should touch the surface on which the doll stands. *Figure 234* shows a rear view of the dress seen at *figure 232*, which is for a child doll. Of course, the larger the doll the more elaborate the dress may be, and the easier it will be to adapt fashion plates for its gowning. Paper dolls have this decided advantage over those of china or bisque, that they may be so adapted as to show perfect grace of figure, which is usually lacking in the ordinary doll.

Clothespin Doll

An ordinary wooden clothespin may be made to serve as a foundation for a paper doll, and if proper care is exercised in the dressing and finishing, no one will suspect at a casual glance what a homely article forms the basis of its construction. *Figures 235* and *236* give a front and back view of a doll made in this way. *Figure 237A* shows the clothespin covered with paper to form the head and body.

The head is painted with oil colors, the features being carefully imitated; and the coiffure is formed of a little tuft of natural hair that is coiled about at the back of the head and surmounted by a broad-brimmed hat, which is bent in two deep curves at the left side and trimmed with stiff, upright folds of paper. The hat with one curve bent is shown at *figure 237B*. The figure is, of course, slightly padded to present the proper outlines of the body, and an underskirt is cut from stiff notepaper according to *figure 237C* to serve as a support for the doll, and also to hold out the skirt, which is shaped like *figure 237D*. The arms are cut from cardboard by *figure 237E*, and the sleeves, shaped like *figure 237F*, are drawn at the curved edge to fit about the shoulder, and above the straight edge to form a wrist frill, as at *figure 237G*. The shoulder frill is shaped like *figure 237H* and joined to a straight band that is arranged in surplice fashion in front. The overskirt draper is like *figure 237I*, and the sash is a straight piece of paper bowed at the back.

FIGURE No. 236.

FIGURE No. 235.

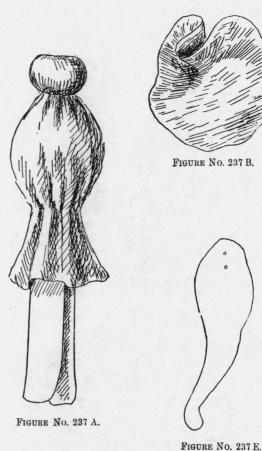

FIGURE No. 237 B.

FIGURE No. 237 A.

FIGURE No. 237 E.

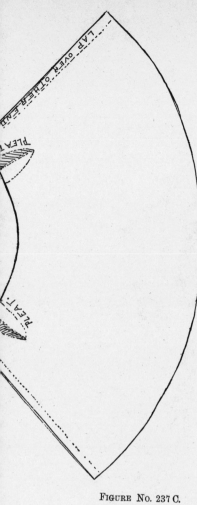

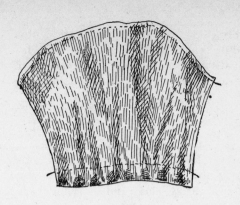

FIGURE NO. 237 F.

FIGURE NO. 237 C.

FIGURE NO. 237 G.

FIGURE NO. 237 H.

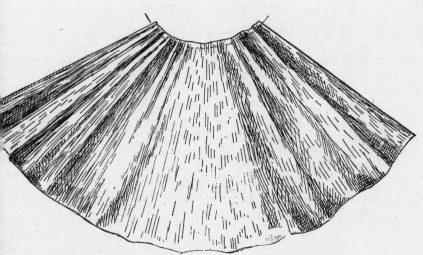

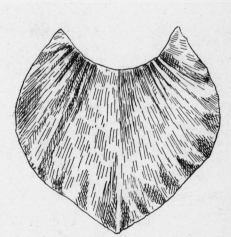

FIGURE NO. 237 D.

FIGURE NO. 237 I.

Bride's Costume

Figure 238 represents a bride's costume made of white crêpe paper and decorated with lace and flowers. The veil is of tulle (silk tulle is best), and a tiny bunch of flowers made of white French tissue paper holds it in place.

The very elaborate doll's costume pictured at *figure 239* is made of pink and black crêpe paper and white French tissue paper. The ruffles are white and are not gathered, but are secured in place with flour paste. The decoration at the wrists is black, and so is the sash, which is evenly fringed at the ends with very sharp scissors. If it is not convenient to obtain black paper, pink may be used instead.

The current fashions may always be easily adapted, especially to the dolls made on clothespins. Such a doll, however, can have but one dress at a time, while a flat paper doll may have a dozen or more, which may be readily fastened on by means of straps of flat silk elastic sewed upon the dress foundation before any of the dress is attached. The head is slipped under the straps, which will hold the dress to the doll much more satisfactorily than paper straps could do. *Figure 240* displays a back view of a dress with straps attached. (1895)

FIGURE NO. 239

FIGURE NO. 238.

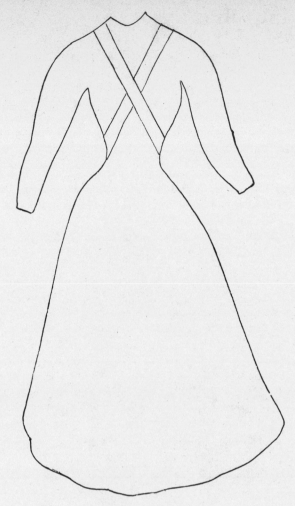

FIGURE No. 240.

For a head, what could be better than a grape. Since the lady must have arms, a straw is stuck in each side. In order that she might be in full dress, a belt of the skin of a rhubarb stalk is furnished. The feet are made of beans and are attached to the flower with toothpicks. A full head of hair is composed of corn silk. Our artist has taken the liberty of gilding the grape with a painted face. (1869)

A "Wishbone" Doll

Among the many invented dolls, there is none more original and odd than the one here shown. The frame (*figure 1*) is a chicken's "wishbone." The head is made

Fig. 1.—THE FRAME.

of black wax, which, when warm, is easily modeled into shape. The mouth and lips are fashioned of red wax. Two small white beads are used for eyes, and when inserted, should be pressed down so that the black wax will fill the holes. The feet are made of black wax, and can be turned in any direction, when as in *figure 2*, the doll has the appearance of walking.

A Horticultural Doll

The starting point is a hollyhock flower which, turned upside down, furnishes in its colored part a very nice skirt, and the green part (calyx), a nicely-fitting waist.

Fig. 2.

227

The clothing consists of a pair of black flannel pants, a scarlet flannel skirt and circular cape, trimmed with a band of black velvet. The cape is finished at the neck with long pointed paper collar, and yellow silk necktie. A cap is then finished with yellow silk tassel and attached to the head with mucilage. (1883)

A CARD OR PANEL DOLL.

A Doll Panel

A rosy-cheeked little girl upon a black panel is one of the novelties of the season. The face, and perhaps figure, are cut from one of the infinite variety of pictures in newspapers or periodicals, and pasted on. Then the puppet is dressed in a real costume; tiny little lace cap, or beaver hat, white skirt, silk dress, cloth sack, even a collar around her neck, and wee bits of slippers, or shoes, made from an old kid glove, on her feet. All is as complete as the outfit of any mother's darling on Broadway, excepting only that her clothes are fastened with mucilage, instead of being sewed and buttoned.

It requires very skillful fingers to make these panels nicely, but when finished, they are a charming remembrance for the children for New Year's and birthdays. (1883)

Lamp Brackets

The lamp bracket may be merely a simple shelf or a very elaborate affair. We like to see such things homemade, and they afford an opportunity for the younger members of the family, both boys and girls, to display their skill. A lady of our acquaintance is quite celebrated among her friends for her handiwork with the saw and knife. She has sent us a very simple and not inelegant pattern for beginners.

Take ½-inch stuff and mark out with the compass a circle 10 inches in diameter. Inside of this, mark another circle ¾ of an inch less. Divide the circle into four parts, as shown by the dotted lines in *figure 2*. Then mark the smaller circles, leaving the cross-bars as shown in the engraving. This forms the back piece. A solid semi-circular piece, *figure 3*, serves for the shelf, and the brace, *figure 4*, is made exactly like one-quarter of the back piece.

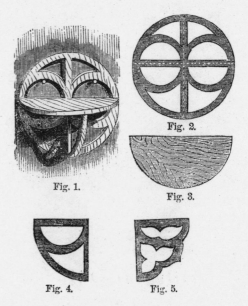

Fig. 1. Fig. 2.

Fig. 3.

Fig. 4. Fig. 5.

The whole can be laid out with the compass and square, and be cut out with a compass saw. The parts may be put together with wooden pins or with glue. It may be suspended by means of two brass-headed nails driven into the wall, as shown in *figure 1*. If the bracket is made of soft wood, the parts may be cut out with a knife.

When one becomes skilled in this kind of work, the pattern may be made more elaborate. In *figure 5* our artist suggests a slight variation which will give an idea for other patterns. When the regular form first given is departed from, it is best to make the pattern on a piece of stiff paper, and carefully draw it out upon the wood. The wood of which cigar boxes are made is often used for small work of this kind.

There is a great deal of power wasted by boys in whittling, and it would be well if these suggestions would induce them to whittle to some purpose. A pair of neat brackets would allow a boy to surprise his mother or some friend with a most acceptable present, and even the father need not be ashamed to bring in from the workshop a pair that he has made. (1869)

Soap Cups

Soap dishes of some kind are indispensable about the kitchen sink or wash room if the housekeeper means to be neat and orderly. The illustration presents cheap forms of these articles. *Figure 1* is a berry bowl, such as is retailed in the market for a few cents. It is turned in a lathe from poplar or any soft wood, and makes a convenient dish for hard soap.

Figure 2 is made from two blocks of inch board, about 4½ inches square, with a hole cut in the middle. Between the blocks a strip of copper or iron screening is inserted, and the two blocks are pinned or screwed together so as to bring the grain at right angles. These dishes can be made at home, and have this advantage over stone china or earthen ones, that they are not easily broken.

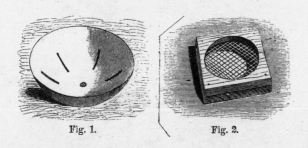

Fig. 1.   Fig. 2.

These illustrations of ornamental and useful articles are given frequently within these pages for the purpose of encouraging their home manufacture. In many parts of the country, where labor and material are plenty, they can be made cheaper than they can be purchased, and making them serves to develop the mechanical skill of the boys, and affords them interesting and profitable occupation. A little workshop, with a turning lathe and a tool chest, is one of the best investments a father can make for his sons. They will spoil some good timber, some screws and nails, and cut their fingers perhaps, but will soon learn to use tools efficiently, and will get an education in practical matters quite as valuable as anything they learn in schools. (1868)

Birdhouse

A correspondent in Danvers, Massachusetts, sends a drawing of a birdhouse made from flower pots and saucers. He says nothing about fastening the parts together, which we should think it necessary to do with a little water lime or other cement, else the birds might find themselves houseless during a violent storm.

The bottom board is nailed to the top of the pole. Upon this is set a five-inch flowerpot which is covered by the saucer of an 8-inch pot. Upon this is placed a 5-inch saucer, and the whole surmounted by an inverted 2-inch pot. The hole can be easily knocked out, and trimmed with a jackknife, the soft burned ware whittling as easily as slate pencil. (1869)

A Rustic Birdcage

Building birdcages is one of the amusements of boys who like to use carpenters' tools, and here is a pattern of a very pretty one. It is a cage for a parrot, but the same style may be followed in making one for smaller birds.

The sticks are all cedar and left "rustic." Other wood with the bark on may be used. The roof is covered with sticks, split in halves and tacked on. The platform with the ladders seen inside will not be needed for small birds. In making a thing of this kind, start with a definite plan. Draw out the parts on a piece of coarse paper in the proper proportion, and then work to measure. Where the pieces of wood cross one another, as in the door, they are "halved together," as the carpenters say; that is, a piece is cut out of each stick halfway through, and one stick is let into the other. But few tools are required—a fine saw, a good knife, and a gimlet for boring. Try to make straight lines and square corners, and endeavor to learn something even in building a birdhouse. (1870)

A Rustic Bird-Cage.

A Boys' And Girls' Birdhouse

We call it a boys' and girls' birdhouse because any boy with ingenuity can make it for his sister, or the two can make it in common.

The foundation of the house is any convenient-sized wooden box. A piece is nailed to each end, cut to the slope it is desired to have the roof. As the roof is to

SWALLOW.　　　NUN.　　　TRUMPETER.　　　　LETZ.　BLACK PRIESTS.　　　　　　BEARDED TUMBLERS.
　　　　　　　　　　　　JACOBIN.　　　(COPYRIGHT SECURED.)　　　　　　　　　FAN-TAILS.

GROUP OF FANCY PIGEONS.—*Drawn and Engraved for the American Agriculturist.*

Fig. 1.—FRAMEWORK OF BIRD-HOUSE.   Fig. 2.—SPLIT STICK.   Fig. 3.—BIRD-HOUSE COMPLETE.

be thatched, it had better be pretty steep, as it will not only shed the rain the more easily, but the house will look better.

The upper end of the pole which is to support the house is made square; it passes through a hole in the bottom of the box, and extends far enough above the ridge of the roof, to form the chimney. A ridge pole is then passed through the upright pole and the end pieces, as shown in *figure 1*.

Places for the windows are to be cut out, but the door may be only a dummy, and painted black. Birds are not very particular how they enter the house, and will go through a window just as well as a door. As we wish the house to have a pleasing appearance, we must cover it so as to represent a log cabin. For this purpose small branches of any straight, easy-splitting wood are to be cut of the proper lengths, and split lengthwise, as in *figure 2*. These, with the bark on, are then to be fastened by small nails all over the exterior of the house, as shown in *figure 3*.

The roof is then to be thatched. Here is how to do it: We should tie the straw into small bundles with twine, making them long enough to reach from one side of the house to the other and able to project well over to form the eaves. Then we should nail the bundles, one by one, to the upper edges of the box, and bind them at the top to the ridge pole, by means of twine. The bundles must be crowded up close to one another to prevent leaking. If this way of putting on the straw does not work, you can no doubt hit upon some other that will.

The house may be divided up to accommodate several families. The lower story may be so partitioned as to form four rooms, with an entrance-window to each, and the garret can have a division across it, and make two rooms, which can be entered by windows in the gable ends. The appearance of the house will be much improved, and it will stand the weather better, if the wood has a coating of painter's oil.

Birds will like a house of this kind better than they will the showy painted things that are often provided for them. When the house is in place, you can put "To Let" on it, if you choose, but the birds will come just as soon without it, and it is very amusing to see the little things out house-hunting. The enjoyment of a birdhouse may be much increased if you put in some quiet place nearby such materials as the birds use in making their nests; cut hay, locks of wool, old curled hair, shreds and ravelings of cloth, feathers, and the like, will all be acceptable.

The whole affair may be made much more ornamental by setting some climbing plants at the bottom of the pole. A hop-vine will grow very quickly, and make a fine mass of green. If strong strings or wires are attached near the top of the post, and their other ends fastened to pegs driven into the ground, you can plant morning-glory seeds and soon have a fine pyramid of vines, which in the early morning will be covered with flowers. (1872)

Easter Eggs

The exchange of eggs between friends, as a token of love or friendship, is a very ancient custom, dating back almost to the flood, for it is a symbol of the ark, as well as of the resurrection, which is the reason that they are presented at Easter. It is moreover a very universal custom prevailing among different nations and reli-

A GROUP OF EASTER EGGS.

appropriate texts of Scripture. For these painted eggs, it is better to puncture a tiny hole with a pin in each side, and blow out the inside, leaving a clear shell, than to boil them. The apertures can be concealed by stars of silver of gilt paper.

In former times, boys used to hold egg contests on Easter Monday with hard-boiled eggs. In Cheshire, England, children go round the village and beg for eggs for their Easter dinner, singing a song addressed to the farmer's wife. Asking for "an egg, bacon, cheese, or an apple, or any good thing that will make us merry!", they end with, "And I pray you, good dame, an Easter egg."

AN ODDLY-COLORED EASTER EGG.

gions. The Jews placed eggs on their Passover tables, the Druids used them in their ceremonies, and the Persians frequently give them as New Year's gifts. If you should happen to be in Russia, a Russian would greet you on Easter morning with "Christ is risen," and offer you an Easter egg. Stranger still, if you were in the Far East, a Mohammedan would also offer a decorated egg. At city confectioners, fancy sugar eggs—some of them of enormous size, and containing panoramas of landscapes and figures, or else filled with bonbons—may be had at all prices, but appropriate homemade ones are worth twice as much.

It is a good plan for the Easter egg colorers of a neighborhood to hold a sort of "bee," and unite in the production of the dyes, thus saving time and money. To dye eggs, onion skins put in the water in which they are boiled will make them a bright yellow; or, if left longer in the solution, a rich brown. Violet ink gives a royal purple. Cochineal will produce pink and crimson. Many pieces of chintz, or bright ribbon that fade easily, if sewed tightly round the eggs, will color them nicely in figures, stripes, or dots. Another way to decorate is to dip an egg into hot water, and then write a name or motto on the shell with tallow. It is then boiled in the solution of dye, and the inscription will appear in white, upon a colored ground.

Those who are skillful with pencil and paint brush can present their friends with really exquisite souvenirs by ornamenting eggs with flowers and butterflies or

Charles the Second once presented one of his favorites with an Easter egg made of silver; and in the British Museum, in London, is still preserved a curious and beautiful one, given almost two hundred years ago to a lady of high rank. It was sawed open, the shell lined with gold paper and decorated with figures of saints done in silk. It opens and shuts and is tied with green ribbons. (1883)

The Game of Croquet

In the spring, sunny days and the green grass remind us pleasantly of the mallets and hoops that were laid aside only with the late frosts. The popularity of croquet (pronounced *cro-kay*) is not difficult to account for. It is one of the few outdoor games which both sexes can share. The implements used in the pastime are simple and cheap, the field for its enjoyment is the yard or lawn adjoining the home, the exercise is gentle and facilitates

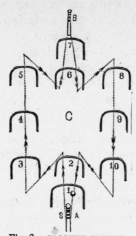

| Fig. 1.—THE MALLET. | Fig. 2.—CROQUET GROUND. | Fig. 3. CROQUET GROUND. | Fig. 4. CROQUET GROUND. |

rather than hinders conversation. It is always at hand—a pleasant relaxation for young and old. It is best known in cities and villages. Many think it deserves a wider range in the country, where the people work quite as hard, and need quite as much a cheerful recreation. All the materials of the game can be got up by any skillful boy who can use a lathe and handle a brush.

The mallet seen in the hands of the player, *figure 1*, requires a thin, round handle about 3 feet in length; the head say 5 inches long, and 2½ inches in diameter—smaller in the middle than at the ends. The bottom of the handles should be painted with different colors to correspond with one of the balls. It takes eight of these mallets to play a full game.

The balls are also eight in number, and should be painted with a single stripe, or all over, of the following colors: blue, pink, black, yellow, brown, orange, green, red. They should be about eight inches in circumference, perfectly round, and should be made of hard-wood—maple, cherry, oak, ash, or walnut.

The hoops, ten in number, are made of wire, about 16 inches high and 12 wide, and painted white, for convenience in seeing, if the game should be prolonged into the twilight, as sometimes happens. Wire ⅜-inch in diameter will answer a good purpose. Rods of wood might be used, but they are not as durable and are not recommended.

The posts, two in number, should be about 24 inches high, and sharpened for driving into the ground. The upper end is marked with 8 divisions, as seen in *figure 2*, by painting in colors to correspond with the balls. This arrangement of colors is to distinguish the two sides in playing, the *alternate* colors being matched against one another. This arrangement brings the light colored balls on one side and the dark upon the other.

The arena, or spot for playing, is a matter of some importance. Any smooth turf will answer, but it is better to have it graded perfectly level for the purpose, as it gives a much better chance for skillful playing. Make the turf thick by top-dressing and frequent mowing, and it will last much longer.

The game begins by choosing sides, the captain of one side taking the blue ball and mallet, and the captain of the other side the pink, and so on in due order. Eight can play, or any smaller number down to two. If only two play they can use two balls each, playing them alternately. The hoops may be arranged in either of three orders, shown in *figures 2, 3,* or *4.* The playing begins at the spot or foot of the arena, and the object is to drive the balls through all the hoops in the direction indicated by the dotted lines and arrows, and to strike the two posts. The side all of whose members do this first wins the game. To "croquet" is to put your own ball against the one you have hit, and holding it firmly with the foot, strike it with the mallet and send off the ball it touches by the communicated force. As you can "croquet" friend or foe and help or hinder the object in view, this croqueting becomes a very important part of the game.

The captain holding the blue ball places it in any direction, twelve inches from the starting stake, and with a blow tries to drive it through the first hoop. It is his stroke as long as he drives the ball through a hoop. When he fails, the captain on the other side plays, and it is his stroke if he drive his ball through a hoop, or hit his enemy's ball. The *hitting* is called "roqueting," and gives him the privilege of croqueting, which he does by sending his enemy's ball as far off the track as possible. When he has missed, the other players follow in the order in which the colors are marked upon the post.

233

Until a player has gone through the first hoop, he is not allowed to have an extra turn, even if his ball has hit that of another.

The player who reaches the turning post first has great advantage for a time, for as soon as he touches it he commences his return journey, and meeting the other players on their road to the farthest part of their journey, he is able to croquet them and considerably impede their progress. When a player has passed through all the hoops he becomes "a rover," and is privileged to rove about all the ground, croqueting his friends and foes. A good player, when thus situated, can prove of immense advantage to his side, and should on no account hit the starting or winning post until all on his side have passed through the last hoop. The game grows most exciting as the last pair approach the winning post and one player by a dexterous stroke hits it and wins the game.

Parlor croquet is played upon a board made for the purpose with the same arrangement of hoops and posts as shown in the diagrams. The mallets, balls, and hoops, of course, have to be much smaller, and the croqueting must be done by placing the forefinger, instead of the foot, upon the ball. The best boards have a rim to them with a steel wire stretched parallel to the sides and ends, against which the balls strike and rebound. This gives opportunity for much more skill in the game.

The rules of the game are quite numerous and differ somewhat in different localities. The essential principles and course of the game have been indicated, and any rules may be adopted that the players can agree upon. They are soon learned from a skillful player. (1868)

About Kites

The kite is a toy which depends upon very philosophical principles. And there is a good deal of skill required to make a good kite and fly it well. Fall is just the time for kite-flying, for the grass is mown and the grain is much of it harvested, so that the fields are clear, and there is room enough to raise the kite without doing any injury.

A good kite is strong and light—and of such a shape that a great surface is exposed to the wind in proportion to the amount of wood in the frame. A square kite, or a diamond-shaped one, or a six-cornered one, are each better than a bow-kite because there is so much wood in the bow that it is hard to make a bow-kite that will fly well in a light breeze.

Whoever makes a kite should take care to make it perfectly symmetrical—that is, just the same on one half as on the other, just as heavy, and to look the same. Select straight-grained pieces of pine wood and have them of very even size throughout, somewhat flat and without splits—as light as you think they will do.

For a square kite, cross two pieces of equal length at the middle of each. Tie them together with waxed shoelaces if you can get them; they will not slip—and it is not best to cut notches or nail them, for this weakens the wood. Then take a stout linen cord, and having notched the sticks on the ends, pass the string around and tie it as tight as you can and not split or make the sticks bow, and drive a small carpet tack into each end through the string.

Next make some paste—which is done thus: Take a tablespoon of flour, put it in a teacup and wet it with a little *cold* water and stir it up till it is as thin and smooth as cream. Next stir it slowly into about a teacupful of boiling water in an old pan. This will make a beautiful, smooth, clear paste, and if you stir some salt or powdered alum into it, it will keep a long time.

When the paste is made, spread a newspaper out on the clean floor, or upon another paper, and lay your kite-frame upon it. Then cut the paper about an inch larger all around than the frame. Beginning on one side, spread a thin coat of paste on the edge of the paper and paste it over the cord; then do the opposite side. Next cut the paper at the corners so that it shall fold smooth, and paste the other edges. Finally paste several narrow strips of stout paper across the sticks to keep the paper from tearing off or rattling. Care must be taken to have the paper very smooth and tight, and if the paste is strong it answers sometimes to dampen the paper slightly but evenly when it is pasted. It will then be tight as a drumhead.

To make a diamond-kite, have one stick about ⅔ as long as the other and let it cross ⅛ from the top of the long one. Otherwise make it like a square kite.

Fasten the line to strings tied to the sticks, going through the paper, so that it may be slipped up and down. The amount of wind the kite holds may be regulated in this way—the higher it is "hung" the less wind it will hold, but the more it will take to hold it. It must always be hung above the middle or it will not go up. Light woolen strips make the best tails—the length of which must be regulated according to the strength of the wind. So also must the strength of the line for a light line will do very well in a nearly still day. But when the wind blows hard, the line must be strong or the fruits of much labor will be lost. (1862)

A Toy Hand Roller

Here are instructions for making a roller, which, moreover, when of rather larger dimensions than that of a toy shop, is a very useful article to run over seedbeds in the garden, where the soil is light, and is almost as easy to make as the toy roller. In the latter, however, we shall want a frame of deal and a turned cylinder of wood. Taking the handle at 2½ feet or 3 feet at most, according to the size of the child for whom it is intended, it may be planed to a width of 1½ inches to 2 inches, and a thickness of ⅜-inch to ½-inch.

The engraving (*figure 27*) is made to scale to show the proportions of the different parts. The handle (*A*) is 3 feet long, the rails (*C, C, B, B*) are 2 feet, the sides (*E, E*) 1 foot. The roller is 9 inches in diameter, and just long enough to turn easily between the side pieces in which its axles are made to run in two holes, which ought to have

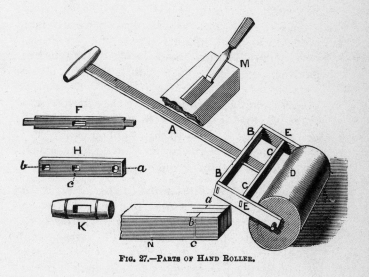

FIG. 27.—PARTS OF HAND ROLLER.

little tubes of tin or brass let in. This is called "bushing" the holes, and is done in the case of real rollers, wooden clocks, and other articles of the kind where the axles of wheels have to revolve in holes bored in the wood framing which holds them together. It is often possible to get bits of brass tubing for such purposes as the present, but tin will do almost as well, and it need not be soldered, but only bent round to meet, and then hammered into its place.

F is a plan view of *B, B,* or *C, C,* which are exactly alike. The central square hole allows the long handle to go through it, fitting well and closely. The ends are to be cut as shown, *i.e.,* with tenons to fit well into mortices in the side pieces, one of which is seen in plan at *H.*

In these pieces *a* is the bushed hole for the roller pin; *b* and *c* the square holes to receive the tenons of the rails *B, B,* and *C, C.* It is as well to make the sides of rather thicker stuff, say, ½-inch, if the rest is of ⅜-inch scantling. The end of the long handle should be tenoned and fitted into a short rounded piece about 6 inches long, like *K,* and pinned through. If the different tenons are made to fit and are glued, there will be no need, in a toy of this kind, to pin or wedge them, as they will be quite strong enough without.

The axle of the roller is made of two pins of stout wire about the size of a pencil, driven in after the cylinder is in place. Bore holes truly central and point the wires slightly. Another plan is to use two long screws passed in from the outside. The heads may be filed off, but it is quite as well to leave them as they are. Paint the roller as you wish. (1883)

A Toy Wheelbarrow

In the following description of a toy wheelbarrow are given such instructions as will suffice for a really useful article fit for work in a garden. Of whatever size it is made, a child's barrow should be of utility to the little gardener, or it becomes a foolish toy, fit only for keeping baby fingers out of mischief. There is no greater pleasure to a child than to take a barrow out of doors and load it with rubbish, and no more healthy amusement can be devised than light outdoor work of this kind, which may also be made to teach many a useful lesson of tidiness and industry.

The ordinary child's barrow (*A, figure 30*) is constructed in the simplest manner that can be devised, and is not by any means a bad one. It might, with one or two modifications, answer on a larger scale, and it certainly has the advantage over those in daily use that it is much less prone to tip over sideways, because the center of

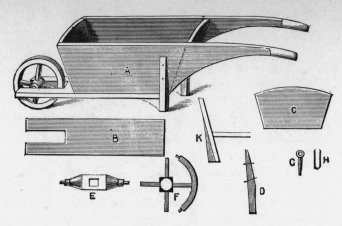

FIG. 30.—ORDINARY WHEELBARROW.

gravity is below the level of the hands. But this is an advantage with a drawback. It is better for wheeling, but renders it difficult to discharge the load at the end of the journey, and hence it is that this design has not gained favor. But for children's use it is perfect, because their difficulty always is to prevent an upset, and if they try to wheel a barrow of ordinary shape fairly loaded they generally capsize the whole before arriving at their destination.

Each side is made of a single board sawn out to the form shown. The front, cut like *C,* and the back of similar form, are then nailed inside these. These front and back boards ought to be thicker than the sides, to make a strong job, because, if thin, you have to use nails too slight to hold all securely.

The bottom, which also forms the bearing of the wheel, is cut like *B,* the wheel running in the slot. By an oversight, the engraver has illustrated a barrow that will tip easily like that used by gardeners. For a child's safe barrow the sides are continued like short shafts to take the wheel, the axle thus lying above the center of gravity of the load. *D* shows one leg sloped off towards the top to suit the outward slope of the side, and so bring the legs into an upright position.

The arrangement of these essential parts of a toy barrow is always faulty, and very soon the legs are seen to have taken up a walking position instead of remaining perpendicular. To prevent this, there should always be a stay of light iron rod (if the barrow is intended for use) attached at one end to the bottom the the leg and at the other to the underside of the bottom of the barrow.

In a mere toy, when it is easy to find stuff wide enough, the side boards may even be shaped like the dotted line, and thus, form the legs. But, if so, these boards must not splay or slope outward much, as they will throw the parts forming the legs too far out of the perpendicular. In this case a bit of stuff can be sloped like *K* and nailed on outside (*K*, the part shaded, being an independent leg similar to *D*, but nailed all the way down, and thus forming a much stronger support than when cut and attached with only a nail or two in its upper end). The parts of the side boards which form the handles are rounded off with a spokeshave, so as not to hurt the hands.

A barrow wheel, if made of wood, is always formed in a peculiar way, unlike any other wheel. The nave, square in the middle, slopes off at each end, and has iron ferrules driven on to prevent splitting, as the pivots are driven in and have to bear the weight of the load and stand the ceaseless strain and jar of wheeling it. Through the middle of the squared part a mortice is cut in one direction to receive the piece *F*, which forms two spokes, and is shaped as shown, fitting the mortice in the middle, and being rounded at the ends to go into holes bored in the rim or felloe.

This being put in place, a hole is now pierced through the axle in the other direction, passing, of course, through the center of the piece just described. This is a round hole, and a portion of rounded ash, or oak, or elm, forming the other two spokes of the wheel, is now driven in tightly, fixing the flat portion securely and completing this part of the wheel. The rim, made of two, or at most of three, separate pieces, as already described, is now fitted on and worked up to a correct form, and an iron tire completes it.

Such is the mode of construction without independent framing, which generally finds favor with toy-makers. Nothing can be better for a child's barrow. (1882)

A Toy Windmill

There is, perhaps, no toy that allows of the exercise of ingenuity as much as the windmill. We meet with it in various forms in the toy shops, and there are many others which it may take until it becomes an absolutely correct model of the well-known machine. The simplest toy windmill is that consisting of four light arms with colored paper attached to the ends, and a pin or small nail through the center, by which these small sails are attached to the end of a light rod, but so as to turn freely upon it. Faced to the wind, the rod held in the hand, the small sails spin merrily enough.

Here, however, described in detail, is a much more interesting windmill, one which will give you great pleasure, although you will have to turn the sails yourself by means of a small handle. It is made to take

apart, and it has a click-clack attachment, to say nothing of a flight of steps, or step ladder, on which can possibly stand the (toy) miller himself.

First of all there is the stand, consisting of a square board about 2 inches each way, with four knobs at the corners to make it stand more firmly. This will be better if made 3 inches square of ½-inch deal, as it has to support the whole structure. It will be still better weighted underneath by attaching to it a bit of sheet lead. It will not then require to be steadied by the hand while working the sails. In the drawing (*figure 33*), which is partly sectional to show the inside of the mill, this stand is marked *A*.

In the center of this board is glued a round turned boss (*B*) to add to its thickness, and thereby give greater steadiness to the pillar which comes next to it. This may be 1¼ inches in diameter, and ¼-inch or more in thickness. In the center of it a hole must be made about the size of a pencil, which must also penetrate through the square board. It will be best made by a shell bit or nose bit used in the brace—a gimlet may split the wood, and will not make so smooth and round a hole.

FIG. 33.—SIMPLE MILL WITH CLICK-CLACK ATTACHMENT.

237

We now arrive at (*E*) a turned pillar, 1½ inches to 2 inches long and about 1 inch in diameter, which is to be turned with two tenons or pins, one to fit the hole just described, the other, a similar one, to enter in the bottom board and boss of the mill itself. This pillar should be made of beech or ash, not of deal; but, if the latter is used, it will be as well to bore holes and glue in these pins made of some harder wood.

C is a boss similar to *B* glued to the center of *D*, and serving a similar purpose. *D* may be 3 inches square, *i.e.*, the same size as the lower board, and ⅜-inch thick. Near the corners, holes are to be bored, but not so large as the others, say, the size of a penholder. It is as well to put a boss also under each of these corner holes, as they prevent the wood from splitting if put with the grain across that of the board to which they are attached.

All the parts described should be made as neatly as possible, so as to fit together without the least shakiness. For a thoroughly good job the bottom board might be of ¼-inch stuff only, with strips ⅜-inch broad glued on, so as to give it the form of a framed panel, which will prevent it from warping. If this is not done, let the stuff be very dry, and use by preference a harder wood than deal. Let it be quite square with nice clean sharply-cut edges.

Thus far we have built up the stand and floor. This may be glued up, of course, if preferred, but one chief pleasure of this kind of toy is derived from taking it apart and building it again *ad libitum*. Thus, if possible, do not glue any part of it until perhaps by frequent use it may have become shaky. It might then be glued together and remain as an ordinary toy.

We now have to plane up the angle pieces (*H*), which also fit by pegs into the bottom where the holes were made for that purpose. Here again, as in the rest of the main framework, deal is not so good a material as beech or ash, but it will do fairly well. The original mill was a German or Swiss toy, constructed of the well-known beautiful white pine of finer grain than deal, and less prone on that account to split.

The pillars may be 3 inches or 3½ inches in height, and are grooved on two adjacent sides, as shown at *F* and *G*, which is the cross section. They may be ⅜-inch wide each way with ⅛-inch groove. This groove a carpenter would plane out with a plow or grooving plane, or with a gauge made on purpose, but it is easy to manage it with a mitering saw and small chisel. An ordinary gauge is, however, a good tool to use to mark the groove out with the grain of the wood; and one made with a cutting edge instead of a mere point (a tool easily made at any time) will do such work most efficiently.

There is such a tool called a string or stringing gauge. It is used to plow out a straight and narrow groove for the insertion of strips of veneer, to form ornamental lines in pieces of furniture. Whenever a gauge is wanted for special jobs, it is quite easy to make them without a sliding head. A bit of hard wood is cut like *K* (*figure 33*), and gauge points inserted at the required distance from the head. They are made thus for marking out sash work and many other such jobs which have to be repeated to the same dimensions. They are also made like *L* in steps. These cannot be purchased, but are made by the carpenter for special requirements to save the trouble of setting and readjusting the sliding gauges commonly seen. It is easy to make one of these to plow out the grooves in the upright posts of the mill.

The object of the groove is to receive the sliding panels of thin board, forming the four sides of the mill, each of which has a little window, and one the door, with hinges of fine wire or of thin leather glued on. These sides are of stuff barely ⅛-inch thick, merely bits of board very truly squared up. They are slid into the grooves in the posts, and then four little beams like *M*, *M*, with holes through them near the ends, slip over the upper pegs of the posts and keep them from spreading, thus securing the structure.

The top beams are to be notched out at their extremities to fit with a half lap upon each other and upon the pegs, so as to form a level surface upon which to set the roof. This may be made of a solid pyramidal-shaped bit of deal, painted in oil colors to imitate tiles or wood. It is made to fit on the top beams by four short pins, of which two are seen in *a,b*. On the summit is a turned ornament or a weathercock. In one part of the floor a trap door (*P*) is made and hinged with leather. Through this the chain falls for lifting sacks. The windows should have glass put in, which may be secured inside where not seen by strips of calico glued over its edges and attached to the boards. Very thin glass should be used to make a neat job of it.

We now have to form the sails and arrange the axle to carry them. The latter is turned with an enlarged part at *O*, or this is turned and made to slip on stiffly. The axle is also made to fit tightly in a wooden cogwheel and a cotton spool (*S*). Its lower end is made smaller, so as to have a shoulder at *X*, which rests against the three-cornered bit (*T*), glued to the wall on that side, and which is necessary on account of the angle which the axle itself makes with the side of the mill. The wheel (*R*) has a wooden spring resting on the cogs to cause the clacking noise when the sails turn. The spring is fastened securely at one end to the inside of the wall nearest to the wheel. The sails or vanes are merely thin pieces of board cut as shown, and rounded at the end to fit into holes in the boss of the axle.

Not being intended to turn by the wind, these may stand quite flat, as they generally do, or they may be turned in the holes to set at any desired angle, in which case the wind will of course drive them, if set out of doors; but this is not meant as an out-of-doors toy, and had better remain as an indoor one for the table. In order to get the axle into place, the side (*H*), through which it passes, has a U-shaped piece cut out of its upper side, the width of which just allows the axle to pass into it, and rest on the bottom. The handle at the opposite end is removed, and this end placed in its block until it rests against the block at the shoulder. The said end then drops down into its U-shaped bearing. This is, of course, all arranged before putting on the roof.

W is a wire loop to guide the chain, so that it may not slip off the end of the cotton spool, which should be turned with large flanges. (Although this "reel" is described as a cotton spool, it should be made on purpose.)

The steps are shown in section, the view giving the inside of the further board forming one side. The other is like it with grooves for the steps, which are to be glued in or fixed with small brads. The upper end may rest against a block by the mill door, or be made to hook on with two wire staples.

This toy is one requiring a little care to make neatly and firm when put together, but will not present any real difficulty. It is a capital toy to construct, and should have a box to hold it. It will make a birthday present for any child from 3 to 5 or 6 years of age. (1882)

A Toy Locomotive Engine

The essential parts of the ordinary toy locomotive will consist of a stand, carrying the axles of the wheels; a boiler of solid wood, turned to size and shape in the lathe; and a funnel or chimney. To this should, however, be added a smoke box, a dome, and a cab for protection for the driver. These additional parts give a far more realistic appearance to the toy, although otherwise of no real importance. The drawing, *figure 39*, will be recognized as the normal type of toy engine.

The part marked *A* is a cylinder of wood, to be neatly turned and smoothed with fine sandpaper. The size is of no great importance, but should be such as to give the whole a handsome appearance, say, 6 inches long by 2½ inches in diameter. After being turned, a flat place is to be made by the chisel or plane on one side of the cylinder, by which it can be attached to the bottom board. The flat thus made should be about 1¼ inches wide on a boiler of the size stated, and the bottom board may then be ⅜-inch thick, 8½ inches long, and 3 inches wide, the extra length allowing of smoke box, with funnel above it, and the cab, of which the bottom will then be 1½ inches in length.

Plane up neatly on one side, if not on both sides, the bottom board, taking care that the ends are truly square. The ends, moreover, of the boiler must either be cut off

FIG. 39.—SIMPLE LOCOMOTIVE ENGINE.

in the lathe or marked with a deep notch made by the chisel and then sawn off with a tenon saw to insure their being at right angles to the length of the boiler. Otherwise the additional pieces at the ends cannot possibly be made to fit accurately, and the whole concern will be a muddled, unsatisfactory affair. Both these end pieces should be like that shown at *B*, but that carrying the funnel should be 1 inch thick; the other, called the cab, may be ¼-inch only.

The latter should stand higher than the other, which need not be more than ⅜-inch to ½-inch above the boiler, and project ¼-inch on the sides. The other board should be exactly the width of the bottom board, and may stand ¾-inch to 1 inch above the top of the boiler. The funnel is to be turned to the shape shown, and may be 2½ inches high, ¾-inch in diameter at the lower end, tapering to ½-inch just below the cap, which should be quite ¾-inch in diameter to look well.

These several parts having been carefully made and sandpapered, they may now be put together with small brads—small, but long enough to hold firmly. The cab board must be attached by brads to the bottom, and by longer ones to the boiler, but the front board, intended to imitate the smoke box, being so thick, will, if nailed at all, need a brad 1¾ inches or 2 inches long to attach it to the boiler. This will not be necessary if it is firmly nailed to the bottom by a couple of 1½ inch brads driven from below into this thicker board.

The dome on the top of the boiler, 1 inch and 1½ inches in diameter, should be turned to shape, and then hollowed out underneath by means of a half-round rasp and file until it will fit closely. It is then to be glued on.

The cab should be made by nailing a strip of thin tin 1 inch wide all round the board (*E*) so as to form a hood or cover. In attaching the tin to the cab use small brass nails if they can be procured, and take care to insert them at equal distances apart. It will be the better plan to make the holes before bending the strip of tin. A tap with a light hammer on a small bradawl will suffice to pierce thin stuff like that recommended. Thicker tin may be used, but the toymaker should remember that if it is stiff and springy, it will be rather difficult to nail it on, as it will often draw one nail while another is being driven in. This may be cut straight or hollowed out like the drawing, and with or without side windows. The board, however, should have two round holes, cut with a ⅜-inch centerbit, as shown at *B*, and if you can manage to fit in bits of glass, so much the better. If not, put pieces of tracing paper, thin horn, or any transparent material, which can be cut out with a pair of scissors.

For axles you can adopt either the plan of having them fixed and the wheels turning on screws or turned wooden pins, or the axles of wood or stout wire may be fixed to the wheels, and turn with them, being attached to the bottom board by passing through wire staples or wooden blocks attached underneath, and drilled to allow the axles to pass freely through them. If the former plan be carried out, it will be better to glue on two axle beams, ½-inch square, to receive the screws on which the wheels are to turn, as the bottom board, being but ⅜-inch stuff, is hardly thick enough to receive the screws.

The wheels must be 1¼ inches in diameter at least, and made from stuff ½-inch thick. Let them be turned up nicely and attached firmly to their axles, or well secured on screws of tolerable thickness and length if the latter plan is adopted. Thin wheels always wobble about as they revolve and no defect has a worse appearance.

Small square blocks, turned at one end to resemble buffers, should be glued on at each end of the bottom board near, but not quite at, the corners, or, if more similarity to a real locomotive be desired, two long strips may first be glued under the bottom board, extending ½-inch beyond it at each end, and to the ends of these strips or buffer beams small mushroom-shaped pieces can be attached by glue. Such is the mode of constructing a toy locomotive of rather good quality, but it cannot be considered finished until painted and decorated.

The smoke box should be painted black, as it always is in a real engine. *A* should be green, because it is not the iron that is visible in this part of a railway engine, but strips of wood or "lagging" as it is called. These are laid close together like barrel staves, with a layer of felt under them, and are bound over by three or four hoops of iron. The object of all this "lagging" is to retain the heat as much as possible by preventing the cold air from striking on the metal boiler and chilling it. This woodwork is usually painted a rich green, the bands of iron being black, though these are sometimes replaced by hoops of bright brass. The dome (*D*) is always of bright brass or copper. The wooden one may be painted to imitate copper. The cab (*E*) may be colored vermilion. The bit of rail (*C*) should be made of brass wire polished. The wooden frame will look well of a dark oak, or of a lighter oak tint veined with a darker color. The wheels may be the same, with, perhaps, the small central circle and a band on the edge colored black. The name should be painted on a piece of tin first colored white, the letters being of a bright vermilion edged on one side with black. This will cause the letters to stand out and appear solid, as the black edge stands as a shadow. It must be all on one side of each letter, not on both, for shadow is cast only in one direction. Buffers black, and the whole varnished afterwards. (1882)

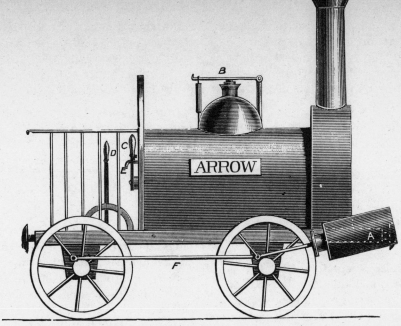

FIG. 40.—LOCOMOTIVE ENGINE, WITH OSCILLATING CYLINDERS.

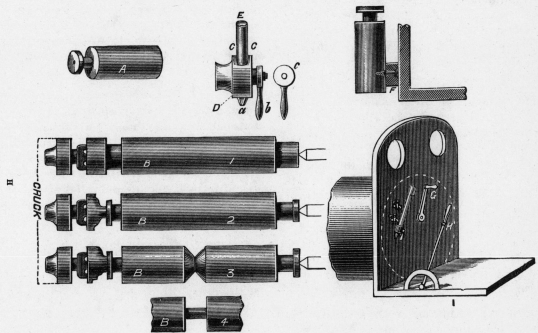

FIG. 41.—SECTIONAL PARTS OF LOCOMOTIVE ENGINE.

A More Realistic Locomotive Engine

The next step towards reality that can be made in a toy engine is to add cylinders, and give motion to the piston-rods.

Retaining the parts illustrated in the previous figure (*figure 39*), we must place two turned cylinders on the outside of the boiler, and, for the sake of simplicity and ease in manufacture, they should be made on the oscillating principle, which will prevent the necessity of connecting rods and guides. An oscillating cylinder is pivoted on a pin at one end, or in the middle, so that it

241

can rock up and down on this pin, and accommodate itself to the motion of the crank to which its piston-rod is attached. This rod in the wooden model will be simply of wire, and no piston will be attached to it—the cylinders, in such case, not requiring to be bored, except with a small hole to allow free movement of the wire.

Figure 40 represents the complete engine, to which a few additional parts have been added besides the cylinder. *B* is an imitation safety valve; *C*, the starting lever; *D*, the reversing lever; *E*, gauge cocks. The wheels are also linked together by side or coupling rods (*F*), giving another source of motion, because the more visible the movement of its parts the more like a real engine will the toy be.

In *figure 41* the cylinder is represented by *A*. It is about 1¼ inches long by ¾-inch diameter, but may be larger or smaller, according to the size of the complete model. At one end is an imitation gland or stuffing box, through the center of which the piston-rod moves. These cylinders, being solid, are easy to turn. Put a bit of deal or beech of suitable size on a prong chuck, and use the back center to keep it in place. Place the rest nearly close—the top of the T a little below the centers—rough down with the gouge, and finish with the chisel, producing in the first place merely a plain smooth cylinder.

Then turn down the small part to imitate the gland, making it on the right-hand end of the cylinder next to the back poppethead. Turn it down merely to a smaller size in the first place, using the chisel to face up the end nicely. Then cut out a notch, and with the chisel angle-work it right and left to widen it, finishing with a very narrow chisel or parting tool, and smoothing with a bit of sandpaper or with a small file. Lastly, cut it off at the chuck end. To do this neatly use the sharp angle of the chisel, and cut a deep notch. Continue to widen this, keeping the cylinder end upright and true as you deepen the cut, and sloping the other to give you plenty of room to work the chisel.

It is as well in all cases like this, where you have to make two things alike and of equal size, to turn them together out of the same piece. In the present instance, if the original piece of stuff is made long enough to produce both cylinders with a half inch, or thereabouts, to spare, you may make glands at each end as much alike as possible, and then divide the piece exactly in the center, forming at this division the ends of the two cylinders instead of only one, working as before directed. Then, while enough substance remains to prevent the parts breaking asunder, finish the cylinder ends with sandpaper, and then give the *coup de grâce*, cutting off where necessary, but taking care to work down all the three parts ready for the final severance, *i.e.*, the stuffing boxes and the cylinder bottom. The

right-hand gland may be worked close to the point of the back poppethead, as the mark made by this point will be just where the hole must be drilled. The two places of severance will then only remain, and little difficulty will be found if care is taken.

In *B* of *figure 41* is represented the two cylinders in process of construction, showing how they are to be worked simultaneously. *1, 2, 3, 4* illustrates them in several stages. The glass gauge (*C*) if also added, may be made very easily of a bit of quill from the wing of a goose. Turn two little pieces of wood to act as sockets and imitate the brass taps like *D*.

The nozzle (*a*) and handle (*b*) are to be made separately, and if the latter is filed out of a bit of beech, like *c*, and a hole drilled through it and the turned piece, a wire nail driven through the whole into the boiler will secure it, but allow the handle to be turned upon the nail. The dotted line shows the position of the end of the boiler. A little glue should be put upon the end of *c* if the handle is to be thus made to move, which will prevent this from gradually working loose. The glass tube (*C*) is inserted in a hole drilled in each of these pieces (only the lower one and a bit of the tube is shown). This hole need only form a hollow recess, as the tube cannot escape or get out of place when once fixed, and will require no cement to secure it. We must now return to the cylinders and their fittings.

The cylinder is to be attached to a block (*F*) by means of a small screw, the shank of which must move easily thereon, and the head must be countersunk, so as not to project in the least. This block is then to be glued outside the frame. This will allow the cylinder to move up and down, but not to come off the frame or board, if the boiler is glued to a board only, as previously directed.

A frame, however, is not much more difficult to make, as the two sides will be glued fast to the boiler, and must, therefore, be quite firm, and no strain falls on the end pieces, which may be notched in the glued or secured by a brad, while it looks better than a mere board.

Let the position of the blocks and cylinder be such as to bring the wire that is to serve as a piston-rod just clear and outside of the wheel. The wheels should now have spokes. The axles should run in neat blocks of mahogany or hardwood glued on under the frame. These axles should be of stout steel wire, flattened at the ends when red hot and inserted in holes which will barely admit them in the nave of the wheel. If a little resin and brickdust is inserted, and the wire heated slightly, it will be rendered more secure. If a wooden axle is preferred, let it be of some hardwood, and glue the axles on tightly.

On one of the spokes of the wheel insert a small screw head, outwards, as a driving pin on which to center the piston-rod, which must be bent into a loop to fit the screw easily. On the same screw, also, center the side rod—a similar pin, in exactly the same relative position, being fixed in a spoke of the second wheel. Neither pin should be more than ½-inch from the center of the wheel, or the stroke will be too long and the piston-rod will be drawn quite out of its cylinder, which latter must have a central hole drilled almost entirely through it. The side rods connecting the wheels, and rising and falling as they revolve, may be of flat tin, painted black. This will look better than mere bits of wire, and is equally easy to arrange.

For the lever handles G will represent the one attached to the back of the boiler to turn on a center screw, and H that to imitate the handle of the reversing gear. These are placed as shown at I, which is a perspective view of this part, representing the back of the engine under the cab or windguard, for the cab is not always used to protect the engine driver, who then merely has a shield of flat plate in front of him with two windows to enable him to keep a lookout ahead. The maker can therefore take his choice in the construction of this part of the engine, and make merely a shield if he thinks it easier to manage.

The safety valve is hardly worthwhile to make with movable parts, but it is no difficult task. The flat top rod can be cut out of tin and pivoted at one end to the short pillar glued to the side of the steam dome, and a little weight can be hung on at the other. Or what will be more like reality instead of the weight, which is only used on stationary engine boilers, an imitation of the spring balance can be made, consisting of a short piece of very small brass tubing, or a bit of brass rod with a loop of wire attaching it to the lever, and another to hook into a small staple on the side of the steam dome. These, however, almost necessitate the use of a little solder to attach the wire loop to the brass rod at its two ends. A wooden imitation will suffice if covered with gilt paper, and this may be also used to cover the steam dome, but it will have to be very neatly done with narrow strips, smaller at one end than the other. (1882)

A Toy Worked by Sand

There is one self-acting toy which is worthy of mention, in which the prime mover is sand falling on the vanes of a wheel from a receptacle placed above it. The acrobatic and similar moving figures are thus made, and are of very simple construction, although the movements of the figure or figures are natural and lifelike if the toy be made with care.

Prepare, first of all, a box of thin board, like those used to contain puzzles, toy bricks, dissected maps, and

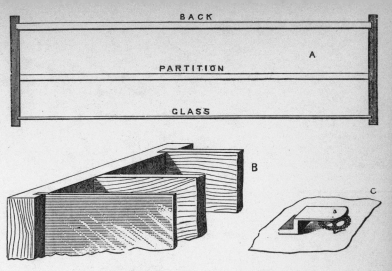

FIG. 50.—PLAN AND SECTION OF SAND TOY.

similar articles. Let it be about 9 inches or a foot square, and 1 inch to 1½ inches deep; not less than the latter if a glass is to be fitted in over the figure, which is the best plan. If a glass is to be used, the bottom of the box, or that part forming the back when it is set on end, as it will be eventually, ought to slide in by means of a groove, so that the interior may be got at if at any time the machinery should be out of order. The front glass ought also to slide in a groove, and there must be in addition a false bottom or partition to which the sides and ends may be nailed and glued. A (figure 50) is a section across the box, and B an enlarged perspective view, in which one side is removed to show clearly this arrangement.

The glass need not stand more than ⅜-inch to ½-inch away from the middle partition. These sliding parts, viz., the glass and back, need not be so fitted, although it will be the best way to make them thus. If considered easier, the glass can be puttied into a neat rebate, and the back nailed or glued on; but in case of a breakage or some little defect in the moving parts, it will then be impossible to get at the interior without breaking the back. All machinery should be so constructed that it may be easily taken to pieces for cleaning and repair, and, wherever it is possible so to plan it, each individual part should be get-at-able without having to disarrange the rest.

The box made as directed will have to stand on one end, and, therefore, the end in question should be made larger than a cross section of the box, so as to form a firm base. This may be moulded round its edges if it can be managed; if not, never mind. In figure 51, which shows the toy complete, an idea will be formed of the sort of finish usually given to it. A little bit of fretwork, for instance, at the top adds to the height and takes away the box-like look of it, and if the whole affair be painted or covered with ornamental paper it adds greatly to its appearance.

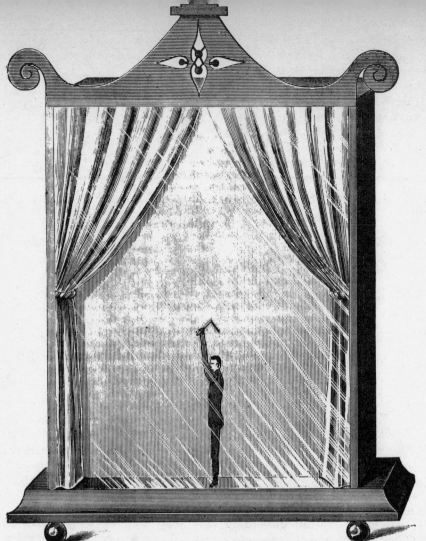

FIG. 51.—SELF-ACTING ACROBAT TOY.

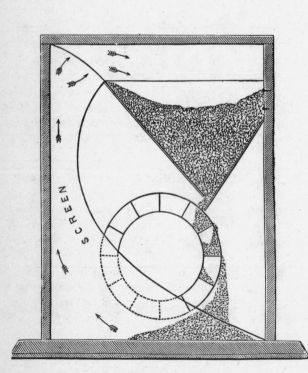

FIG. 52.—INTERIOR OF BOX.

SCREEN

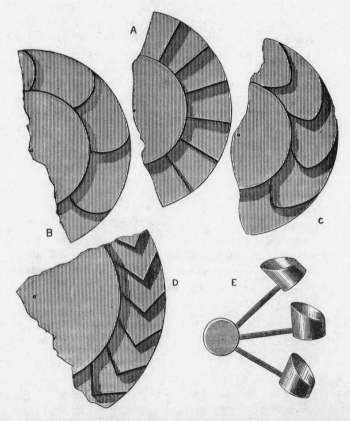

FIG. 53.—DIFFERENT FORMS OF BUCKETS.

Now for an insight into the works. The object is to make the little cardboard Leotard behind the glass go through his acrobatic performances. This will serve as an example, but many similar figures are made—a smith at his anvil, a carpenter using his saw or plane, a cobbler sewing a shoe, or a group of figures may be contrived, if we make our machine powerful enough to give the required motion.

Figure 52 shows the interior of the box. It contains a wheel of stiff cardboard, wood, or very thin tin, as the prime mover. Card is commonly used, and will answer very well, being also easy to cut and manipulate. Any liquid glue will be the best adhesive.

The first thing to make is the wheel, similar to the driving wheel of a watermill, and the bigger it is the more power you will get. First consider what room you have for it, because on its axle, which will project through the front of the case, the arms of the figure are to be fastened. This axle must, therefore, be high enough to let the feet of Leotard clear the ground, and the lower you can put it, while bearing that necessity in mind, the better, as it will give a greater fall to the sand and leave you more room for the reservoirs containing it.

If the case is made 9 inches high, 7 inches wide, and 2 inches deep, which is ample for a single moving figure, you can have a wheel with a 4-inch diameter, its axle being 3 inches from the bottom of the case, which will do very well. The wheel may be made with two round discs enclosing the floats between them, or of one only with slits cut into the edge in which to insert the floats; but in any case the thing to aim at is a wheel that will run lightly and easily.

The floats, too, may be mere flat pieces, or so made as to form what in a water wheel are called buckets, so as to contain a certain portion of sand. Flat ones generally move the figure more quickly and with greater regularity of action, but in this case we should rather aim at irregularity because it will give a more lifelike appearance to the figure. With buckets the result usually is that the figure remains nearly, but not quite, still while the bucket is being filled, and then, when it becomes sufficiently heavy to over-balance, the wheel moves rather suddenly a little way, and thus it continues to turn with a sort of hesitating motion, which is imparted to the figure. The latter then appears as if trying unsuccessfully to turn over its bar, and then, by a sudden effort overcoming the difficulty, it makes a quick somersault, hesitating again at the next movement. A little variation in the size of the buckets again will prevent too regular and undeviating motion, which is to be avoided. In attempting this, care must be taken not to add more than absolutely necessary to the stiffness of the moving parts. These should have plenty of freedom of action without undue looseness, or they will fail to work efficiently.

In constructing a wheel with two discs, 3 inches or 4 inches in diameter, commence by striking out two circles with compasses on a piece of Bristol board, and cut them out neatly to the line, taking care also to preserve the center marks, which is the place where the axle will come. If you get your wheel eccentric and lopsided, it will probably refuse to rotate, and be useless.

Make a small hole through the centers, and run through both a bit of wire or small knitting needle, securing the discs upon it by a dab of glue. Adjust the discs nicely at a distance apart of about ¾-inch.

The needle will hold the discs steadily while proceeding with the buckets or floats. If they are to be flat, cut out ten for a 3-inch wheel. Let each be 1 inch long and a little wider than the space between the discs, so that each edge can be folded sharply in order to glue them to the discs. If ⅛-inch is turned up, it will do very well. Mark with compasses before the discs are mounted, the place where each float is to come, or take a narrow strip of paper that will just go round the wheel, and double it again and again until the required number of measurements is got, or just consider the 4-inch wheel to be 12 inches in circumference, or the 3-inch wheel 9 inches, and divide these to suit your convenience, for ten, twelve, or any number of floats can be used; only they must not be placed too far apart. Instead of ten put eight, at 1½ inches apart, on a 3-inch wheel, which will be easier. But here again, no harm will be done by irregularity, so that you need not be absolutely correct in dividing the discs.

Glue on one end and let dry, which will take but a few seconds. Then put in the one exactly opposite to it, and next the two which will subdivide the spaces thus made. These will render the wheel stiff and strong, and enable you with greater ease to insert the others halfway between these. The floats or buckets need not be of stout card, as numbers make up strength. Card a little stiffer than thin postcards, but less stout than the best, will do well enough for the purpose. If thicker stuff is used, draw a penknife along the lines where the fold is to be made, so as partly to cut the cards at that point. It will then bend up quite sharply and make a neat joint. There should be no difficulty experienced in making such a wheel as described, and it can hardly fail to be satisfactory if the directions are followed.

A similar wheel, with only one disc, may appear easier to make, but is hardly so in reality. Cut out one disc, then, of stout card, as thick at least as a stout postcard, and divide it into as many parts as you will have floats. At each of these points draw lines in the center radial lines, and with a pair of sharp scissors cut slits on these lines all round, in which to insert the floats. You must not merely snip the card, but cut out a little piece at each slit so as exactly to admit the floats, and this will need sharp scissors (or a razor blade) and nice cutting. If the slits are the least bit too wide the floats will be too loose to be secured by glue—if too narrow, the floats will stand awry, because the edge of the disc will bend in forcing them into their places.

For those who prefer bucket wheels to floats, here is a description of two bucket wheels, in which instead of floats upon which a shower of sand is made to impinge, this material is made to fill in turn certain receptacles, until by their weight they overbalance the empty ones and cause the wheel, on the rim of which they are fixed, to revolve. The form of buckets has varied extremely in the case of water mills, but the ordinary shape now used in overshot wheels is that of curved floats fitted between discs of iron. These discs, however, do not reach to the axle, as in the cardboard ones described, but form two rims only, the rest of the wheel being made up with arms or spokes.

Such buckets we can readily contrive in cardboard simply by bending the floats, as shown in *figure 53, A, B, C, D*, in which three different forms are given. But in *E* a very simple plan is suggested, in which common pillboxes are the buckets, which can thus be obtained ready-made. They can be attached by glue to a disc, or between two discs, or to the end of arms or spokes, the latter making a very light wheel. But in order to facilitate the emptying of each bucket as it gets to its lowest position, it will be as well to cut away the little boxes on one side, so as to make them slope off like *E*. There is plenty of choice given therefore to the machine maker, and a selection can be made of that which appears easiest.

A light tin wheel offers great facilities to one who can solder, because thin tin is as easy to cut as card, and when bent will remain so. The least touch of solder, moreover, will secure the parts of such light articles as described here.

The difference between floats and buckets, in regard to power, depends on the fact that with the former a good deal of sand is wasted, and that only the impetus of the falling column of sand is utilized. But in the case of buckets, we get this impetus, and, in addition, the weight of the sand that accumulates in each. Either will work the very light cardboard figures used in these toys, so that it does not much matter which plan is adopted.

The remainder of the mechanism consists of a reservoir for the sand, a funnel-shaped affair, ending in a shoot which delivers the sand accurately upon the wheel, and the little athlete or other figure made with jointed limbs, whose hands are attached to the axle of the moving wheel, goes through its performance. If more than one figure is used, silken bands are passed over pulleys from the main axle to those with which the figures are connected. The latter are often replaced by mill wheels amid painted scenery, ships sailing, trains moving along a railway, and other devices.

In *figure 52* the whole interior is seen complete. To start the movement after it has ceased, owing to the whole of the sand having run out, the box is slowly turned over, by which the sand falls against the sides of the box, and is returned to the reservoir, which should be as wide as the box is deep so as to ensure its catching the whole of the sand when the box is inverted. A screen of card or tin as shown is sometimes placed to assist this, but if the reservoir fits the whole of the upper part, only a little of the sand will escape, being returned to it from the heap which it forms on the floor below the wheel. The reservoir must fit close to the box, and be glued to it as shown.

These sand toys, when neatly finished, are almost too good for a nursery; but they always afford amusement, and are capital presents to children who have passed beyond the age of systematic toy-breaking. As an exercise of ingenuity in the toymaking department, they are exceedingly satisfactory objects to work upon, and give plenty of scope for cleverness in design and skill in manufacture. They also form an excellent introduction to mechanical engineering of a more important character, standing, as it were, halfway between mere ordinary toys and those actuated by clockwork, steam, or electricity. (1882)

The Egg Pig

The engraving shows how a few lines added to the drawing of one object may change it into another. An egg is an easy thing for any boy or girl to draw on a slate or paper.

Near one end of the egg place a dot in a circle, and attach a coiled line to the opposite extremity. Above the eye draw the ears, and a snout below, and with the addition of the feet, you have a pig that is "fat enough to kill." If you take the egg endwise, the face of the pig may be drawn within the circumference of the shell, and then, by making the short legs, the fat animal will be facing you. Try it, and see. (1883)

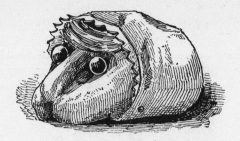

A "Peppery" Face

Not long ago was found a pod of the common garden pepper, dressed up to resemble—well, what do you think? The engraving is an exact reproduction of the general appearance of the dressed fruit as it was left for consideration. It is wonderful how two tacks for eyes, and a little red flannel for a hood, with proper edging and some tow, will transform a simple ripe red pepper into a very odd-looking thing. (1883)

A New Plaything

Young people who are afraid of harmless snakes may, perhaps, overcome their dislike by making such a one as seen in the engraving.

Take a straight piece of soft pine wood 2 feet long. Whittle it into the form of a snake, supposing him to be stretched out and frozen stiff. Next cut out a little groove

Fig. 1.—THE SNAKE COMPLETE.

along the top of the back, and another exactly under it along the belly, just wide and deep enough to allow a piece of fine strong cord, like a small fishing line, to lie in below the surface as shown at C, figure 2. Also bore a

hole to pass the line through the head from the top to the under groove.

With a fine saw, cut down through on each side of the snake, nearly to the middle, making the cuts exactly opposite, and an inch apart, except at the head and tail, each of which may be left about 2 inches long. *Figure 1* shows nearly how these cuts should be made.

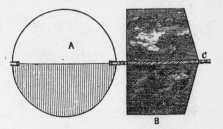

Fig. 2.—SECTION OF BLOCKS.

Then cut the front edge of each division, beveling about one-quarter of an inch down to the center. This will separate the snake into inch pieces. B, *figure 2*, gives the shape of each piece, looking from the top. A, *figure 2*, represents the back end of each piece.

Arrange the pieces in proper order in a straight line, from head to tail, and, with a fine brush, partially fill the top groove with glue. Then pass the cord through the hole in the head piece, crowd it down snugly into the glue, bringing each piece close up to the one before it.

Turn the snake over, glue the under groove, and fasten the other part of the string down into the groove of the belly part, throughout the whole length, the same as on the top part.

Leave it until perfectly dry, and you will have a wooden snake that will squirm alarmingly. Two pin heads for eyes, and a little paint skillfully applied will complete the resemblance to nature, and make an amusing plaything. Do not selfishly use it to frighten the timid. (1867)

Street Toys

If you were to walk down Broadway you would be surprised at the number of men—all of whom look strong and healthy enough to do a good day's work—who are engaged in selling childrens' toys from little stands placed at the street corners, or upon the steps on some building. If you passed by these venders day after day, you would notice that the stock frequently changes. A dealer will for several days offer figures that tumble heels over head. After a while he will have those which dance at the end of a rubber string, then again,

An Amusing Toy

Almost any boy can whittle out from a soft pine stick two figures like those shown in the engraving. The body and head of each are made of a single piece about half an inch thick. Two thin pieces a little curved in the middle, for the elbows, represent the two arms joined

An Amusing Toy.

together as in wrestling. The legs are each made of one thin slip of wood, and are attached to the body by pins, so as to hang loosely. The arms are pinned on at the shoulders in the same manner, and the figures are thus made to look like two boys in a position for wrestling. They can be painted, if convenient, or merely marked with ink, to suit the fancy.

When all is ready, pass a thread about six feet long through the holes in the arms near the elbows. Fasten one end of it around the leg of a table or chair near the floor, and hold the other end in the hand. The images should be two or three feet from the lower end of the thread. Now by gently twitching the string the images will be made to wrestle in a very comical way; sometimes one will go down, then the other, then both, and by a little management they can be made to perform an almost numberless variety of very queer antics, to the great amusement of the little folks. (1868)

A New Popgun

The boys in New York and vicinity are amusing themselves with a new toy sold at the shops which is easily made with a jackknife and gimlet or small hand tool for boring holes.

---

some kind of tops will be for sale, until they in turn will be replaced by a new fashion in toys.

One of the recent toys consists of a pasteboard man without any legs and a pair of pasteboard boots hung by threads to the figure. At first sight, one is puzzled to know what to do with such a toy. At the back of the toy is an elastic band, shown in the engraving, *figure 1*, by a dotted line. Two fingers are slipped between this elastic and the figure, and one of the boots put upon the end of each finger, and you have a Highlander. The fingers represent the bare legs which are considered necessary to a Highlander when in *full dress*; the knuckles make capital knees, and when by moving the fingers the image is made to walk or dance, the effect is laughable. The figure should be painted to represent the gay colors of the Highland costume, but one recently acquired was dressed like a jester or clown.

There is another toy just now popular—a puzzle. It is a coil of brass wire of the size of *figure 2*, upon which a ring is placed in such a manner that two wires of the coil pass through the ring. The puzzle is to get the ring off the coil. It cannot be screwed off by turning the coil, as that is prevented by having the ends of the wires of the coil soldered so as to prevent the ring from going off in that way. One could *show* you in a few seconds how it is done, but to describe it is quite another matter.

Let us begin by putting the ring on. Suppose you have a coil of wire and a ring like those shown in the engraving, but both separate. Put the ring over the top of the coil and bring it between two of the turns of the coil; then give the ring a turn or a twist from left to right, and it cannot be taken off without turning the ring back again from right to left. The manner of passing two or more turns of the coil through the ring is easily found out by trying. (1870)

A New Popgun.

Bore a hole lengthwise through a straight pine stick, say 6 inches long, and whittle it into the form of a small cannon, as shown in the engraving. Fasten a small peg on each side of the cannon, and make a rod to fit the inside of the bore, but about an inch shorter; leave a knob on the end of this stick. Tie each end of a rubber band to the pegs, and stretch the middle part of the strip around the end of the knob on the rod, as shown in the illustration. Drop a pea into the mouth of the cannon; draw the rod back, take good aim and let fly; the India rubber spring will force the rod forward, and send the pea out with considerable force.

Be careful! (1868)

Amusing Toy for the Little Ones

Cut out from wood the figure of a dancer, somewhat like the one here given. It will be easier to form the head, body, and arms separately and afterward glue them together. The legs should be quite thin, and hung so as to play loosely upon a wire running across a hollow place cut in the bottom of the body, as shown by the dotted lines in the figure. Keep them separated by a small slip of wood placed between them on the wire.

When this is done, take four strong bristles, each about an inch long, and insert them as pins for the image to stand upon. They should be long enough to just keep the feet of the image from touching the floor, or whatever it is set upon. It will improve the image to

paint it in bright colors. Place it upon a tea tray or cookie sheet, letting it stand upon the bristles, then whistle or sing a tune, and at the same time drum with the fingers upon the pan. The image will dance about in a way to give great amusement to the little folks. (1866)

A Curious Fan

Introduced recently is a Japanese fan which is calculated to afford some amusement. At first look nothing

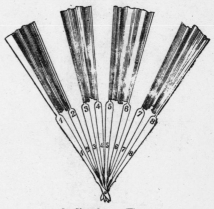

A Curious Fan.

out of the common way was seen. It opens and closes like any other fan when spread from left to right; but on spreading it the other way, from right to left, it seems to fall to pieces, as shown in the accompanying engraving. The following is a description of the arrangement so that ingenious young craftsmen may make one to puzzle their freinds with.

First make the splints or sticks for the frame in the ordinary manner. Cut paper or silk for the covering in strips 2 or 3 inches wide at the top, according as the size of the fan is to be large or small. The cover strips should be tapered so that they may fit smoothly when the fan is spread out. The shape of the right taper can be determined by laying the splints upon the silk at the top, and bringing their ends together.

Next lay one splint (4) *upon* the right hand edge of the silk, and another splint (3) *under* the opposite edge of the silk, and fasten them there with gum or paste. Make 10 pairs in this way, one pair of splints in each, and number the splints, 1, 2, 3, 4, etc. For the outside parts have one wide and one narrow splint (1, 8).

Make a hole in the lower end of the splints, through which a wire is to be passed to hold them in place. Put the wire through the splints, in the following order: through No. 1, 3, 2, 5, 4, 7, 6, 9, 8, 11, 10, 13, 12, 15, 14, 17, 16, 19, 18, 20. Fasten the wire by riveting it at the ends to prevent the splints slipping off and the fan is complete. (1868)

THE BOTTLE IMP.—*Engraved for the Am. Agriculturist.*

A Homemade Bottle Imp

Probably most of you have seen in one form or another, the amusing toy called "The Bottle Imp." It usually consists of some kind of glass image which stays at the top of the water in a tall narrow glass jar. At the command of its owner, it will go to the bottom, remain there for a long time, rise to half way, and do other amusing things.

Sometimes the jar is much larger, and contains a beautiful balloon, entirely of colored glass, and must be worth several dollars.

An ingenious Frenchman has shown children how to maek a neat toy to cost but little. The glass figures and the balloon are hollow, though they may have a little water in them, and are light enough to float. Each one has a minute hole in the foot or elsewhere, and when the sheet of rubber tied over the top is pressed, a little water is forced into the body of the figure, or into the balloon,

and become heavier, both sink in the water. When the pressure is removed, the elasticity of the air drives the water out of the figures, and up they go.

To make an imitation, the most important parts needed are a walnut (English), and a bottle with a mouth wide enough to admit the nut. Carefully halve the shell, take out the kernel, and then join the parts with sealing-wax or glue, being sure it is quite water-tight. Then bore a little hole, not larger than a pin head at the bottom—see dotted line at *o*. The wooden man will be too light, and you will need to give him a bit of lead, *p*, to keep him steady. Attach some fine wire to the nutshell, by which to suspend the figure. After all is adjusted, tie a piece of sheet rubber (a piece of old rubber glove will do) over the mouth of the bottle, and press on the rubber. The figure will then sink and rise according to the amount of pressure. (1883)

Making Shadows

These boys are having a fine time making shadow-pictures upon the wall. A great deal of amusement can be made in this way, not only to divert young children, who are always pleased by these shadow-pictures, but older ones can get much entertainment from them. Almost every one knows how to arrange his fingers to form the shadow of a rabbit, a fighting cock, and a bleating calf, but these are not by any means all the pleasing shadows that can be made.

In order to have the shadows show to the best advantage there must be a white wall, or in absence of this a white cloth pinned against the wall. Then there must be but one light in the room, and the shadow will be all the more distinct if this is a strong one. You must recollect that in shadows it is only the outline that shows and in forming them with the hands it makes no difference how the rest of the fingers are fixed if those engaged in producing the shadow are in their proper places. Also, the nearer the hands are held to the wall the sharper will be the shadow. A little ingenuity and patience will enable one by the use of one hand or both to produce very amusing shadows.

Quite pleasing are what are called Chinese shadows A sheet is hung across a door between two rooms. The spectators are in one room, in which there is no light, and the shadow-makers are in the other, in which there is a very strong light. The lower half of the door has a blanket or other screen, through which the light cannot pass, across it, and the performer is hidden below this. When he lifts his hands above the screen, the shadow

250

falls upon the sheet. But Chinese shadows are not usually made by the hands; figures cut from stiff paper or pasteboard are used and operated from below. As an outline only is required, the joints and all other parts may be made very rough. Any ingenious boy or girl can get up figures of men, women, and animals, to make these shadows, and cause them to have lifelike movements, taking care that the hands operating them are carefully concealed below the dark screen. The exhibition of Chinese shadows can be made more amusing if a dialogue is kept up as if it came from the figures. It would not be difficult to illustrate some story or dialogue in this way and thus furnish a pleasant entertainment. (1872)

"SHADOWS ON THE WALL."—*Drawn and Engraved for the American Agriculturist.*

Index of Projects